3/13

DATE DUE

	7/7/12
MAR 3 - 2000	
MAR 2 1 2000	
APR 0 8 2000	
MAY 1 4 2000	
MAY 3 1 2000 JUL 2 6 2000	
JUL 1 2 2000	
AUG 4 - 2000	
FEB 2 8 2007	

DEMCO, INC. 38-2931

DEC 3 0 1999

ACTORS TALK

ACTORS TALK

*Profiles and Stories from
the Acting Trade*

DENNIS BROWN

LIMELIGHT EDITIONS
NEW YORK

First Edition December 1999

Copyright © 1999 by Dennis Brown

Published by Proscenium Publishers Inc., New York.
All rights reserved under International and
Pan-American Copyright Conventions.

Library of Congress Cataloging-in-Publication Data

Brown, Dennis, 1945-
Actors talk : profiles and stories from the acting trade / Dennis Brown.
p. cm.
Includes bibliographical references and index.
ISBN 0-87910-287-X
1. Acting. 2. Actors--Interviews. I. Title.

PN2061.B76 1999
792'.028--dc21

99-053523
CIP

Manufactured in the United States of America.

THIS BOOK FOR

CLARENCE AND ARIELLE OLSON

and

DAN AND DOROTHEA PETRIE,

FAITHFUL FRIENDS

CONTENTS

INTRODUCTION 3

1. THE CHOICE: Stacy Keach 7

SIDES: *Lessons*
Joan Plowright   George Grizzard   Christopher Walken 31

2. EVERYBODY WANTS TO DO A MUSICAL:
Edmund Lyndeck   George Rose   Richard Chamberlain
Barry Bostwick 37

SIDES: *11/22/63*
Harve Presnell   William Biff McGuire   Joyce Van Patten 63

3. ATTICUS: Gregory Peck 69

SIDES: *Getting Started*
James Garner   Sam Neill   Louis Gossett, Jr. 103

4. WAND'RIN' STAR: Sterling Hayden 107

SIDES: *Being There*
Cameron Mitchell   Bert Convy   Roberta Maxwell 129

5. ACTOR LADIES
Lillian Gish   Beulah Bondi   Jessica Tandy 137

SIDES: *Child Actors*
Jackie Cooper   Billy Dee Williams   Patty Duke 165

6. BE A CLOWN: Danny Kaye 171

SIDES: *The Audition*
Fritz Weaver   Jon Voight   Christopher Walken
Geraldine Page 193

7. OUTSIDER: Paul Winfield 199

SIDES: *The Mysterious X*
Dorothy McGuire   Kevin Kline   Frank Langella 223

8. CYRANO: José Ferrer 229

FOR FURTHER READING 265

INDEX 271

A SELECTION OF PHOTOGRAPHS FOLLOWING PAGE 88

ACTORS TALK

INTRODUCTION

The first actors in my consciousness were movie stars.

When I was a youngster growing up in St. Louis, grade school was little more than a week-long respite between movies. An ideal weekend meant being allowed to go to the movies Friday night, Saturday matinee, Saturday night and Sunday matinee. So many movies, seen and since forgotten. But I'll never forget Robert Taylor and Alan Ladd and William Holden. These larger-than-life pretenders-to-reality imbued my daily routine with glamorous, fanciful imaginings.

As I grew older and live theater began to supplant the movies in importance, faithful touring players like Tom Ewell, Eva LeGallienne and John Raitt were welcomed as old friends. Not *real* friends, of course. I always yearned to know where the actors went after the curtain came down.

When you're young and enraptured by theater and film, you think that you too want to be an actor, simply because acting is the most visible part of those worlds. Not until you actually enter those professions do you realize how many employment opportunities there are. So it was with me. Flush with the success of high school acting triumphs, I assumed I was bound for the Great White Way. But at Illinois Wesleyan University, my dream of pursuing an acting career was quickly dashed (which means it *should* have been; no regrets there). Instead, after graduation I toiled as a publicist, first in regional theater, then for CBS Entertainment.

At last I began to learn where actors went after the curtain came down. On occasion they went out with me. On one of my first television-movie sets, Rip Torn eagerly accepted an invitation to dinner, not because he relished my company but because he knew my corporate credit card would pay the bill. "After all," the Ripper rationalized, "actors are just a bunch of pirates."

Pirates, yes, and cowboys and court jesters, and Toulouse-Lautrec and Martin Luther King, and Hester Prynne and Blanche DuBois, and has-been boxers and men in gray flannel suits.

Sure, some actors could be annoyingly self-centered and hands-on. But as I grew older, the glamour that had sustained me in youth gave way to something more subtle: appreciation. Appreciation that actors were able to do something I could not. (If you think acting looks easy, try it.) And appreciation for their contribution to the written word. Actors are the bestowers of life. They are the life-givers.

We're all familiar with the celebrated, if slightly apocryphal, exchange between Ernest Hemingway and F. Scott Fitzgerald about the rich being different from you and me. ("Yes, they have more money.") Well, actors are different from you and me too: They *become* you and me. Actors are a balm, because they remind us that, though our emotions are uniquely our own, the dark, twiny trail along which we are hacking our way has known other pilgrims. There is no sensation, none, that has not been felt before.

But how can actors become us, when we don't know who we are ourselves? Call it fancy footwork; call it alchemy. (You'll be surprised at how often the words *magical* and *miracle* occur in these pages.)

Actors Talk introduces the reader to an eclectic assemblage of eleven actors whose varied careers span the twentieth century. (One began acting in 1901; another won a Golden Globe Award just last week.) Some have been interviewed ad nauseam; others have never before been profiled between hard covers. Yet they all allowed themselves to be cajoled into discussing the art and craft of their lives, and they responded with articulate clarity.

Because actors are storytellers foremost, what follows is a veritable cornucopia of stories ... stories about naïveté and insecurity, about choices made and lessons learned. Stories lived, and now shared.

The emphasis, I hope, is on what they have to say rather than on what I have to say about them. In Act One of *Cyrano de Bergerac*, at the end of the "nose speech," after the poet-swordsman describes his prominent protuberance eighteen different ways ("inquisitive . . . insolent . . . eloquent . . . "), Cyrano concludes,

INTRODUCTION

I say these things,
Lightly enough myself, about myself,
But I allow none else to utter them.

So it is with actors. They don't need me to rationalize their existence; let them speak for themselves.

CHAPTER ONE

THE CHOICE

"I'm not satisfied just being Mike Hammer. . . .
If I don't play King Lear, I won't have accom-
plished what I was put on this earth to do."
—STACY KEACH

In his memoir *Dear Me*, Peter Ustinov describes the uneasy alliance that existed between Charles Laughton and Laurence Olivier
on the *Spartacus* film set. Laughton "overflowed with an almost car-
nal glee at the process of acting," Ustinov reports. But to Olivier,
Charles Laughton was a Hollywood sellout who had exchanged his
soul for a great art collection and sundry other accoutrements of
wealth. When *Spartacus* was filmed in 1960, Sir Larry was still striving to be Great Britain's first theatrical peer. Ustinov recounts how
between scenes Olivier would pore over his grocery bills in an attempt to find money-saving errors that would help him to survive
within the confines of his living allowance.

Actors often talk about "the choices" they must make while developing a role, but a far more critical choice occurs early on when,
like Olivier and Laughton, they must determine what kinds of words
they are willing to savor in their mouths.

All too soon, successful actors learn about the inverse ratio between great words and low fees, about the trash that arrives wrapped
in dollar signs. "When you get hot," one young stage actor come-to-

film remarked, the harsh glare of discovery still blinking in his bleary eyes, "you're suddenly sent this crush of scripts. It's an embarrassment, there are so many. They come accompanied with offers of huge sums of money. Invariably, the ones with the most money are the most formulaic and cliché, movies where your mind is merely massaged while your solar plexus is attacked. It's very frustrating."

Stacy Keach never enjoyed the frustration of having to unbury himself from under piles of scripts. But Keach personifies the choice that every idealistic young actor must confront. He was raised in Hollywood, yet his ambitions lay east. He didn't want to sell out, but he didn't want to be left out. When early success did not propel him along the path he had hoped to travel, he found himself wracked by the vice that presses in on every young actor's soul.

Keach was thrust into national prominence as America's response to the noble tradition of British classical acting. The English had long given American actors a collective inferiority complex. In the 1960s, the revered triumvirate of Olivier-Gielgud-Richardson was reinforced by a frisky new generation that included Richard Burton, Albert Finney, Peter O'Toole, Nicol Williamson. What classical actors did America have? Well, there was Stacy Keach and . . . well, there was Stacy Keach.

Once his career took off, he seemed tireless, ubiquitous, playing Hamlet, Peer Gynt and Falstaff in Central Park, taking on Eugene O'Neill Off-Broadway, making movies. And everybody liked him. The word on Stacy Keach was: *nice guy*.

I first met him on the set of *The Blue and The Gray*, an eight-hour mini-series propelled by historian Bruce Catton's writings about the Civil War. As the CBS publicist assigned to that ambitious project, in autumn 1981 I spent nearly two months on location in northwest Arkansas. Normally local press are not allowed to visit a film set until the publicist is on hand to babysit. But the day I arrived, I was taken aback to find three television crews and two print reporters already pursuing stories. All the activity was being coordinated by our accommodating star—Stacy Keach. That was a first.

Six months later we convened in Washington, D.C., for a preliminary *Blue and The Gray* press conference. The day he was scheduled to return to Los Angeles, Keach arrived forty-five minutes late for his limo ride to the airport—highly unusual for the punctual actor. With a shaken voice, he explained that earlier that afternoon he had entered the hotel health club to take a whirlpool, only to discover an unconscious man, with neither pulse nor heartbeat, in the pool. Employing artificial respiration, Keach restored the fellow to life. But because they were alone, he couldn't leave him, not even to call for help. Not until another patron entered the health club was Keach able to alert the front desk. Only after the medics arrived did the actor think about catching his plane.

A nice guy.

Success in *The Blue and The Gray* begat success in additional television projects, culminating in his role as the macho private eye in *Mickey Spillane's Mike Hammer*. Then, in April 1984, America's young Olivier was arrested at London's Heathrow Airport and charged with importing cocaine. Keach was sentenced to serve nine months in Reading Prison, the same penitentiary where another celebrated theatrical personage, Oscar Wilde, had been incarcerated at hard labor in 1895.

Ten years after that arrest, we sat on the terrace of Stacy Keach's six-acre Malibu domain, watched the thick mist hover over Catalina Island, and chronicled the rise, fall and reclamation of an American actor.

Let's start at the beginning, I suggested. You were born . . . .

"June 2, 1941, in Savannah, Georgia. My father was an actor, but when I was born he was teaching theater at Armstrong Junior College in Savannah. When I was six months old, Dad got work at the Pasadena Playhouse, so we moved to California. Then when I was five, he became a talent scout for RKO Pictures in New York, and we moved to Flushing, Long Island. My brother, James, was born a year later. The baby was very demanding in terms of my parents' time, so they sent me to live with my grandmother in Taft, Texas, a tiny little town outside Corpus Christi that might have been the model for *The Last Picture Show*. That's where I started going to the movies. It cost nine cents to see a double feature. After a year in Texas, we moved the whole family out to Sherman Oaks, in the San Fernando Valley."

What brought your father back to California?

"He developed a weekly radio show for NBC called *Tales of the Texas Rangers* that starred Joel McCrea. He produced and directed that for five or six years. He was also acting. He'd do guest shots, bad guys and sheriffs, on TV shows like *The Lone Ranger*."

What are your memories of growing up in Los Angeles in the 1950s?

"It was a different era. There were still orange groves in the valley. I especially remember the holidays. Nobody out here went Christmas caroling. Then one December my grandmother thought that we should all go caroling to raise money for the church. It was a chilly night, I remember, because we had to bundle my brother up. We went from door to door. Then we reached John Wayne's house. He lived down the block, and he invited us in. What a thrill! I mean, *what a thrill*! He was giving a party, so they served us food and we sang Christmas carols for his guests. Zsa Zsa Gabor was there. Every other house had given us quarters, but John Wayne gave us five dollars!

"Halloween was also a fun time, because my dad would take great pleasure in making me up to be these wild characters. His enthusiasm for makeup and disguises was infectious. From him I caught that disease of wanting to be someone else. That's when I decided I wanted to be an actor. In the tenth grade at Van Nuys High School, I played the Stage Manager in *Our Town*, which was a big challenge for a young kid. I didn't know how to pantomime making ice-cream sodas or indicating the size of a tree, and my dad showed me how to do those things. I watched him and learned from him, and I was a huge success."

So in high school you heard that applause and said, "This is what I want to do"?

"That's true, as far as it goes, but it went further than that. My dad was always creative. When he wasn't acting, he was writing a script or trying to sell an idea for a game. But this is a cyclical business, and there were many down times when he was out of work. So when I was growing up, there was a lot of tension in our house. For me the release from that tension was to become someone else. I developed such a rich fantasy world that I actually had a problem with the truth. It reached a point where I didn't know who I was unless I was playing someone else."

What happened when you told your parents you wanted to become an actor?

"I thought my father would be thrilled to learn that his son wanted to follow in his footsteps, but when I told him, he said, 'Oh no, you're not going to be a professional actor. Be a lawyer or a doctor. Be like Walter Pidgeon.' But I didn't want to be Walter Pidgeon. I wanted to be Marlon Brando or James Dean. But to placate my parents, I went off to college at Berkeley as a political science and economics major, with an edict from home that I couldn't do any school plays until I got a B average. Well, good luck. Berkeley was tough! I studied eight, nine hours a day just to stay in school. Gradually the grades did improve; so at the end of my freshman year, I finally acted in a play.

"My sophomore year I was still an economics major, very unhappy, but acting more and more. Then I took a course called Economic Statistics that blew me out of the water. That did it. I said, 'No more of this; I am not interested.' And I called home and announced that I was changing my major to English and dramatic art. My parents were not happy, but I was adamant. That summer I went off to Bedford, Massachusetts, for a season of stock, having fallen in love with a young girl who also went there. Returned to Berkeley, changed my major, acted in plays and began to thrive. My grades went up, and I became very popular on campus because I was 'the actor.' "

About this time, didn't you have an experience at Berkeley that influenced the direction of your acting?

"When I was a senior in high school, one of the questions on a quiz in drama class was, 'Who is the world's best Shakespearean actor?' And I couldn't answer the question. When the teacher returned the tests, next to that question she had written the name *Laurence Olivier*, and I didn't know who Laurence Olivier was.

"So when I was at Berkeley, I saw an ad that the local art house was going to show Laurence Olivier in *Richard III*. I didn't plan to, but I watched that film three times in one day. I went into the theater at one o'clock in the afternoon, and I came out at eleven o'clock that night a changed man. I knew that that was the kind of work I wanted to do. From that day on, I only wanted to play those roles that would challenge and stretch me. Shakespeare does that. If you can get your mouth around his words, you can do just about anything.

"I also thought to myself, what a great thing if I could do classical work as an American actor, because nobody was making a career of playing those roles in America. I had this naive, idealistic revelation that I could bring the classics to American audiences, who were dying to see them. Not true. They aren't. But Olivier really did change my mind about the direction in which I wanted to take my career."

You actively pursued that ambition, because the very next summer you went to the Oregon Shakespeare Festival.

"I had a great time doing Antipholus of Syracuse in *The Comedy of Errors* and a couple of smaller roles. It went well, and they asked me back the following summer to play Henry V and Mercutio. Henry Hewes wrote an incredible notice in *Saturday Review* that compared me to Christopher Plummer. That fall I went to Yale Drama School. While I was there, I auditioned for Joe Papp. He had seen the review, and he asked if I was a member of Actors Equity. When I said no, he said, 'You will be. You're going to be in *Hamlet* this summer in Central Park.' That production got me my Equity card. In the summer of '64 I played Marcellus and the Player King to Alfred Ryder's Hamlet, with Julie Harris, Nan Martin, Howard da Silva, John Randolph. A dream production, right? But it wasn't, because Alfred Ryder couldn't do it. A lot of drinking; he'd forget lines.

"While we were playing in the Park, Richard Burton was doing *Hamlet* on Broadway. So Papp arranged for Robert Burr, who was Burton's understudy, to replace Ryder. It was all so rushed. I met Robert Burr for the first time onstage. In the second scene, we entered the court, and he looked at me. He said, 'Marcellus?'

" 'My good lord—'
" 'I am very glad to see you.'

"Shakespeare always comes through for you. After the performance Richard Burton and Elizabeth Taylor came to the theater and schmoozed with the entire company, so I got to meet them both. I said to myself, 'I've made it!' I wasn't even playing Hamlet, but as a young actor, this was heaven."

That fall you moved to London to study acting on a Fulbright scholarship at the London Academy of Music and Dramatic Arts. Pretty heady stuff for an ambitious young actor.

"In terms of absorption, that was the most exciting year of my early career. The Royal Shakespeare Company was doing *Marat/Sade* with Ian Richardson and Patrick Magee. They were doing *The Homecoming* with Ian Holm, *Richard III* with Ian Holm, *Hamlet* with David Warner. The Old Vic was doing Zeffirelli's extraordinary *Much Ado About Nothing*. Olivier was doing *The Master Builder* and *Othello*. I saw it twice. Albert Finney was doing *Black Comedy*. Colin Blakely was in a great production of *The Crucible* directed by Olivier. I saw *Julius Caesar* with Patrick Stewart wonderful as Cassius."

Your ambition to pursue great theater must have been keener than ever.

"I was chewing at the bit."

Yet when you returned home, didn't you find yourself in the midst of an unprecedented debacle?

"At that point in my life, my definition of happiness was to be able to act the roles of my choice in a regional theater for two hundred dollars a week. For me, that was *making* it. So, even before I returned to the United States, I accepted a job in a new acting company at Stanford. But I stopped off in New York, auditioned, and got the part of Mr. Horner in *The Country Wife*, which was to be part of the historic opening season of the Vivian Beaumont Theater at Lincoln Center. I couldn't pass that up. All the expectations were tremendous for the maiden voyage of this extraordinary new space designed by Jo Mielziner. We had no idea that the space was not going to work.

"In order to play the lead in *The Country Wife*, I had to act several small roles in the opening production, *Danton's Death*. After a year of having been exposed to productions at the Old Vic and the Royal Shakespeare Company, I didn't have to rehearse very long to become very disillusioned very quickly. *Danton's Death* was probably the most disastrous opening in the history of the New York theater. But let's face it. Any four-play season that includes *Danton's Death*, *The Condemned of Altona* and *The Caucasian Chalk Circle* does not bode well."

You left that company a little bloodied?

"I ran! I did a season at Williamstown. I did a couple plays at the Long Wharf. Then a guy who had been with me at Yale said he had a play that he wanted to produce in New York. He said, 'You'd be perfect for the lead. It's called *MacBird!*' He finally got the money together, and we opened at the Village Gate in February of 1967. Using the themes from *Macbeth*, this play suggested that Lyndon Johnson was responsible for the Kennedy assassination. Paul Hecht was John Kennedy; Bill Devane was Bobby Kennedy, and I—buried under several pounds of makeup—was LBJ."

MacBird! was your first taste of fame. Yet with success, everything you'd been working for suddenly took a right turn.

"I still wanted to achieve something artistically. Didn't care about money. Wanted fame, sure, but didn't want to pursue it. I still wanted to do something unique, something that nobody else had ever done, which was to be a classical actor in America. At the very least, I thought that being the lead in an Off-Broadway show might parlay itself into the lead of a Broadway show, but it didn't. Instead I ended up doing the last thing in the world I wanted to do. I was cast in my first movie, *The Heart Is a Lonely Hunter.*"

So now this would-be classical actor finds himself in Selma, Alabama, playing a downbeat, drunken drifter in an Alan Arkin movie—

"And I realized I knew absolutely nothing about screen acting. The production company took over the Selma movie theater to show the dailies. I'll never forget the first time I saw myself on this big screen. I was mortified. I thought I was overacting like crazy. The amazing thing is that I look back at that movie now, and I say to myself, 'That's a really good performance.' "

What happened to turn the performance around?

"I realized that screen acting had nothing in common with the kind of acting I'd been doing for the past seven or eight years. I had to learn to stop giving 'a performance' and just 'be.' When I was in front of James Wong Howe's camera in Alabama, I was simply a downbeat drifter. It wasn't easy for me, because I like to keep building on to the character. But in *The Heart Is a Lonely Hunter* the simplicity worked, and that drifter became a very human fellow."

During all those early years, your parents had opposed your career choice. What did Dad say after he saw you up on the silver screen in *The Heart Is a Lonely Hunter*?

"He said, 'When are you going to get the kind of role Clark Gable would have been cast in?' To him, I was just playing a supporting part. It wasn't the lead. Once it was clear that I was in this business to stay, he kept telling me, 'Listen to your dad. I know the ropes. This is how to do it. You come out to Hollywood; you get an agent; you make yourself available.' Even when I was doing *MacBird!*, he was telling me, 'You've got to be out here, you've got to be available.' Whereas of course I was the rebellious son, replying, 'I'll show you. I'm doing this my own way.' "

In 1968 your way was to once again bury yourself behind tons of makeup and play Falstaff in *Henry IV, Parts I* and *II* in Central Park.

"One of the best bad reviews I ever got was from John Simon: 'What Stacy Keach lacks in spirit, he makes up for with spirit gum.' That's great."

At this same time, an important movie role came your way. *End of the Road* was supposed to do for you what *The Graduate* had done for Dustin Hoffman the preceding year—the difference being that Dustin Hoffman never played Falstaff. Which came first, *End of the Road* or *Henry IV*?

"They were simultaneous. We shot the film in Great Barrington, Massachusetts. I would finish shooting at five o'clock in the afternoon. I'd get in the station wagon. I'd sleep for one hour in the back. Then I'd apply my makeup for Falstaff in the front seat. I would arrive at the New York Shakespeare Festival in makeup. They'd stick me into my padding and my costume, and I'd go out onstage. I'd play Falstaff in front of that wonderful Central Park audience. Then

I'd get in the car and drive back to Great Barrington that night, sleeping in the back, get to the inn, and get up at five o'clock the next morning to begin shooting."

This is a young actor flexing his muscles, showing off.

"Right. I loved it."

What went amiss with *End of the Road*?

"We set out to film John Barth's novel, which is a social satire set on a college campus. We had a terrific screenplay by Terry Southern. But Aram Avakian, our director, had his own agenda, and I don't think anybody ever knew what it was. What finally ended up on the screen is simply not the movie we shot. Some of it was way ahead of its time, and some of it is brilliant. But it's not the story we were trying to tell. *End of the Road*, which was supposed to explode on the American scene like another *Graduate,* instead was withheld for two years. When it finally did come out, it received an 'X' rating because of the abortion scene. Women fainted, it was so graphic. Aram would not listen to anyone who spoke in such mundane terms as 'This scene is unwatchable.' This was 1968, remember, the summer of the Chicago riots. Vietnam was tearing the country apart. To Aram, who was heavily into politics, that scene was symbolic of the abortion of America. But with the 'X' rating, the film had an extremely limited release. To this day, it has never been shown on television.

"But I learned something from that film. After I saw the finished product, and realized how different it was from the story I thought we were telling, I learned that the key to successful screen acting is knowing that each moment exists and lives for itself. Till I saw that film, I'd been approaching my screen roles the same way I approached stage roles. I was making building blocks, where something I do in scene two pays off in scene six. But in a movie, if the director cuts me out of scene two, I wind up looking like a fool in scene six. It was a painful lesson, but I learned that a film actor has to play each moment for what it is: moment-to-moment reality."

Next you played Edmund to Lee J. Cobb's King Lear at Lincoln Center. Then you starred in Arthur Kopit's *Indians* at the Arena Stage in Washington, D.C.

"Not quite. While I was still doing *King Lear* I got a call from my agent: 'Mike Nichols saw you do Falstaff, and he thinks you're right for a couple roles in *Catch-22*.' So I go up to Mike Nichols' apartment, and the casting director says, 'You could play either General Dreedle or Colonel Cathcart. But either way, you're going to be in the movie.' I floated out of this room. Didn't even have to audition. I'm going to be cast in what's destined to be the biggest movie of the year, from the director of *The Graduate*.

"The months roll by, and I hear that I'm going to be Colonel Cathcart. But two weeks before we're supposed to fly to Mexico I still haven't heard anything about the final deal. But everybody's so enamored of being in this movie that nobody's questioning things. I then get a call from my agent, saying, 'I've got bad news for you. Mike Nichols doesn't think you're right for the part.' I was crushed. Later that day Nichols attended a private screening of *End of the Road*. The next day my agent called back and said, 'You're in the movie.'

"The entire star-studded cast flies down to Guaymas, Mexico, travels two hours to the hotel, a remote, beautiful location. The next morning the company assembles and Mike Nichols walks us through the sets, telling each actor in great detail what he'd be doing where. We walk into Colonel Cathcart's office, and I'm excited. I want to know where he'll be sitting, and all my details. Mike says, 'We'll work that out later. Let's move on.'

"We sit down for a reading. The minute the first sentence is read, Mike begins to laugh. That was the funniest thing he'd ever heard. Every subsequent line, he laughs. Everybody wants to please the director, so the cast joins in. Everybody's laughing at everything.

"I read my first line. Absolute silence. And I start to sweat. I was beside myself with anxiety. After the reading I went to Alan Arkin, who I knew from *Heart Is a Lonely Hunter*, and I said, 'Something is very wrong.'

"He said, 'No, no. Relax. Everything's fine.'

"Two days later, I'm out looking at the bulletin board, and a voice comes up behind me: 'Can we talk to you, Stacy?' It's Mike Nichols and John Calley [one of the film's two producers]. I knew this was it. We went up to my room. They sat me down and said, 'You're simply too young for this role, and we're going to let you go. But we can't get you out of here till tomorrow.'

"I was destroyed! And Jon Voight, God bless him, heard about this right after it happened. I had never met Jon Voight till the flight to Mexico, but he came over, and he hung out with me all night, just rapping, keeping me from slitting my wrists. I don't want to be overmelodramatic about this, but Jon Voight saved my life. Even after I was back in the States, he called periodically, kept checking on me. I've never forgotten it. I'll always be indebted to him."

It's amazing, what actors can do to themselves. Surely you made that situation worse than it was.

"I look back objectively on that experience now, and I realize there was nothing personal involved. But as a young actor, you can't help but take it personally. Any time you're fired, you have to take it personally.

"I'll tell you. Most of us watch too much television, and a lot of us watch too much sports on television. But if you watch sports, you see coaches and managers getting fired every year, and by the following season they've landed in another job. I think that's very healthy for people to know. But for me, that was a rough one."

Doubtless you returned from Mexico with your confidence shattered, believing you'd never work again. How long was it till you did return to work?

"Five days after I got back to New York, I had a call from Robert Altman, who asked me to come talk to him about a movie he was going to direct. So I went and talked to him, and he was crazy as could be. I loved him, and he offered me what became the Donald Sutherland role in *M*A*S*H*. But before I was able to give him an answer, the next day the Arena Stage called and offered me Buffalo Bill in *Indians*, which had been done at the Royal Shakespeare Company. I opted for *Indians*. We were a big hit at the Arena. Then we moved on to New York.

"I will never forget the excitement of being on Broadway for the first time. As Buffalo Bill, I used to ride this mechanical horse that was actually slung over my shoulders. It had springs and a black skirt to disguise my legs. It was a magical thing. For my entrance I'd come in and run around, then rear back and throw up my hat. At the very first preview, my very first performance on Broadway, I was so nervous that, when I reared back and pulled my horse's reins, his neck snapped. I broke his neck! During the opening monologue I had to climb out of my costume, holding this dead horse in my hands."

Indians became the second big turning point in your career.

"Right. But it also became the next major disappointment of my career because, despite fairly good reviews and good business, we closed after four months."

And once again your being successful in the theater led, not to more theater, but to more movies. After *Indians* closed, you filmed *The Traveling Executioner* and *Doc*.

"In the early 1980s I made a movie with Orson Welles. He was a very easy guy to talk to, but the one ground rule he set was that he didn't want to talk about his career. Then, as he would open up, of course the stories would begin to creep in about the problems he had filming *Chimes at Midnight* and *Macbeth* and *Othello*. And I really began to relate to his career, because this man—despite all his artistic achievements—never achieved any commercial success at all. But the difference between the 1930s and the 1970s is enormous. In the '30s, if Welles wanted to stage *Macbeth* or *Dr. Faustus* or *Julius Caesar* on Broadway, it could be done. But by the time I got to Broadway, those options were gone. All you had to do was look at Dustin Hoffman and Al Pacino to realize that film was now the dominant medium. The larger your status in the business, the wider your range of choices. But to be large, you had to be large in movies. So I made *Doc*, which was a failure, and I made *The Traveling Executioner*, which was hardly a success, but John Huston saw it, loved it, and offered me the lead in *Fat City*. The script was not great, very depressing, but I was so flattered that John Huston had sought me out, there was no question about my accepting the role of this has-been boxer.

"John trusted actors tremendously. He'd say, 'You and Susan [Tyrell] go in there and work out your blocking, then I'll come in and change it all.' That's how he directed. But he always started with the actor's impulse. He liked to shoot rehearsals, which I love doing. It's a crap shoot, because an experienced actor has learned to hold his performance on the first take. You ease your way into a scene. You make sure that the camera operator and the sound men are doing their jobs properly before you feel free to let go. This is all part of learning that on a film set the actor is only one of many people involved in the creative process. Some people will tell you that the director is the most important person on the set, but the truth is that the most important person on the set is whoever happens to be most important *at that moment*. The greensman might spend days sitting on his duff. But if we suddenly need to disguise a telephone pole with a tree, until that pole gets hidden, the greensman is the most important person on the set.

"John and I would play backgammon between takes. Ray Stark, our producer—and a great producer—got very upset because we were behind schedule, so he'd come in and take the backgammon board away. Whenever this happened, John became like a child. [Keach does an uncanny imitation of Huston's drawling voice.] 'Now, Ray. Come on now, Ray. Give me back the backgammon board.'

"*Fat City* is a good film, but twenty minutes were cut. Twenty minutes longer, *Fat City* is a great film, a classic. Unfortunately, twenty minutes longer made it twenty minutes more depressing."

You must have been a little depressed yourself in January 1973 when the New York Film Critics, after already having voted you Best Actor of the Year for *Fat City*, actually changed their voting rules in mid-meeting and denied you your victory. Instead they voted the award to Laurence Olivier for *Sleuth*.

"I couldn't believe it! I was beginning to feel that I couldn't get a fair shake in this business. I get cast in a big Mike Nichols movie, and I get fired. I star in a hit Broadway play, and it closes in four months. I finally film an award-winning role, and the critics change the way they vote. All these setbacks were becoming the story of my life."

The next part of the story is *Hamlet*, because in 1972 you returned to Central Park, where you started as a spear-carrier, only now you were playing the title role.

"That production actually began earlier that year at the Long Wharf. Toward the end of the run in New Haven, Joe Papp called and said, 'I want to bring *Hamlet* into town. I want to do it in the Park.' I was thrilled. Then he said, 'But I don't want to take that production.' So I had this great dilemma, because Arvin Brown, who ran the Long Wharf, was my good friend. But Joe said, 'I'll get you the best cast that any Hamlet could hope for in America.' And he did."

It was after this production that you said, "The whole secret to being a great Hamlet is to make sure you have a great cast around you." You had James Earl Jones, Colleen Dewhurst, Sam Waterston, Barnard Hughes, Kitty Winn, Linda Hunt, Charles Durning, Tom Aldredge, Raul Julia, Christine Baranski as a courtier.

"Unbelievable. A dream come true."

What are your most vivid memories of that production?

"It was a richer, deeper *Hamlet* than at the Long Wharf, though I think lots of actors will tell you that their second Hamlet is best. But one memory from that summer has nothing to do with the play. One afternoon while we were rehearsing at the Delacorte Theater, Robert Ryan turned up, unannounced, and asked me to come over to his home on Central Park West and spend some time with him. Bob Ryan spent much of his career playing psychopaths and killers in movies like *Crossfire* and *Bad Day at Black Rock*, but off the screen he was one of the sweetest men I've ever known. The preceding year we had done *Long Day's Journey into Night* together Off-Broadway. It was during the time I was preparing to film *Fat City*. Bob had done a terrific boxing picture called *The Set-Up*, so he taught me his moves. This man was so supportive. Things were beginning to happen for me. *Fat City, The New Centurions*. But Bob knew from his own career that, regardless of how many movies I made, I wasn't going to be Clark Gable. So one day, to sort of prepare me for the future, he said, 'I've made seventy-eight pictures. Maybe ten were good. That's a high ratio of success. Don't count on any more than that.' It was good advice.

"In the fifteen months since *Long Day's Journey*, Bob's wife had died of cancer. When he showed up in Central Park, Bob was dying of cancer too, and we all knew it. He looked terrible. So I went over to his home, and we reminisced a bit. A few months later he was dead. It broke my heart. Thank God I saw him and shared that last meeting."

Hamlet opened. Clive Barnes wrote in *The New York Times* that you were "one of the great Hamlets of our time. . . . Keach must surely be the finest American classical actor since John Barrymore."

"It was a very successful production. After it opened and was so well received, I remember saying to myself, 'Well, that's it.' I had no goal beyond playing Hamlet. I had no vision for my career beyond Hamlet, because deep down in my own insecure being, I never really believed that it *would* happen. But once I did reach what I thought would be the pinnacle of an actor's career, the shocking thing was that *nothing* happened."

How can that be?

"That's what I kept asking. And I had plenty of time to ask it, because there was not one single job offer as the result of *Hamlet*. This is when I asked my agent, Sue Mengers, 'Why isn't anything happening in my career?' and she said, 'Nobody's casting *King Lear* this week. Come out of your ivory tower. Forget the classics. Get back out here to Hollywood.' She was giving me the exact same advice I'd been getting from my father, only now it was costing me 10 percent.

"And of course, true to form with my career, *Hamlet* turned into a big disappointment. It was so successful that Joe Papp decided to move it to Broadway. But he insisted on moving it intact, with no cast changes. James Earl Jones already had work for the fall, so he couldn't stay with it. On the loss of that one actor, Joe scuttled the Broadway production. I wanted to scream at him, 'It's called *Hamlet*, Joe, not *Claudius*.' But there was no talking to Joe; he was not a good listener. So that created a rift between us, and I never worked at the Public Theater again."

Eventually you did return to Los Angeles, but it wasn't for the movies. You played *Hamlet* a third time, at the Mark Taper Forum in 1974.

"Big mistake. I was very unhappy with the production, unhappy with Hollywood's disinterest in live theater, unhappy that America cared more about *Barney Miller* than *Hamlet*, unhappy that I was unable to parlay the classics as a steppingstone to freedom in my career choices. I had lots of unfulfilled expectations. Disillusionment had taken hold. It was after the Los Angeles *Hamlet*, when I felt that everything I touched turned to shit, that I began to get involved with drugs in a serious way."

After *Hamlet* you went off and did an action-adventure television series called *Caribe*, which only lasted for three months in 1975. After it was canceled, you got very defensive about your decision to have done it.

"Sure I did, because *Caribe* was a big, big step in the wrong direction. Not because it was a TV series, but because I did a bad TV series. My friends wouldn't talk to me. They thought I was selling out. And they were right. I knew what I had done. I had chosen to compromise my values. I'd gotten tired of trying to create that niche that nobody cared about. During that same period I was getting more involved in drugs, and denying that they were hurting me. 'I can handle this stuff.' Also, it was during that period, soon after the Mark Taper *Hamlet*, that I bought this little estate out here in Malibu."

Which means that you needed to earn more than two hundred dollars a week at a regional theater.

"A lot more than two hundred dollars a week."

So in essence, you're looking for stardom to open up your choices; but as your lifestyle changes, you're also limiting the choices you're able to make.

"At the time, I didn't see it that way. I assumed that for every *Caribe* there would be another Falstaff or Peer Gynt."

Yet after *Hamlet* in Los Angeles, you stayed away from the stage for four years. Finally you went down to Long Beach and starred in *Cyrano de Bergerac*. Therapeutic for you?

"Very! Very, very, very. Got me back. Spreading my wings, feeling my oats. For the first time in years, I felt passion again. Before I did the play, a friend of mine arranged for me to meet José Ferrer. I had a fabulous time talking with him about *Cyrano*. He gave me some great advice. He said, 'My dear boy, make sure you have light in the balcony scene.' He warned me that, although that scene is set at night, in order for the poetry to be really effective, you've got to be seen."

Drugs through *Cyrano*?

"Yes."

Would you stop while you were doing the play?

"No."

Now let me back up a minute. In 1971, before you made *Fat City*, and before you starred in *Hamlet* in Central Park, you and your brother, James, costarred in a television drama about the Wright Brothers. The two of you enjoyed working together, so you began to look for another story involving brothers.

"That's right. That's when we said, 'Now that we've done the Wrights, let's do the Wrongs.' So we began to look at outlaws, and decided upon Jesse and Frank James. Nine years, we worked on that project. We spent so much time developing *The Long Riders* that we ended up with three film scripts. Along the way we had the notion to cast other acting brothers as historical brothers, so the Carradines played the Youngers and the Quaids played the Millers."

Here's my question: The film was your idea. You and James spent nine years developing that Western. At what point did you two lose control of the movie?

"The day we made the deal. Once Walter Hill signed on as director, he took charge. Directors don't really want to tell somebody else's story. They want to make it their own story. I've worked with some great directors, and I've worked with some of the worst. But it wasn't till I did some directing myself that I learned the tremendous pressures the director is under. Perhaps it's because of those pressures that he needs to feel responsible. It's very difficult for most directors to give credit to others. Their egos get involved, which is so sad and unnecessary, because the truth is that a good idea doesn't care who had it.

"Nevertheless, after having spent nine years researching Frank and Jesse James, finally getting *The Long Riders* filmed was a tremendous catharsis. Once again the main disappointment on that film is that there's forty minutes of fabulous footage that'll never be seen."

In the 1980s you moved more and more into television. First you played the romantic lead in *The Blue and The Gray*. Then you were cast as Mike Hammer.

"Finally I was playing the romantic parts my father had wanted me to play all my life, the parts Clark Gable would have played. But I realized that those roles weren't so much acting as they were the projection of an attitude. Once I did them, I said to myself, 'Fine, I've done that; now where's the next Quasimodo?' "

You must have been struck by the irony that in January 1984, the night *Mickey Spillane's Mike Hammer* premiered on CBS, your competition on another channel was Laurence Olivier as King Lear.

"I think others were more struck by that irony than I was. I was simply an actor trying to earn a living. I had never set out to become the American Olivier. But what I just said about Clark Gable being typed to an image was equally true of me. The media typecasts actors, typecasts writers. Once you have success at something, God forbid you should try to do something else, because you're pinned to the mat like a dried-out butterfly. Their label of 'classical actor' became a yoke around my neck—"

Wait a minute. How can you say you didn't set out to become the American Olivier?

"It's true that the example of Olivier deeply influenced the path that I chose to tread as an actor. But after I saw him in *Richard III*, the promise I made to myself was *not* to become the best classical actor in America, as the press kept writing; the promise I made was to be *the best actor I could possibly be*. For me, classical roles were a means to that end, and I pursued them as long as I could. But an actor thrives on variety. Name me an actor other than Richard Burbage who built his career on Shakespeare and then stayed exclusively with Shakespeare. At some point, you have to acknowledge that an actor is not above meeting mortgage payments and putting bread on the table.

"Doing *Mike Hammer* allowed me to continue living in this house. Wherever I go in the world, people recognize me from *Mike Hammer*—"

I can't dispute that. I remember the night in 1989 when we had dinner in St. Louis following your performance as the King in *The King and I*. The TV series had been off the air for more than two years. Now you had your hair dyed black and slicked back in an Oriental style. But when we walked out of the restaurant at 1:15 in the morning, this dude across the street looked up and called out, "Hey, Mike Hammer."

"You cannot turn your back on the impact of that kind of recognition. But I'm not satisfied just being Mike Hammer. I still have to do *The Kentucky Cycle* and, one day soon I hope, the Scottish play, and *King Lear*. If I don't play King Lear, I won't have accomplished what I was put on this earth to do.

"I eventually met Olivier, by the way. I was in London filming *Luther*, and it was arranged that I go backstage after his performance in *Long Day's Journey into Night*.

He was very gracious. He said, 'Hello, hello.'

"I said, 'Sir Laurence, my name is Stacy Keach.' I was beside myself! He offered me a glass of champagne. We sat there and chatted for a bit, just the two of us. Then his dresser walked in, and he said, 'Oh Mildred,' or whatever her name was, 'I'd like you to meet Stanley Kreech.'

"Stanley Kreech!? I could feel the eggs running down my face, but I wasn't about to correct His Lordship. So I, from that moment on, was Stanley Kreech. I met him a couple times later, once on the set of *Jesus of Nazareth* in Morocco, and he called me Stacy. I was so relieved."

Now you're doing *Mike Hammer*. On April 4, 1984, three months after the series premiered, you were arrested at London's Heathrow Airport on a charge of importing cocaine. What were your emotions that night?

"It was an interesting combination. That first night in jail, of course there was a sense of fear. But an even stronger emotion was relief that it was over. I knew this was the end of the terrible nightmare I'd been through. The self-delusion, the hiding, the hoarding, the pretending were all over."

Are you saying that the shock of having been arrested was enough to end your cocaine addiction?

"No, though I did stop for a long period after the arrest. Then I gave into it. When that happened, I knew I was in big trouble, so I saw a doctor. He put me on some drug that only made me sick. By now it was December, and I was just days away from the sentencing."

You mean to say you were going to have to go into prison cold turkey?

"Yes, except that I didn't know I was going to prison. I'd been led to believe that I was only going to get a slap on the wrist. My attorneys told me that everything had been worked out behind closed doors. I flew to England on a Tuesday for a Friday court appearance, thinking I was going to be back home shooting *Mike Hammer* on Monday. Nothing could have been further from the truth. When the judge pronounced a sentence of nine months and I was taken straight from the courtroom to Reading Prison, I was in shock. I was in a state of denial. I couldn't accept the fact that it was happening. I remember walking into the prison and hearing radios in the cells blaring out news stories about me. The entire experience was surreal."

Were you put into a cell immediately?

"Actually, I was not. I had thrown my back out doing a stunt on *Mike Hammer*. The pain was so severe that I had to be taken to the courtroom on a stretcher in an ambulance. When I stood for my sentence, it was everything I could do to stand up."

Didn't that elicit some sympathy from the judge?

"He didn't know. I didn't allow anyone to know I was arriving in an ambulance. The judge had no knowledge of my back problems. I thought that would make me sound like a whiner. That's not my style. So when I arrived at Reading Prison, I spent the first three weeks on my back in the hospital ward.

"Nothing moves more slowly than time when you're in a prison hospital on your back. But during those three weeks, I tried to put matters into perspective. I was determined to make this a positive experience. I wanted desperately to be away from the cocaine that was controlling my life, and I knew that prison would rid me of it. As it played out, the shock and trauma of that unexpected prison sentence were so severe that I never missed the cocaine for one second, and I haven't missed it since. I've never ever had a hankering for it."

After three weeks in the infirmary, they moved you into a cell?

"I was going to be the new library trustee, so they put me into a cell with the then-librarian, who was going to teach me the paperwork and cross-referencing. He was a complete con artist, this guy. The minute he got out, he went straight to the newspapers to try to make some money with fabricated stories. But I was in the London papers every day. It was endless. They had me running a drug ring inside Reading Prison."

Here in America, we don't know much about English prisons. You couldn't have had any expectations except the worst.

"Fortunately, the worst was never there, because the turnover was very great. Reading Prison was a holding cell for a lot of cons. Although it was rated as a minimum-maximum security prison, which is at the heavy end, there was not a lot of violence inside. I didn't even see those hardened criminals, because there was no mess hall. Everybody ate in their own cells behind a steel door.

"You get a real cross-section of life in a prison. Some of the guys were totally illiterate, and I would read to them the letters that their families had written, and help them to write letters home. But there were also a lot of very intelligent inmates who were there because, like me, they had gotten involved with drugs. For those guys the library was very, very important. They would hoard books in their cells. Then it would be my responsibility to get them back. Guys would actually fight over books. They would be intensely interested in any new book we received. There were six or seven guys, real readers, who were always asking, 'Put that book aside for me, and I'll get you an orange.' We lived by the barter system. Fruit was very big, though tobacco was the most important commodity."

Once you got into the routine, was every day the same?

"Pretty much, except that they had different colors. One weekend a month you were allowed a visitor. On Sundays there was church. And I kept very active. I filled my days. And thank God the governor, Brian Hayday, a wonderful man, allowed my mail to come in. I received over seven thousand pieces of mail."

Television?

"One night a week for forty-five minutes."

Movies?

"One night a week. As librarian, I was in charge of the movies. Mostly they wanted to see action pictures, so one night I showed *The Long Riders*."

Lights out at a certain time?

"Seven o'clock. But I could go to the library every night. I had the run of the place. Not because I was Stacy Keach, but because I was a librarian trustee. That was the key to the entire experience. The governor didn't show me any favoritism, except in this respect: He put me in the library. As the librarian, I was entitled to a typewriter. That typewriter helped to keep me sane."

Did you ever get in trouble while you were there?

"The coffee incident."

Were you innocent or guilty?

"I was definitely innocent. *Definitely* innocent! The whole incident occurred because one of the screws didn't like me."

What happened?

"You have to understand: Each prisoner has a mentor guard, who he reports to. As the librarian, one of my responsibilities was to provide coffee and tea for my mentor guard, Mr. Snell. One morning I ran out of coffee. So I went from the library to the officers' mess, which was just across a long hallway, to get coffee. Mr. Snell allowed me to do this, even though it wasn't policy. While I was in the mess, this screw came in. He said [affecting a Cockney accent], 'What are you doing in here, Keach?'

"I said, 'Just getting coffee for the library, sir.'

" 'But you're not supposed to be in the officers' mess. You're on report.' "

Why didn't Mr. Snell vouch for you?

"On this particular day, he was off. The next day the guard did confront Mr. Snell, but he couldn't say he allowed prisoners to go into the officers' mess, because he was violating a rule. So I was caught in a political situation.

"When you're on report, they wake you up at five o'clock in the morning. You stand at attention in your Skivvies waiting to be called out. They take you down below to this room in the depths of the dungeon, and the governor is sitting there with two guards flanking him, and you stand in the middle of the room and express your testimony. You testify. Then you return to your room, and they deliberate for a couple of hours, and then they tell you whether or not you're on report. Eventually the governor let me off. But that incident terrified me. Only a week earlier, the same screw had nailed a kid, a young offender, for taking a bite out of a cheeseburger, and he got three months added to his sentence. This was the one occasion in prison where my being an actor helped me to hide my true emotions.

"To tell you the truth, it occurred to me that my self-assured performance at my testimony might be the last time I ever had occasion to act. By the time I left prison in June '85, having served six months of my nine-month sentence, I had fully accepted the notion that I would never work again as an actor in my entire life. I would write, I would teach. I would do whatever I had to do to live.

"What actually happened was a nice surprise. CBS treated me very well, for which I'm eternally grateful, and they put *Mike Hammer* on for another season. Then the TV mini-series *Hemingway* happened, which was probably the most important film role of my career, even though it wasn't seen by a lot of people, because it was syndicated. Meanwhile, I got a call from Congressman Charles Rangel's office asking me if I would come to Washington and testify [before the Select Committee on Narcotics Abuse and Control, chaired by Rep. Rangel, Dem., N.Y.] about what had happened to me. I said I would welcome the opportunity. Then I got a call from Nancy Reagan, who asked, 'Would you help me?' So I became very active with antidrug speaking engagements. And I went on all the talk shows and told my story. I never said that I got a bad deal. I said that I had a problem; I didn't deal with it; I got caught; I paid for it; and I'm back. The one by-product in all this was that the press finally stopped writing about me as 'America's classical actor.' Now they had a new label for me. Here it is ten years later, and they still love to talk about prison, as if that's the only thing that ever happened to me.

"But really, I started life over. Prior to prison, I was too preoccupied with my career to want children. I think I was drawn to women who also didn't want children. But once I got out of prison, I realized that my house here in Malibu was made for children. I remarried; we've adopted two beautiful kids; and now finally, after twenty years, the sound of children's voices has made this domain a true home."

One thing didn't change, and that was your love of the classics.

"If anything, that love grew. In prison I reread much of Shakespeare. Once I realized I was going to be allowed to resume acting, I knew I had a rendezvous with the role that had started me down this path, Richard III. I always said I was going to do it, and I had opportunities to do it, but I always shirked away. Richard had been burning in me for so long. So I went to the Folger Library Theater in Washington, D.C., and took him on. It was thrilling and terrifying at the same time. It was more than just playing a role; in effect, it was bringing my career full circle. I know it's the best work I've ever done on the stage. Once upon a time, I would have dwelled on the fact that we couldn't move it to Broadway or that the whole world couldn't see it. This time around, the overriding thrill was that *I did it*."

What else do you want to do that you haven't done?

"Lear, of course. But I'm past the point where I want Dustin Hoffman's career. I'm very happy with my own. I really am. For all its ups and downs, it's my career. I'm a war-torn old soldier, and I will continue to go on until I die. Maybe I've finally become my father's son, because every time a show closes or a film ends, I'm on the phone to my agent saying, 'I'm available.' There are days when I wish I was a little less available, but there are other days when nothing would drag me away from the kids. It took me a long time—too long—to realize that an actor's career need not be a choice between art and commerce; it should be a balance."

As the years elapsed, the balancing act continued. *Macbeth* in

Washington, D.C., was offset by twenty-six hours of *Mike Hammer* in syndication. Supporting parts in feature films were balanced by the national tour of J. B. Priestley's *An Inspector Calls*. But essentially, the new roles were simply more credits to tack onto the bottom of an already-lengthy résumé. Then he was invited to be part of the first American cast (with David Dukes and George Wendt) to star in the international hit comedy *Art* in London. *Art* was important, because it returned Stacy Keach to England.

"The worst thing that happened to me as the result of the drug bust," he said in early 1999, not long after his return from London, "was not being able to work in England. The first time I tried to go back was in 1988, three years after my release. I was offered the role of Magwitch in a six-hour mini-series of Dickens' *Great Expectations*. I was in Warsaw, ready to fly to London. I had my work permit. And at the last minute, the Home Office said no.

"Now, there was nothing in my conviction that specified that I would be barred from coming back to England. But there was a discretionary, unwritten law that if you were convicted of the importation of controlled substances you would not be allowed back into the country for ten years. That was not explained to me in any way, shape or form. I only found out about it by virtue of trying to get back in to work.

"Losing Magwitch crushed me. It crushed me! He's one of Dickens' most memorable characters. Then, after *Great Expectations*, time and again I tried to work in England, and my requests were always refused. Finally, eight years after I was released from prison, I learned about this ten-year ban.

"So when *Art* happened, it was like a purge, or an epiphany, to finally return. We rehearsed in the upstairs rehearsal hall at the Old Vic. Working in that historic space, you could feel the presence of the great actors who had rehearsed there through the decades. Even when you'd go to the john, you'd think to yourself, Sir John used this john.

"Then, when we opened in the West End and the press welcomed me back with open arms, it was fabulous. One night during the run, I even had a reunion backstage with Brian Hayday, the governor at Reading Prison. He's become a dear friend."

The rise, fall and reclamation are all behind him. Stacy Keach is back in the world of take-a-meeting, do-a-play, film-a-pilot. But hovering like a specter above the hubbub and the new choices to be made is an actor's unspoken, unfulfilled covenant with himself . . . and the awareness that Lear still beckons.

SIDES:
LESSONS

"Suddenly the script reads, 'Enter Jane.'
And Jane has no second name."
—JOAN PLOWRIGHT

"Uta said, 'But George, he never went through the
pain of finding out where the laughs are.' "
—GEORGE GRIZZARD

"Even if you're bad and you fail, nothing happens.
That's a great lesson for actors."
—CHRISTOPHER WALKEN

When a producer doesn't want to go to the bother or the expense of giving an auditioning actor the entire script, he provides the actor with "sides" instead. Sides are short, for they are only those specific pages that contain the auditioning actor's lines and cues.

Here then, and between the chapters to come, are some sides, some brief Polaroid-like anecdotes and theorems that have continued to resonate in my mind long after I first heard them. These first three sides include some lessons learned by actors . . . and by me too.

Because I don't observe the world through an actor's eyes, often I'm struck by the startling originality of a statement that to an actor is the result of simple observation. Consider this assertion from **Joan Plowright**, the Lady Olivier. Back in 1961, the same year she married Sir Laurence, Plowright's Tony Award-winning performance as Angela Lansbury's sensitive daughter in *A Taste of Honey* was the talk of Broadway. Although Joan Plowright was one of England's most promising young actresses, marriage promptly altered her priorities. But after Olivier died in 1989, she resumed her career at full throttle. The week before we spoke in 1993, she received an Academy Award nomination for her role in *Enchanted April*.

"I am, at the moment, in a lovely position of being offered more scripts than I have time to film," she said. "I don't know how long it will last. But for the time being, I get to choose."

What sort of scripts are you looking for? I asked.

"I'll tell you what I'm not interested in," she replied. "Some scripts arrive, and the people around me say, 'You should be in this big film, playing opposite all these wonderful men.' And when I read the script, my character is not in any way three-dimensional, nor does she have an identity or a history. You know the kind of script I mean. There are male characters with names like *Jim Parkinson* and *George Anderson*. Then suddenly the script reads, 'Enter *Jane*.' And Jane has no second name. She has no real reason to be there except that she's a girl Jim Parkinson and George Anderson know. They *do* have second names. So right now, I'm in the enviable position for an actress of being able to restrict my acting choices to characters with second names."

Since talking to Plowright, I have checked every script that's crossed my desk to see if the female characters have second names. It's astonishing to discover how many do not.

George Grizzard has starred on Broadway in plays by Arthur Miller, Tennessee Williams, Lanford Wilson and Robert Anderson, but he's most associated with Edward Albee, having won a Tony Award for his performance in *A Delicate Balance* (1996) and having created the role of Nick in the electrifying original 1962 production of *Who's Afraid of Virginia Woolf?*

"Back in '62," Grizzard recalled, "I was out in Los Angeles working. I had a week off, so I drove up to San Francisco. I stopped in Palo Alto because my good friend Alan Schneider was teaching there, and directing one of his many productions of *The Good Woman of Setzuan*, or one of those Brecht things that I always hated.

"So I stopped in, and Alan said, 'Listen, I have this play I want you to read.' And he handed me what looked like the New York City phone book. This manuscript was so thick, I couldn't believe it was a play. But it *was* a play, called *Who's Afraid of Virginia Woolf?* During rehearsals Arthur Hill kept saying, 'When do you think he's gonna cut it?'; and I kept saying, 'Arthur, I don't think he is.'

"But there in San Francisco I read it. And I thought, this is a brilliant play, and a hateful part. Nick is the kind of person that Edward Albee truly detests. So it was tough to rehearse it, and it was tough to play it. I was grateful for the opportunity to be in

Edward's first Broadway play. But it was not an acting experience that gave me any fulfillment, because every time Arthur Hill and Uta Hagen would stick another knife in me, the audience would laugh more. It was as if I was there to be destroyed. It's painful to be laughed at and hooted down, because I take everything personally. I really *am* that character when I play it.

"I was the first of the original four actors to leave the production, simply because I was already committed to play *Hamlet* in the opening season at the Guthrie Theater in Minneapolis. After I left *Virginia Woolf*, I returned to see it. Obviously, the actor who replaced me did not receive the quality-time rehearsal that the original cast enjoyed. So I don't mean this as a put-down, but I missed some of the moments that I thought had been happening onstage. After the performance I mentioned this to Uta Hagen, and she said an interesting thing. Uta said, 'But, George, he never went through the pain of finding out where the laughs are.' He *knew* where the laughs were, because he had seen it several times before he went into it.

"Uta taught me a lesson that night, but it was not a lesson I'd care to repeat."

I first met **Christopher Walken** in 1968, when he was playing Romeo in Stratford, Ontario. During the ensuing years, even as he began to find his way into such movies as *Annie Hall* and *The Deer Hunter*, for which he won an Academy Award, Walken continued to seek out demanding stage roles.

Why is it, I once asked him, that invariably after an actor fails onstage, he'll defend his work by suggesting that the part "stretched" him?

"But it's true," Walken asserted. "The role that I came away from with the most muscle was the one that I failed in: Macbeth. It's probably the most terrible role ever written, *terrible* in the literal sense of terrifying and enormous. This is a role that makes as many requirements on you as anything could. I played it at Lincoln Center for ten weeks [in 1974], eight shows a week, and I did not succeed at all. I wasn't even permitted to open by the producer. Ten weeks' work, and we never even got reviewed, except by John Simon, who sneaked in on his own and wrote something mean.

"The year after that terrible failure, I jumped at the opportunity to go out to Seattle to play *Hamlet*, which was a very different sort of experience. It's very hard, oddly enough, to really screw *Hamlet* up. The play is so fascinating by itself that even if you are bad, the audience's tendency to walk out is not nearly so much as with the other Shakespearean plays. I mean, you can be doing a bad *Timon of Athens*, and there'll be nobody left when the curtain comes down. But almost any time a viewer gets to see *Hamlet*, he's going to have some reason to be glad he came. There's so much going on. It has a lot of lighter scenes where the audience can have a good time. But *Macbeth*, you know, there are not a lot of laughs in *Macbeth*.

"As things turned out, we rehearsed *Hamlet* in such a way that I never got to perform the entire play from beginning to end during rehearsals. Even in dress rehearsal things were always going wrong, and we'd stop to fix them. So I never knew whether or not I had the *juice* to get through it, and I was quite concerned. Our first performance was a student matinee. I said to the director, 'Nobody even knows how long it's going to take,' because we'd never gotten through it in less than six hours.

"And he said, 'Well, just forge ahead.' English director. Duncan Ross. Very good. Knew a lot about the play.

"So I walked out, and I said my first line, and I kept going, and things went wrong—lights, things that we would have stopped for in rehearsal—and then it was over. I remember sitting in my dressing room after the performance saying to myself, 'If you died now, you would have played Hamlet!' Which is a more remarkable thing than you can imagine. I mean, I couldn't imagine it, and I'm an actor. It's an exhilarating experience, sort of like climbing a mountain.

"I didn't have that kind of exhilaration when I did *Macbeth*. But I never regretted doing it for a minute, because I came away from the production with this tremendous insight about myself and about acting that I could not possibly have gotten anywhere else. It was taking on that monster and being trounced by it, but still learning something. *That's* what actors mean when they talk about stretching.

"I started out in this business as a dancer. It's a perfectly analogous thing. When you step up to the bar, you stretch until it hurts. And you do it again; you do it again; you keep doing it until you get another inch there. And the next time you're dancing, you're able to kick just that much higher.

"What was going on in *Macbeth* was psychic stretching, personality stretching. A production like *Macbeth* teaches you that, even if you're bad and you fail, nothing happens. That's a great lesson for actors, because most actors are terrified of doing something wrong and falling down. And I don't mean onstage after the audience is seated and the critics come in. This applies to the first moment of rehearsal, where you either plunge in or you're tentative. Because you almost always strike the theme of your performance early on.

"But if you fail a few times, what happens? The critics give you terrible reviews, or you get booed. I was booed in *Romeo* at Stratford. So what? It's not as if somebody takes you out in the alley and beats you up. You go home; you're depressed. But nobody really hurts you. You learn that getting bad reviews is not all that serious. Next time you'll do better. Failure teaches you that you never get anywhere being careful. I don't know of a more important lesson for any actor to learn, and keep relearning."

CHAPTER TWO

EVERYBODY WANTS TO DO A MUSICAL

"Acting students get enough theory in the classroom.
I want them to know how dangerous it is."
—EDMUND LYNDECK

"Standing ovations have become one of the hazards
of being an actor these days."
—GEORGE ROSE

"Everyone told me Holly Golightly *was going to be*
the biggest musical of the decade, and I was so
naive, I believed them."
—RICHARD CHAMBERLAIN

"Theater . . . [has] become like a blood sport . . .
we use up performers."
—BARRY BOSTWICK

Everybody wants to do a musical. Even a veteran Shakespearean actor like Stacy Keach, when he's not wearing Richard III's ponderous crown, welcomes his summer stints performing musical royalty in *The King and I* and *Camelot*. And why not? In musicals the emotions are so heightened that an actor can approach the same intense feelings he experiences when playing the Bard. Indeed, in the twilight of his career, even Laurence Olivier had hoped to gambol through *Guys and Dolls* (as Nathan Detroit, to Christopher Plummer's Sky Masterson) at England's National Theatre.

So it should be no surprise that an inordinate number of the actors who inhabit these pages received early experience in musicals, or dabbled in musicals, or pursued starring roles in musicals:

• José Ferrer was in contention for two now-classic Broadway roles: the King of Siam in Rodgers and Hammerstein's *The King and I* and Fred Graham in Cole Porter's *Kiss Me, Kate*.

• At age seventy-three, Lillian Gish made her Broadway musical debut in the short-lived *Anya*. Undaunted, she sang on Broadway again in *A Musical Jubilee*, alongside such stalwarts as John Raitt and Tammy Grimes.

• Gregory Peck pursued an active quest for the title role in the film version of *Man of La Mancha*.

• Jon Voight's first Broadway credit was in *The Sound of Music*, where, as the young Nazi, Rolf, he sang "Sixteen Going on Seventeen."

• Christopher Walken began as a dancer in such Broadway musicals as *High Spirits* and *Baker Street* (which starred Fritz Weaver as Sherlock Holmes).

• Even the admittedly unmelodic Paul Winfield celebrated the joys of "Cairo, Illinois" in the movie musical *Huckleberry Finn*.

For many of us, the adage can be amended to read: Everybody wants to *see* a musical. If I have an abiding affection for musicals, it's because, as a child growing up in St. Louis, Monday nights meant going to the Municipal Opera with my grandparents. Not every Monday night—but often enough to ensure a sense of event as we entered that enchanted twelve-thousand-seat enclave in Forest Park, where the audience was cooled by roaring airplane propellers, where the mighty stage was dwarfed by towering oak trees and where, on humid nights between Memorial Day and Labor Day, the sultry skies were alilt with the melodies of Romberg and Kern and Rodgers and Hammerstein. Even the moon smiled over the festive proceedings. Or was it humming?

Our only enemy was rain. How vividly I remember, at age eight, being rained out of *Show Boat* just as William Warfield began to sing "Ol' Man River." And surely no one who attended the final performance of the Royal Ballet's *Romeo and Juliet* in August 1967 will forget the sight of Rudolf Nureyev, mop in hand, assisting the crew as they dried out the stage after a sudden shower.

But more often the evenings were perspiringly clear, and *Annie Get Your Gun* and *Can-Can*, both starring the prodigious Dolores Gray, and *West Side Story* and *Brigadoon* remain indelible memories. Not only the hits were hits. Musicals that I otherwise never would have seen, like *Wish You Were Here*, *Happy Hunting* and *Mr. President*, played well in Forest Park. And every few years *The Wizard of Oz* would return, with the beloved Margaret Hamilton frightening the children, then the grandchildren, of those children who had first been scared by her Wicked Witch on the screen.

In retrospect, it seems ordained that my first professional job would have been at the Muny. During the summer of '62, at age seventeen, I served as a gofer for the resident scenic designer. The season premiered with an extravagant musical adaptation of *Around the World in 80 Days*, complete with hot-air balloon, live elephant and a steamship that was dismantled onstage. Cyril Ritchard starred as Phileas Fogg. But the evening's most versatile performer was Edmund Lyndeck, the Muny's resident character actor, who played five roles: a French travel agent, a Hindu elephant guide, a Barbary Coast gunslinger, a London confidence man and the Maharajah of Panjipur. As if Lyndeck didn't have enough to do, he also understudied Ritchard.

During the preceding five seasons I'd seen Lyndeck in nearly fifty musicals: always different, always believable. Now that I was actually working with him, I was startled to realize he was only in his thirties. From Lyndeck I soon learned that the seemingly glamorous acting trade was not without its hazards. Physical hazards.

Many of his injuries had occurred right there on the Municipal Opera stage. He still grimaced at the memory of his 1960 appearance with (pre-*Laugh-In*) comics Dan Rowan and Dick Martin in Victor Herbert's *The Red Mill*. "Delightful men and talented comedians, those two," Lyndeck said, "but they do leave wounded actors in their wake. They were not accustomed to the theater. They didn't know the ways of it. One of them was supposed to hit me over the head with a breakaway bottle. Instead he took a real bottle and clobbered me. I blacked out.

"Later that same night I found my dressing-room mate writhing on the floor in pain. In one scene, he too was supposedly knocked out and was lying on the stage floor. Rowan and Martin were supposed to step over him. Instead, one of them accidentally stepped on the tenderest portion of his anatomy. They were dangerous to be around."

Lyndeck's next accident occurred the following summer in *Calamity Jane*: "I walked offstage into the dark wings and stepped on a nail sticking out of a board. I bled a lot, so I was taken to the hospital. Fortunately, my character was out of the show for about an hour, so I made it back in time for the next scene."

The nail puncture had barely healed when Lyndeck found himself cast as the villain in another sagebrush musical, *Destry Rides Again*. During the climactic scene, as Lyndeck held the townspeople at bay in the Last Chance Saloon, he grabbed a shot glass and furiously slammed it onto the bar. "The glass went right into my hand, which began to bleed profusely," he said. "Anne Jeffreys made her entrance and almost went into shock when she saw this bloody mass, but I had to finish the show." As soon as he did, he was rushed to the hospital again. "Now, if I'm asked to talk to a class of young actors at a university, I try to tell them about the real world of the theater. Acting students get enough theory in the classroom. I want them to know how dangerous it is, and how careful you have to be."

In 1969 Lyndeck was cast in the original Broadway production of *1776*: "Most of us thought that a musical about the signing of the Declaration of Independence, especially one with seventeen character actors, only two women and no dancers, would last a week at most. Instead it turned out to be one of those theater miracles and ran for three and a half years"—during which, Lyndeck played six different roles, ranging from the second-youngest (Thomas Jefferson of Virginia) to the second-oldest (Stephen Hopkins of Rhode Island).

"There are very real dividends to being in a hit," he said. "I'll always remember the night we performed for President Nixon. *1776* was the first musical ever presented at the White House in its entirety. When the invitation arrived, our producer, Stuart Ostrow, said he would not accept it if even one member of the cast objected. You have to remember that *1776* was running on Broadway at the height of the Vietnam War. The company included actors of wildly varying political convictions. Howard da Silva, for example, who played Benjamin Franklin, had been blacklisted in Hollywood for refusing to answer questions put to him by the House Un-American Activities Committee regarding his alleged Communist sympathies. I thought we might have as much trouble getting a unanimous White House vote as did the original signers of the Declaration. Amazingly enough, everybody voted yes. I'll never forget how charmingly da Silva spoke with President Nixon after the performance. But the next morning he was out in front of the White House, picketing for peace."

As the venal Judge Turpin in the 1979 Hal Prince-Stephen Sondheim musical *Sweeney Todd, The Demon Barber of Fleet Street*, Lyndeck's throat was slashed nightly by Len Cariou. "They actually had to add hazard pay to the salaries of those of us who slid down the barber chair into Mrs. Lovett's basement," he said. "I sustained a few injuries during that nightly ride, though fewer than I had expected."

No, the greatest hurt associated with *Sweeney Todd* was not physical. "The Judge sang a song called 'Johanna,'" Lyndeck recalled. "It was a very, very difficult number, and we worked hard on it during rehearsals. I sang it for the first three previews. But the musical was running long, and something had to go. By that point in my career I'd had some directing experience. I was able to look at the production objectively and ask myself, 'What would I cut?' My unhappy answer was that I would cut 'Johanna.' So when Hal escorted me to the rear of the theater to gently break the news, though it still hurt, I was already prepared."

Into the Woods, Stephen Sondheim and James Lapine's foray into the dark world of fairy tales, was cause for another injury. "When Phylicia Rashad succeeded Bernadette Peters as the Witch," Lyndeck said, "I was playing the Narrator. There comes a moment in Act Two when the fairy-tale characters must make a sacrifice to appease the avenging Giant. Rather than surrender one of their own, the Witch offers up the Narrator. Phylicia had only been in the show for about a week when, at the Saturday matinee, she hurled me offstage with such force that I smashed into the theater wall and got a concussion. Here, I've been in the theater all my life, and it's still a risky business."

Thirty years after our first meeting, I asked the first actor I ever knew, What do you say now when you speak to young actors?

"I tell them to work," Edmund Lyndeck replied. "Work *wherever*, but *work*. I recall an incident several years ago when I was acting at a theater Telly Savalas owned in Connecticut. An actress and I were perusing the Broadway audition notices in the trade papers, and she bemoaned, 'What are we doing up here, when we could be down in New York auditioning?'

"And here we were, working! It's true that there are always actors who want to reach for the golden ring, who set out to be stars.

But that was never as important to me as the sheer act of working, and plying my craft. Especially now that Broadway is phasing down, and there aren't as many available jobs, it seems more important than ever to go where the work is. If you do, you'll be amazed where it might take you."

Do you still warn young actors about the profession's inherent hazards?

"Yes, with this addendum: I remind them to keep their insurance premiums paid up."

Hard to believe now, in an era when most stars won't stay with a Broadway show for more than six months, but there was once a time when stars signed run-of-the-play contracts and then spent another season on tour.

That's how a young boy living in St. Louis, more than a thousand miles from Times Square, could see such Broadway performances as Geraldine Page and Darren McGavin in *The Rainmaker*, Cyril Ritchard in *Visit to a Small Planet*, the crafty Sam Levene in *Seidman and Son*. Best of all were the musicals: Ethel Merman in *Gypsy* and the inimitable Tammy Grimes as *The Unsinkable Molly Brown*. To this day, nobody else breathes like Tammy Grimes; nobody phrases like Tammy Grimes. She was a revelation.

And time and again there was the felicitous opportunity to see George Rose, that consummate craftsman whose very presence in a play ensured stylish precision. Rose passed through St. Louis in *A Man for All Seasons*, *Canterbury Tales* and *Coco*. I also happened upon him in Detroit with *My Fat Friend*, and I saw him on Broadway as the Gravedigger in Richard Burton's *Hamlet* and in his Tony Award-winning romp as Alfred P. Doolittle in *My Fair Lady*. (That same season, Burton took over the male lead in *Equus*. In her memoir, *The Bright Lights*, Marian Seldes describes the night when an inebriated Burton insisted that George Rose was the greater of the two actors "and should be playing star parts." Rose protested "that he was indeed a character actor and played just what he expected to." But Burton's appreciation was well placed, and Rose's star roles would come.)

The following year, in 1977, he returned to St. Louis to make his Municipal Opera debut with Len Cariou in *Kismet*. I knew both men and was pleased to serve as unofficial host and occasional chauffeur during their two-week stay. On the evening after the first day's rehearsal, Rose and I supped at his hotel dining room. He was feeling slightly guilty, for, having been cast on short notice (he was a last-minute replacement for TV star Hans Conried; Cariou was a re-placement for TV star William Conrad), Rose had not had time to memorize his lines in advance. "Back in 1952," he explained, "I ap-peared with Noel Coward in a revival of George Bernard Shaw's *The Apple Cart* in honor of Queen Elizabeth's coronation. That produc-tion was a time of absolute cloudless joy. Sir Noel was the most im-peccably professional person that you could wish to meet. He ar-rived at the first rehearsal word-perfect, which made all of us so ashamed of ourselves that we rushed home and learned the entire play in one night. We could have opened in ten days. That experi-ence proved to me that one could and should come to the first re-hearsal word-perfect. And I didn't come to the first rehearsal of *Kis-met* word-perfect, and I'm rather ashamed of myself because I've bro-ken my own rule."

He stopped slicing his pepper steak long enough to revel, just for an instant, in the past. "But to play with Noel Coward at the Theatre Royal, Haymarket—that puts a stamp on you. You are then a West End actor. You're all right."

After dinner Rose was anxious to return to his suite, not to be-gin memorizing his role, but rather because he had discovered a leak in his bedroom closet. "Hazards of the road," he said dismissively. I was happy to keep him company until the hotel plumber arrived.

"Listen!" he suddenly barked out. Try as I might, I couldn't hear the closet drip.

"No, not that," he chided. "The chambermaid has turned on the telly." He dashed into the bedroom to silence the intrusive voices, calling back over his shoulder, "In the sixteen years I've lived in America, I've never owned one, and I'll be astounded if I ever do."

Your career has not been unsullied when it comes to television, I challenged. Just last year, more people saw you on CBS during your two-month stint as Mr. Hacker, the butler on *Beacon Hill*, than in your forty years on the stage.

Rolling his eyes in compliant dismay, Rose sank into the sofa, where he was set upon by his two rambunctious schipperke dogs.

What are your most vivid memories of *Beacon Hill*? I asked.

"*Vivid* is not the word that springs immediately to mind, I'm afraid. *Frustrating* and *depressing* would be more accurate adjectives. The original pilot I thought was good. It had an overall consistency of style that was first-rate. But television just deals in formulas; and if you step outside the formula, you're asking for trouble. The CBS formula was action in the first ten seconds or viewers will switch off and we will lose a customer for cupcakes. We were told by our producer, 'The American public is not interested in character development,' which means that you're not interested in human beings. So you must have the cliché. If you only have one goal, which is that your program must reach the largest possible audience instead of being the best possible quality, then you're up the creek from the start. No wonder we were canceled after two months. American television is totally abject; it's totally servile; it's the worst television outside of Portugal."

Even as Rose delivered his tirade, he spoke with the keen, controlled authority of an exceedingly proper British gentleman. In fact, his roots were anything but. He was born in a small farming village in south-central England in 1920, the only child of the town butcher. "I was a failure at school," Rose said, "because I was not permitted to participate in the activities that really meant something to me. I loved music. Instead I was forced to study things I couldn't understand, like algebra. All mathematics were totally beyond me."

So he quit school and eventually moved to London, where he entered a music academy to study piano. One day a notice on the bulletin board sought offstage singers for a production of *Peer Gynt* at the Old Vic. Rose applied and was accepted. Then, though he feared the odds were stacked against him, he remained at the Old Vic to try his hand onstage. To his astonishment, he developed into an accomplished Shakespearean clown.

"I came from a background which I thought was totally remote from any possibility of being an actor," Rose explained, "but it turned out to be absolutely full of possibilities because, in actual beliefs and quality of life, my remote area of Oxfordshire had probably not changed very much in the three centuries since Shakespeare's time. The things that Shakespeare writes about in his country people are very, very real to me."

And yet, I suggested, you are no longer parochial in any way.

"But you see," he clarified, "a man from the country, a farmer, a man who is dependent on the earth, is not parochial, because he deals with things that are universal. I think the city man is far more likely to be parochial, because he's divorced from those things that are universal."

Over the years Rose broadened his base beyond Shakespeare and became a versatile character actor. "What I didn't realize when I became an actor," he said, "was that, due to the First World War, practically an entire generation had been wiped out. So all the young actors of my age group were forced to learn how to play character parts much older than ourselves, simply because those actors were not there anymore."

During the 1950s Rose was much in demand, playing support to the likes of Olivier, Gielgud, Redgrave, Coward and the Lunts. In 1961 his life turned inside out when he went to New York to repeat his role (eight roles, actually) as the Common Man in *A Man for All Seasons*, Robert Bolt's historical drama about Sir Thomas More.

"I didn't think the play would run in America," Rose confessed. "I remember quite distinctly saying, 'Broadway audiences won't like this; I'm only going for the trip.' I thought five thousand people would come three times, and it would last three months." Instead, *A Man for All Seasons* was a hit. After 647 performances in New York, Rose continued with the play on tour. He withdrew only after John Gielgud cast him as the Gravedigger in Richard Burton's *Hamlet*. Because Burton's torrid romance with Elizabeth Taylor was still sizzling, the production was the object of massive scrutiny. Dick and Liz married during the play's tryout in Toronto.

"Elizabeth loved being around that production," Rose said. "The theater was a world that she'd never been part of. For this little girl who'd grown up amidst all the razzmatazz and nonsense of Hollywood fan clubs and fan magazines to suddenly see a group of actors going through highly detailed work day in, day out—I don't think she'd ever been exposed to that. It was a world in which she saw that very few extraneous things mattered, that the actors came and rehearsed the play, and that all the show-business whoopsie which consumes celebrity simply wasn't there. I think she was fascinated. She was also extremely generous. Both she and Richard couldn't have been nicer to the company.

"There's something very honest about Elizabeth, and I think it comes through in a lot of her work. For instance, in one of her best performances, in a terribly underrated movie called *Reflections in a Golden Eye*, there's a great earthiness about her, a great kind of unpretentious, uncomplicated, forceful woman. And there is something of that in Elizabeth."

With two consecutive hits under his belt, Rose chose to remain in the colonies. He specialized in American productions of British plays, such as the witty and perceptive *My Fat Friend* by Charles Laurence, in which he costarred with Lynn Redgrave and John Lithgow as an acid-tongued homosexual.

"It was one of the best-cast plays I've ever been in," Rose said. "We just missed hitting the bull's-eye on Broadway, which was a pity, because the production was superbly well done. It worked like one of the most beautiful Fabergé toys."

Then why was it, I asked, that when I saw the play in Detroit I seemed to be the only person in the audience who was laughing?

Rose rolled his eyes again, then embarked upon another tirade: "*My Fat Friend* is an absolutely moral play in every sense. But members of the Detroit audience were so shocked at seeing a homosexual character on the stage that they could no longer grapple with the play. They felt that they were being affronted personally."

You actually felt hostility from the audience?

"Tremendous hostility. One of the critics told me that he got phone calls berating him for having given the play a good notice. Those are very dull people. And if you have jokes about French cooking and Glenda Jackson and Edith Piaf, and they don't know who Glenda Jackson and Edith Piaf are . . ." His voice trailed off, as if in defeat. Then, with a renewed burst of energy he charged, "You are restricted to three jokes with that audience: booze, adultery and money. Outside that range, don't bother. Certainly don't try to make jokes about Madame Bovary. *My Fat Friend* is a very, very funny play. But it does assume a certain know-how in an audience."

Canterbury Tales fell prey to the same pitfall. Despite the fact that Rose's antics stopped the show nightly, and despite the fact that the musical had been a huge hit in London, it only eked out a brief Broadway run. "Great disappointment," Rose said. "Again, a show that was unable to find an audience, because you can't do a musical about Chaucer if the audience doesn't know who Chaucer is. *Canterbury Tales* is a highly sophisticated show. But if you can't appreciate that vulgar kind of Rabelaisian, medieval humor, you're not going to laugh. It's the 'booze, adultery and money' syndrome. Yet my experience has taught me that the more sophisticated people are, the more they enjoy low humor."

Why is that?

"I think it's because, as [G. K.] Chesterton said, nonsense and vulgarity are a God-given holiday from the intellect. But if you have no intellect, then you've nothing to take a holiday from, have you?"

Coco, the 1969 Alan Jay Lerner-André Previn musical about French designer Coco Chanel, was a more accessible venture. There, Rose's chief function was to support Katharine Hepburn. "Not a very difficult job," he said, "because she's an extraordinarily good actress. That same role in a straight play would have been pedestrian. But musicals are a highly technical form. So when the role is part of an ensemble that includes thirty of the most beautiful girls on Broadway, Cecil Beaton clothes, two revolving stages and a thirty-piece orchestra, not to mention a charming solo number in the second act, then it becomes very much worth doing.

"We played a season in New York. Then when we toured, we encountered some of those same dull subscription audiences. They would sit in absolute silence through a musical comedy, and then at the end of the evening give you a standing ovation. In fact, standing ovations have become one of the hazards of being an actor these days. An audience that doesn't know how to join in, but wants to show how much they've liked you, will stand up at the end of the show. But the actors will have had a wretched evening because the audience didn't know whether to laugh, how to laugh, if they *should* laugh.

"And it's all because of *that!*" He hurled an accusing finger at the television set across the room. "To my mind, the invention of television has had a universal and devastating effect on theater audiences, in that it requires very little attention. Television just buzzes, squawks and flickers away in a corner. In many homes it's become a kind of Muzak; the majority of people hardly notice it. Then when those same people get to the theater, they're burdened by an inability to concentrate on a text.

"But you see, to me, theater is essentially a listening experience. To watch actors is essentially listening. Drama is still very much a branch of literature. But if people cannot concentrate on the spoken word, we're in deep trouble.

"When I was young, all the music halls in London were still open. Right up into the 1950s, you could still see vaudeville. So audiences were used to collaborating with real people. They knew the rules of the game. After all, it's called a *play*, isn't it? It's a game one plays on an audience. But an audience that doesn't know its part makes for a highly unsatisfactory evening. Believe me: There is no acting without an audience. People forget when they go to the theater that they also have a job as an audience. And to not know that job, to not know the enjoyment of playing that role, is to me very sad."

A week later *Kismet* opened on one of the most sweltering nights of the summer. Unfazed by the ninety-degree temperature, George Rose's impious Wazir transformed the villain into a delightfully craven coward who trembled with fright at every sudden noise. It was pure W. C. Fields. Then, an hour into Act One, the musical was abruptly halted. An ominous voice blasting through boom boxes admonished us to vacate the theater. We soon learned that a bomb threat had been phoned in. A half hour later, as policemen combed through the Muny in search of the nonexistent bomb, I happened upon an unperturbed Rose walking his dogs across the street from the theater in Forest Park. He shrugged off the intrusion as a trifling nuisance: "Hazards of the road, dear boy. Hazards of the road. Come back tomorrow night."

In ensuing years, Rose would continue to excel in musicals. He was Captain Hook to Sandy Duncan's Peter Pan and Major-General Stanley in *The Pirates of Penzance*. After a triumphant engagement at the Delacorte Theater in Central Park, *Pirates* moved to Broadway for a two-year run. Perhaps opening night at the Uris Theater was a mere formality. Yet Rose did an amazing thing. Halfway through his big number, "I am the very model of a modern Major-General," he halted the song, announced to the audience that he was having trouble with his new false teeth and requested that the orchestra begin again from the top. *That* was confidence.

At dinner with the actor well into the *Pirates* run (he would, of course, remain for the duration), I mentioned that *A New Leaf*, written and directed by Elaine May, in which Rose costarred as Walter Matthau's haughty butler, had recently aired on television. "I loved working with Elaine May," he enthused. "I'm sure she thought I was going to be rigid and stuffy, and I turned out to be malleable and willing to improvise, which she liked. But I'm not by nature an improviser. I find that actors improvising are usually a pain in the ass. For instance, I thought *Annie Hall* was a disaster. I know everyone loved it, but for me all that improvising between Woody Allen and Diane Keaton was like watching two drunks at a party who didn't know when to shut up. If you want to see an exemplary example of a clean, economical comedy performance, in which not a syllable is wasted, watch Barbara Stanwyck in *The Lady Eve*.

"At any rate, I did improvise in *A New Leaf*, but I don't want to improvise in the theater, because it merely exposes the improviser. I have learned through the years that if people have anything to say, they don't improvise. They write it down. It's the improvisers who usually have nothing to say, and it comes over very clearly. Do not believe that the spontaneous is necessarily the real. This is a highly unsophisticated attitude towards life."

And the opposite of improvisation is . . . ?

"Technique, of course. Stravinsky said that in the last resort the only way to judge an artist was by his technique. The other things could vary. But when you see a technique at work, you know that that could only have been produced by an artist. There's no such thing as a first-rate artist without technique.

"I'm a great believer in technique, but I fear this attitude is no longer in vogue. I recently did a seminar for New York University, and I was horrified by the questions I was asked: 'How much of the character do you take home with you?'

"I thought to myself, but don't you realize that the character is contained in the words of the writer? Where else would the character exist? It doesn't exist outside the pages of the text. Then Al Pacino tells *The New York Times* that when he played Richard III he limped in real life. This, to me, is *total* amateurism. It makes me very angry. It is the things to which one pays attention outside oneself that develop you as an artist. Yet today there is an appalling and profane heresy that, if you refer back to your own neuroses, if you refer back to your own pathology, you automatically become a superior artist. *Nothing* could be further from the truth."

Two years later, in 1983, George Rose teamed again with Len Cariou, this time in the Alan Jay Lerner-Charles Strouse musical, *Dance a Little Closer*, which closed on opening night. Two seasons after that, Rose was back in full throttle, cavorting through *The Mystery of Edwin Drood* (later shortened to *Drood!*), for which he received his second Tony Award. During a *Drood!* hiatus I bumped into him at a testimonial luncheon for José Ferrer. We met for dinner two nights later.

"*Dance a Little Closer* had much to recommend it," he said. "But then, I tend to be very protective about my failures. I think only twice in my career have I been in shows that I didn't think were good enough for me. So if I choose to be in a play, you can bet your life it's worthwhile your coming to see it. Otherwise I'm not going to be in it, for the simple reason that I couldn't face doing it eight times a week."

It's not as if you have to worry about working, I suggested. You could act fifty-three weeks a year if you so chose.

"Don't kid yourself," Rose scoffed. "I still remember back in 1972 when I was in Simon Gray's *Wise Child* with Donald Pleasance and Bud Cort. It was a brilliant, brilliant morality play, complex and wonderful, but requiring just a little bit too much imagination on the part of the critics. They seemed to think it was a play personally directed against them. The critics decided to hit the play hard, and it closed after four performances. I didn't work for a year after that. If I believe in long runs, it's because I've been in this business long enough to have learned that you never know where your next job is coming from. So I'm in no hurry to give up the ones I have."

Is that why you're still with *Drood!*?

"It's fun! I even improvise! Plus, I dearly love to tour." He paused; then, with the hushed authority of one who had crossed it numerous times, he intoned, "The size of America! That's why these periodic discussions about establishing a national theater are so foolish. People forget: This is not a country; it's a continent."

A moment later he reverted to his assured self: "Sure, for the foreseeable future I'll stay with *Drood!* Next summer we play the Muny Opera in St. Louis. I'm looking forward to that. Then when we're not touring, I have time to visit my new home in the Dominican Republic. It's a charming villa. You must come for a vacation."

I never saw Rose again. Eleven months after our dinner, the sixty-eight-year-old actor was bludgeoned to death in the Dominican Republic. There's no explaining these things; such senseless brutality defies understanding. Suffice it to say that, when George Rose died, a style of theater that so many of us cherish lost a touch of velvet-lined spleen, a touch of crisp joy.

There are all kinds of deaths in the theater. Deaths of actors; the demolition of historic buildings. But no demise is as traumatic, as mourned, and sometimes as gleefully anticipated, as the death of a new musical.

Why do they fail? Collaboration is a mystery without a formula. Which is why every time an actor is cast in a new show, that period between the day he's hired and the onset of rehearsals is a charmed reverie in which he is allowed to wallow in the fantasy of impending glory. But once the rehearsals begin, and the egos take over, the odds for success begin to diminish daily. Unless you're there, as part of the process, you really don't know what's going awry.

Consider:

In March 1962 *All American*, a big, splashy musical with direction by Joshua Logan, music and lyrics by Charles Strouse and Lee Adams (fresh from *Bye Bye Birdie*), book by Mel Brooks (yes, *that* Mel Brooks, seven years before he won the Academy Award for his screenplay to *The Producers*), and starring Ray Bolger, opened at the Winter Garden Theater—and closed ten weeks later.

According to Gerald Bordman, in his valuable encyclopedia *American Musical Theater: A Chronicle*, "In Ray Bolger they had a beguiling dancer and comedian. But the book by Mel Brooks . . . was inept and ultimately dragged the rest of the evening down with it."

Not so, says Anita Gillette, who starred as the ingenue (and whose string of bad luck went on to include *Mr. President* [thirty-three weeks, when it was expected to run a decade], *Kelly* [one performance] and *Jimmy* [eighty-four performances]). "Mel Brooks' original book was *funny!*" she asserted. "However, during the out-of-town tryouts we had to change the whole show around to suit Ray Bolger, and the entire production got all screwed up. Mel didn't have the clout in those days. He fought as much as he could, but he was overridden, just as Josh Logan was overridden. Ray Bolger had all the muscle. It was a great loss, because this was the only Broadway musical Mel ever wrote, and it was wonderful. But it was three feet off the ground, and Ray Bolger was very much planted on the ground. Of all my flops, I was sorriest about *All American*."

So . . . who are you gonna believe?

It's when musicals don't die far away on the road, when (like *Dance a Little Closer*) they never leave New York at all and simply preview or, worse, limp battle scarred back into town and then expire, *that's* when musicals become the stuff of legend.

Surely the mother of all Broadway musical failures was the 1966 adaptation of Truman Capote's novella *Breakfast at Tiffany's*, which had opened in Philadelphia as *Holly Golightly*. With direction and book by Abe Burrows (*Guys and Dolls, Can-Can, How to Succeed in Business Without Really Trying*), music and lyrics by Bob Merrill (*Carnival!, Take Me Along*), and television stars Mary Tyler Moore (fresh from *The Dick Van Dyke Show*) and Richard Chamberlain (*Dr. Kildare*) in the leading roles, it seemed can't-miss.

It missed.

When the musical was deemed mediocre in Philadelphia and Boston, producer David Merrick commissioned Edward Albee to rewrite Burrows' script. The revised production, retitled *Breakfast at Tiffany's*, opened at the Majestic Theater and was abruptly shuttered after four previews.

Although the two stars returned to the comforting embrace of television, nineteen years later Richard Chamberlain still paled as he recalled that painful Broadway initiation. "When I signed for the show, everyone told me *Holly Golightly* was going to be the biggest musical of the decade," he said, "and I was so naive, I believed them. After our first couple of weeks out of town, everybody knew we were in trouble. The old pros knew; the dancers knew. But I didn't know. I thought it was going to be terrific. The audiences in Philadelphia and Boston were very polite. So I had this illusion that we were liked, which we were, to a mild degree. But Merrick and Abe Burrows knew it wouldn't get good reviews from the New York critics.

"Then when Edward Albee came in and rewrote it, he did some interesting things, though he didn't do anything very interesting for my character. But still, I was rooting for the show. It was the same show, as far as I was concerned.

"So when we started previewing in New York and the audiences really hated us, I'd never experienced anything like that. I mean, I'd had this golden career up till then. Everybody loved me the minute I walked into *Dr. Kildare*." He embroidered his innocence with a sweet laugh. "I thought that's the way the world was."

Explain to me how it feels when you're onstage and you know the audience dislikes what you're doing.

"Imagine that you were the child of a large, loving family. And you walked in one day and they all said, 'You little shit, you're so boring and ugly, get out of here!' That's what it felt like."

Is it true there were previews when the audience talked back to you?

"Every preview! The degree of hostility from the New York audiences was absolutely shattering. I've never seen it in a theater in my whole life, ever. Not as an audience, not as a performer, not as anything. I have never seen people yell at actors onstage. I later realized that part of the reason was because Edward had darkened the musical so much, and audiences weren't ready for that in the 1960s. They were barely ready for it in the '70s when Sondheim started doing it. So they didn't despise us as performers so much as they despised the darkness, the heaviness, the nonentertaining quality of what Edward had written. He actually stated that his job was not to entertain the audience."

But Edward Albee wasn't onstage; you were. The audience was out after you.

"That's how it felt. I was terribly hurt by those four performances. Mary, who was doing wonderful work, used to go off and cry in the wings between her scenes, it was so horrible. It was desperately depressing. Then when Merrick suddenly closed the show, I felt as if I'd lost somebody from my own family. I was green enough to have gotten very attached to the musical. After it closed, Merrick took those ugly ads and gave those interviews. Oh, he'd done the public this great service by closing the show before it opened, as if he had no responsibility whatsoever. I thought he was a real pig about it all."

After the musical closed, where did you go to lick your wounds?

"I stayed in New York. You get over it. Actors in New York are much more mature about failure than actors in Hollywood. Theater people look out for their own. I ran into Ruth Gordon on the street one day, and she said, 'Darling, it happens to all of us.' I had a reaffirming letter from Cyril Ritchard, whose apartment I was renting at the time, saying it's lucky you've experienced this now, because this is part of the business. Angela Lansbury gave me a big hug someplace unexpected. These people were wonderful to me. Their sensitivity was very healing."

In time you returned to television and became known as the king of the mini-series. Weren't you injured on the set of *The Thorn Birds*?

"I broke my hand. In retrospect, it was a foolish accident. I was angry with myself.

Jean Simmons was one of the stars. I admire her so much, and I thought her work was so beautiful in that production, and underappreciated, in the sense that she was not playing a showy part. It took a great deal of inner depth to play the role as she did. Consequently, she received less attention than Barbara Stanwyck, who had a much flashier part. But I thought Jean Simmons was absolutely brilliant, and I wanted to be good with her.

"We had a very important scene to play, and it was a low-energy day for me. One has these ups and downs whether one likes it or not. And I couldn't get it right, and I was furious with myself, and I finally hit this camera seat—and broke my hand! I've since learned, even when I'm down, to focus what energy I have and get myself going. But I can say without hesitation that the pain I felt from my broken hand was nothing compared to the hurt that resulted from *Breakfast at Tiffany's*."

We're picking up a pattern here. Even Edmund Lyndeck would acknowledge that the loss of a solo hurts more than a nail in the foot.

During the Off-Broadway run of *Colette*, Barry Bostwick was accidentally stabbed in the leg by Zoe Caldwell. He also broke his elbow after a precipitous onstage plunge in *The Robber Bridegroom*. But when asked about the pitfalls of his profession, he brushed aside those physical wounds and replied, "Most of the hazard that you encounter in the theater is emotional hazard."

When Bostwick was growing up in San Mateo, California, just south of San Francisco (like so many young thespians of his generation, he made his acting debut in a high school production of *Our Hearts Were Young and Gay*), friends and admirers told the lanky, six-foot-four-inch actor that he resembled young Jimmy Stewart. It seemed like a good starting point. What's more, Bostwick could sing.

After college graduation, in 1967 he moved cross-country to New York, arriving in Manhattan just as *Hair* was ushering in the rock-musical revolution. During the next couple of years he appeared in many a *Hair* clone:

• In 1969 he and the equally unknown Bette Midler were both replacements in the Off-Broadway musical *Salvation*.

• In 1970 *The House of Leather*, a rock musical set in a New Orleans brothel before, during and after the Civil War, closed in one performance.

• In 1971 *Soon*, a rock opera, closed after three performances.

But in 1972 Bostwick struck paydirt with *Grease*, a rambunctious paean to the 1950s. *Grease* was cast with a dozen high-octane actors, but Bostwick's turbo-charged Danny Zuko dominated the evening. After a sellout run Off-Broadway, *Grease* moved uptown.

(Twelve years later, on a London film set, Richard Burton and I discovered that we had both attended Saturday matinees of *Grease* in June 1972, during the precarious early weeks of its Broadway run. "The theater wasn't half filled," Burton said, "but I will never forget Barry Bostwick's performance. It was sustained by the kind of galvanizing energy one all too rarely witnesses in the theater.")

Although *Grease* propelled Bostwick to Broadway stardom, he eventually discovered he didn't want to continue in musicals.

"I'm not all that eager to do them anymore," he explained; "and the reason is very simple: Musicals use up performers.

"When I was in *Grease*, they only gave us seven days' vacation a year. At the end of the first season, I finally got my first vacation. I was involved with one of the actresses, so we flew down to Puerto Vallarta. I remember getting into the hotel room and being stunned when I saw my reflection in the mirror. I was like a cadaver. I was hollow. It took six of those seven days to restore myself to a point where I could recognize myself. And on the seventh day it was time to fly back to New York to do *Grease* for almost another year."

Now, an asterisk . . .

On December 1, 1973, while *Grease* was rockin' and rollin' at the Royale Theater, another Broadway musical (*Rachael Lily Rosenbloom*, but don't try to remember the title) was aborted after eight previews. The show's choreographer, Tony Stevens, and his assistant, Michon Peacock, frustrated at having been buffeted about by insensitive directors on this and other musicals, conceived the idea of an all-dancers company. With choreographer-director Michael Bennett as their benefactor, the first step was to invite selected dancers to a marathon workshop where they could discuss their lives and careers. Only after Bennett optioned the rights to the evening's audiotapes for one dollar each (and then dropped Stevens and Peacock from his scheme) did it emerge that he planned to use the tapes as the genesis for a new musical about dancers. The world would come to know that new musical as *A Chorus Line*.

During two workshops, Michael Bennett relentlessly shaped his musical from this mass of raw material. For the second and final four-week workshop prior to opening at the Public Theater, he selected Bostwick (who by now had left *Grease* and had completed filming on *The Rocky Horror Picture Show*) for the male lead. As Zack, Bostwick would portray the role based on Bennett himself, that of a director-choreographer who is holding auditions.

"Since I was going to be playing the director," Bostwick said, "the deal I struck with Michael was that I would get to sit in at meetings with his creative team and observe them putting the show together. And it did play out that way for a while. But pretty soon Michael became nervous with me looking at him all the time. He felt I was passing judgment on him. I don't think I was. I was only observing, but even that upset him. I was also asking a lot of questions, which is part of my nature. In retrospect, I think I was inadvertently asking him to explore a side of his personality that he was not comfortable with. I had no idea how offputting that kind of questioning and observing can be. But after three weeks I was shut out, probably because he felt I was learning too much, getting too close. He wanted to keep me as a figure off in the distance."

Distance is the operative word, because that's how Michael Bennett wanted to see his alter ego in *A Chorus Line*—as a distant character.

"There were some rehearsals," Bostwick continued, "in which I was genuinely moved by what was happening onstage, and I would go with that feeling. Then Michael would say, 'No, you can't get involved. Stay distant.' He didn't want to use what my essence is as a human being. Instead he kept trying to turn me into him. At the same time, I was trying to turn him into me. In 1975 I was still looking for approval as an actor. I wanted *some* element of sympathy in the characters I played. And Michael Bennett had that sympathy. I spent enough time with him to see it. But onstage he chose only to show the dark side. Much of our conflict was based on the fact that I was trying to find something soft in him, something accessible, and he kept shutting the doors, saying, 'I'm *not* going to deal with that'; 'I *don't* want to talk about that'; 'That's not a side of my personality I want to show.' What Michael was asking me to do was to give up a long period of my life to just be this shadow." A literal shadow, a mere voice, for Zack soon became a godhead figure, sitting in the rear of the auditorium through much of the performance, addressing the dancers through a microphone.

"I didn't know Zack was going to end up in the audience," Bostwick said, "because nobody knew. These things all evolved during the workshop. They kept talking to me about Zack's song, which was going to come after the character who got hurt [Paul] left the stage. Finally one day Michael took me aside and said, 'He's not going to have a song; it's just not right.' "

Were you upset to lose your big number?

"Not really, because I never had it. It was never written. I have to be fair here: Michael hadn't promised me anything in terms of where the show was going to end up, because he didn't know where the show was going to end up. I had joined the project on trust. Nevertheless, at that point I knew I didn't want to be in a musical where I was in the audience most of the time. Zack had evolved into a character who expressed himself dancing, which is the element of musical performance with which I am least comfortable. After me, they never cast another actor in the role; they cast dancers who could act a little bit."

So by the time the workshop was ending, you knew you didn't want to continue?

"Michael and I both came to the decision at the same time. It was like breaking up with a woman, where you go to say goodbye, and she says it first. I was going to sit him down and tell him, and before I could . . ."

Did you ever regret your decision?

"No, simply because that role would not have allowed me to do what I did best at that point in my life, which was to entertain. Have you ever been to a rodeo and seen them put a strap around the belly of a bucking horse before he's ridden into the ring? Once the horse throws the rider, a clown comes along and releases that strap, and the burr is removed from the horse's belly. Zack wasn't the clown, and he wasn't the rider. Zack was the burr in the side of the horse. I can be a burr in a TV movie that's going to film for X number of weeks, and then you move on. But if you're in a Broadway hit, you live with that show. I knew how consuming it was, because I had just done *Grease* for almost two years."

Came the day when you went to see *A Chorus Line*. Be objective now: What did you think of the finished product?

"I'm not taking away from the uniqueness and the brilliance of that musical, because it's there. It was based on an inspired idea. But in my objective opinion, it was better at the workshop. They threw out a lot of good stuff. When I saw the finished product, so many wonderful moments were gone, and I realized they had overworked the damn show. They were too self-indulgent with their own creation."

Meanwhile, as *A Chorus Line* began to carve out its niche in theater history, a smaller, less ambitious creation was taking shape. *The Robber Bridegroom*, Eudora Welty's novella set in the Mississippi Territory in the 1790s, had been adapted into a musical. *The Robber Bridegroom* also found its form in a workshop, with Raul Julia as gentleman robber Jamie Lockhart. John Houseman, founder of the new Acting Company, saw it, liked it and toured it across America with Kevin Kline and Patti LuPone, newcomers both, in the leads. In October 1975 Houseman even slipped *The Robber Bridegroom* into New York City. Its two-week engagement at the uptown Harkness Theater was successful enough to stimulate a Broadway production the following season—but not with Kevin Kline in the title role. He was not yet "box office." So Barry Bostwick was signed.

"I welcomed that opportunity," he said. "*The Robber Bridegroom* had the same ensemble feeling that *Grease* had. Everyone involved was about the same age, which creates a cushion of safety. It doesn't happen very often. I would suspect that people in *Hair* and *Godspell* shared that same feeling. In 1976 I was still enthusiastic about musicals. I still needed to prove myself by pulling out as many stops as I could. During rehearsals I added as many elements to Jamie as I could, like playing the banjo and the fiddle. I also tried to add things that made the role more physically dangerous. I started swinging on a rope."

And it was the rope that led to your accident?

"Right. It occurred at the gypsy runthrough before our first preview. It was that one performance to which they invited every actor in New York City. Everything was going great. The audience was loving it. I flew across the stage on the rope a couple times. Then, about ten minutes before the end of the show, I got halfway through my swing and the rope snapped, and I was hurled twelve feet down to the stage. I landed on another actor, Trip Plymale, and hurt his shoulder. Thank God he was there, because I might have killed myself if I hadn't glanced off of him.

"We had a raked stage, with two steps in back, and I fell out of sight behind the steps. When I went down, there was that strange confusion in the audience when people don't know if what they've just seen is part of the show. At the same time, onstage there was that horrible moment when reality intrudes upon fantasy and the other actors were asking themselves, 'What do we do now?' Nobody could do anything, because I had the next line—and I was out cold. We couldn't bring the curtain down, because we didn't have a curtain. So the stage manager went onstage, said there'd been an accident, and asked the audience to leave. The paramedics arrived, and I remember being put on a stretcher and taken up the aisle and out the front door of the Biltmore Theater in my full costume with all these audience members still milling around.

"They got me to the hospital, and the only serious damage was a broken wrist and elbow. The doctors wanted to set my arm and wrist in a cast, and I said, 'No, you've got to do something else. I can't continue in this show if I'm in a cast.' So we found the guy who did this sort of work for the New York Jets, and he constructed a lightweight, removable splint that we could cover with a sling.

"Almost overnight I was compelled to reconceive my entire character. The first thing I had to do was to eliminate every physical activity. I couldn't play the guitar; I couldn't play the fiddle; I couldn't play the mandolin. All the flashy stuff I had added, and that I thought was really making a difference, had to go. So I was very saddened by that, thinking, there goes my performance, I can't impress the audience with my uniqueness. But what really happened is that the injury forced me to simplify everything. Had I not had the accident, I would have given a much more superficial, 'look-at-me' performance that probably wouldn't have had half the effect of the final version. Even after my wrist healed, I never reinstated any of that stuff.

"Of course, I didn't realize this at the time. When I finally got back into the show for the last three previews, I was in a lot of pain. Some of it was physical. But there was also emotional pain, in part due to losing 'my performance' but also because the producers had refused to delay the previews. For the first few previews, my understudy was out there. If I wanted the part, I had to hustle. I felt like an athlete who had just been drugged and now was being thrown back out on the playing field. I think that happens in theater. It's become like a blood sport in some ways. As I say, we use up performers."

Though the show ran for the better part of a season, no recording label wanted to produce the original cast album. Bostwick refused to accept that. He produced the album himself and arranged for its release through CBS Records.

Why did you do that?

"Because I thought it was a special show that needed to be remembered. You can't remember a shadow. Other than *Grease*, up till then I had been in so many musicals that had closed in one or two nights, that I refused to allow someone else's lack of energy to prevent this from happening."

The Robber Bridegroom ran for 145 performances. Two months after it closed, Bostwick won the Tony Award as Best Actor in a Musical.

Now a sense of geometry enters the dynamic. During the run of *The Robber Bridegroom*, Bostwick obliged producer-director Hal Prince by reading the supporting role of an egomaniacal film star, Bruce Granit, at a backer's audition for Prince's new musical, *On the Twentieth Century*. But when, after the needed millions were raised, Prince asked Bostwick to play that same role on Broadway, the actor declined. The part was too small for an above-the-title Tony Award winner. Instead Bostwick went off to Hollywood and charmingly sang and danced his way through the Dick Powell role in Stanley Donen's *Movie Movie*. So who was cast as Bruce Granit? The unknown, not-box-office former robber bridegroom, Kevin Kline, whose inventive performance in *On the Twentieth Century* catapulted him to stardom and earned him a Tony Award. Two years later Kline returned to Broadway as the Pirate King in *The Pirates of Penzance*. Who played the Pirate King in the national tour? Predictably, Barry Bostwick.

In the 1980s he turned away from theater and worked primarily in television. There were lots of mini-series (Spider in *Scruples*, John

Gilbert in *Moviola*, the title role in *George Washington*, a Golden Globe-winning performance in *War and Remembrance*) and made-for-television movies. The problem with made-for-television movies is that even the best of them are fast forgotten. Not that they don't offer actors unusual dividends. During the filming of *Red Flag*, in which Bostwick portrayed a jet pilot, he got to know the film's technical adviser, sound barrier-breaking General Chuck Yeager.

"Chuck was always there with his hands in his pockets, observing," Bostwick recalled. "He was in life very much as he was later portrayed by Sam Shepard in the movie *The Right Stuff*. He was a man who always seemed to have more knowledge than everybody around him but didn't care to share it. It didn't need to be shared. He was a man who instilled confidence."

When Bostwick flew in a supersonic F-4, "I got sick every thirty seconds. Back on the ground, Yeager said to me, 'Flying a jet is just like making love to a woman.'

" 'It *is* great,' I told him, 'if you like getting ill after sex.' "

Nick & Nora, in which he starred as *Thin Man* private detective Nick Charles, was Bostwick's first Broadway musical in fifteen years. Although he was cast in the spring of 1990, production was delayed that summer after he caught malaria in Indonesia. By November the original producers had pulled out, and the musical was canceled. Two weeks later *Nick & Nora* found new producers, but it was postponed a season.

Nick & Nora previewed—and previewed—for two tedious months. When I saw the fifth preview in October 1991, I was astonished: The realized production was essentially the same script I'd read more than a year earlier. During all those months of valuable delay, Arthur Laurents had done no appreciable work on his book. *Nick & Nora* finally opened in December to ineluctably fatal notices and closed at the end of the week.

"The day the reviews appeared," Bostwick said, "not a single person in New York phoned me. I felt like a leper, or as if there had been a death in the family. But actually, those final performances after the reviews came out, and after Arthur Laurents left town, were entertaining. Audiences really liked it. And you came to realize that what had been so distracting and debilitating was that during the two months of previews, while we were performing the show at night, we were also restructuring it by day. That's two months of going out onstage and saying lines and singing songs that were intrinsically wrong for the piece. During the course of that, it was impossible not to become disappointed and angry.

"*Grease* and *The Robber Bridegroom* were both small shows that became big shows because of a gradual, evolutionary, step-by-step process that allowed them to find themselves without the pressures of an arbitrary deadline. *Nick & Nora* was my first big, made-for-Broadway musical. For me, the only constructive thing that came out of it was the demand to ask myself if I really need this sort of stress in my life anymore. Every performer loves the idea of starring in a Broadway musical. But to be onstage in that world is a risky business. There is a constant clash of egos, of people trying to control other people. It is edgy and dangerous, which is why people go to live theater. As a member of the audience, we think there's always the chance that something can go wrong. The theater is like the circus. Without the ego, you don't have the nerve. And without the nerve, you can't perform.

"This is why I don't run to musicals anymore. I've lost *that* kind of ego. I don't have that need to control others, because I have control over my own world, the world of my home, my family, my dogs, my pottery. I'm quite satisfied playing the mayor of New York City on *Spin City*, working normal hours, and being home at night with my kids. I still have the need to act, but the needs are more internalized. In 1997 I had a serious bout with prostate cancer. When I found out about it, we didn't waste any time. We went right in and cut it out, and now everything's fine. But after a life-threatening experience like that, I'm more concerned with my need to explore the human spirit than with wanting to get out onstage and see who can tap dance better than the next guy."

But isn't the very concept of *to act* a means of getting outside yourself?

"Not in musicals. Musicals are about promoting the most glib, the most flashy, the most entertaining part of yourself. When you go see Barbra Streisand in *Funny Girl*, that's not Fanny Brice up on that stage. You're seeing a performer who is out there swimming in her ego. When people get to be my age and still do musicals, at least part of the reason is because they feel they still have to prove themselves. I feel that need too, but not to the point of exhausting myself onstage.

"Part of the actor's journey is the evolution through many levels of self-discovery. When we're young, we set up images of these phenomena in our lives, the Clark Gables and the Jimmy Stewarts. We think we're going to become the next Jimmy Stewart. Eventually we appreciate that Clark Gable and Jimmy Stewart *are* phenomena. They're against all the rules of nature, and we will never become them. Once you make that discovery, you begin a new journey, which is to become the most honest, most spontaneous, least-judging Barry Bostwick that I can be. If that turns into superstardom, then that's just a quirk of nature. But it is no longer a goal."

SIDES:
11/22/63

"The decision was made—and I agreed with it—
that life does go on. The time to gird your loins and
accelerate is during a tragedy."
—HARVE PRESNELL

"In the audience the sobs grew so loud, it was like
an enormous wake."
—WILLIAM BIFF McGUIRE

"The play opened on a dark scrim, and as the lights
began to come up, all you heard was Naomi's voice
singing 'He's gone away.'"
—JOYCE VAN PATTEN

Every generation knows a crucible, a defining moment that transcends joy, or even grief, and reminds men and women, strangers and comrades, enemies and friends, that we are more alike than we are different. In time, that moment passes, and pettiness is restored to its place of prominence. But for those who were there, mere mention of the event elicits a hush as they recall personal responses that are forever seared into memory.

• For my grandparents' generation, such an event occurred on May 21, 1927, when Charles Lindbergh landed *The Spirit of St. Louis* in Paris and shrank the world.

• For my parents' generation, the collision with destiny occurred on "December 7, 1941, a date which will live in infamy," when the Japanese attacked Pearl Harbor and propelled the United States into World War II.

• My generation's day of infamy was November 22, 1963, when President John Kennedy was assassinated in Dallas. Even now, more than three decades later, so vivid are the images of that weekend that it's bewildering to comprehend that I have friends who weren't yet born on 11/22/63.

Here are three reminiscences of that numbing November Friday—from Hollywood, Broadway and a point in between.

The Unsinkable Molly Brown, starring Tammy Grimes and **Harve Presnell**, opened at the Winter Garden Theater on November 2, 1960, during the final week of the presidential election campaign between John Kennedy and Richard Nixon.

"That was an exciting time in America," Presnell recalled, "and especially so for me. *Molly Brown* was my first Broadway musical, and it had all the earmarks of being a hit. While we were trying out in Philadelphia, Kennedy came through town campaigning. We were staying at the same hotel, and I met him. *Molly Brown* went on into New York and opened. Five days later JFK was elected president by the narrowest of margins.

"Now jump ahead three years to November 22, 1963. I was filming *The Unsinkable Molly Brown* on Lot 3 at MGM with Debbie Reynolds. Again, an exciting time, because it was my first movie. While we were in the midst of filming the restaurant scene where Molly puts a lamp shade on her head and acts foolish for European royalty, someone came onto the stage bearing the awful news that the president had been shot. We all took a moment of silence, and then the decision was made—and I agreed with it—that life *does* go on. The time to gird your loins and accelerate is during a tragedy. Rather than sit back and drown in doldrums over this horrid event, which had already passed and was now history, we chose to accelerate. So we went on with the scene. I can assure you that the assassination was heartfelt by every person on that set, but I also can look at the movie today and not even detect a bump in that scene."

William Biff McGuire starred in the first play I ever saw on Broadway. In August 1963 he was Bob McKellaway, the befuddled publisher, in Jean Kerr's hit comedy, *Mary, Mary*. Three months later, in November '63, McGuire and his wife, Jeannie Carson, were starring as Arthur and Guenevere in a national tour of *Camelot*.

While *The Unsinkable Molly Brown* was the last Broadway musical to open before John Kennedy's election, Lerner and Loewe's *Camelot* was the first Broadway musical to open after his election. Audiences immediately seized upon the felicitous coincidence and linked the sumptuous tale of King Arthur and the beautiful Guenevere with the vigorous young president and his stylish first lady.

"On Friday morning, November 22, we arrived in South Bend, Indiana," McGuire recalled thirty-four years later, the same week he received a Tony Award nomination for his performance in Horton Foote's Pulitzer Prize-winning drama *The Young Man from Atlanta*. "We checked into our hotel, had a bite to eat, and then, as was our regular habit, Jean and I went out looking for antiques. We were in the process of buying a Chinese horse and rider when the music on the radio in the antique shop was interrupted by an announcement that the president had been shot. By the time we got back to the hotel, the news was very bad, and his life had ended.

"Then the question became whether or not to do the performance that night. I thought, and Jean did too, that the best thing was to go ahead and do the play. We felt that it might help everyone on both sides of the curtain to unload their grief and to cope with this feeling of loss. So that night we went to the theater. We didn't know how many people would show up, but the house was jam-packed. It was an evening that had such subtext to it in everything that Arthur and Guenevere said. Then came the final scene, where the young boy appears out of the shadows and tells Arthur that he's run away to join in the fighting. But because Camelot is now in shambles, Arthur instead advises him to go home and tell the world about Camelot. Then Arthur reprises the title song, which begins,

> *Each evening from December to December*
> *Before you drift to sleep upon your cot,*
> *Think back on all the tales that you remember*
> *Of Camelot.*

"When that song started, you could hear sobbing in the auditorium that grew and grew. As the actor playing King Arthur, having to hold in my emotion and get through those final lyrics,

> *Don't let it be forgot*
> *That once there was a spot*
> *For one brief shining moment that was known*
> *As Camelot . . .*

it was almost impossible to hold back my tears. In the audience the sobs grew so loud, it was like an enormous wake.

"At the very end of the play, the lad goes off, and I yell, 'Run, boy!' As the curtain came slowly down, there was no sound except sobbing. Then there was applause, grateful applause. Then more silence. It was one of the most extraordinary nights I've ever spent on any stage, because *in the play* we were reenacting the mythology of King Arthur; but *in this performance*, we were a part of living history, a microcosm for America, with an audience that believed that King Arthur had just been shot in Dallas."

In June 1993 **Joyce Van Patten** sat in a tranquil church cemetery in tiny Walker's Mill, Pennsylvania, just east of Pittsburgh, on the set of *Breathing Lessons*, a Hallmark Hall of Fame television film starring James Garner and Joanne Woodward.

"I'm a cemetery person," Van Patten said. "They're very soothing."

I reminded her that *Spoon River Anthology* was set in a cemetery, but she didn't need reminding, for *Spoon River* was an affectionate, if all too brief, talisman in her career. Born and raised on Long Island, Van Patten has been acting on Broadway since she was a child, in such plays as *Tomorrow the World*, *The Desk Set* and *A Hole in the Head*. But *Spoon River Anthology* had come into town the long way 'round.

"That production came from the imagination of Charles Aidman," she said. "*Spoon River Anthology* is a collection of short poems by Edgar Lee Masters. They convey the fears and hopes and disappointments of these dead people who are now off buried in the cemetery on the hill and mostly forgotten. Charles had grown up loving this book. So he got me, Betty Garrett and Robert Elston doing the poems as acting exercises. We did them in class at Theatre West in Los Angeles. Then he added original songs by Naomi Hirschhorn, and suddenly we had a first act. Then Lamont Johnson saw it and said that if we could come up with another act, he'd mount a production at the UCLA Theatre Group. And we did, and he did, and then Joe Cates brought us to Broadway. The whole project was loving hands at home; and before you knew it, we were a big hit at the Booth Theater. We had wonderful audiences who came back three and four times.

"In November we had to move to the Belasco, which was too big a theater for our play. Then later that same week, on Friday President Kennedy was shot. All the shows on Broadway were closed that night. But the next day the Saturday matinee was astounding. Jules Fisher had done the lighting, which was extraordinary. The play opened on a dark scrim, and as the lights began to come up, all you heard was Naomi's voice singing 'He's gone away.'

"We four actors were still offstage. The shock of hearing those three words—the same words that we'd heard every night for months, but we'd never heard them like this—the impact was overwhelming. Then we went out onstage and started the play, and the audience laughed so hysterically that they were almost uncontrollable. They laughed at things that weren't funny. They laughed in the wrong places. It took us a while to realize that the production was serving as a catharsis for all of us.

"After the assassination, people were too distracted to go to the theater. We eked out our run until January, and then we closed. Everything changed that Friday. The world was never really the same again."

CHAPTER THREE

———

ATTICUS

———

"I like actors. I think they're good, fine, intelligent,
openhearted, generous souls, every last one of them. . .
. It's courageous to try to become someone else."
—GREGORY PECK

The first time I laid eyes on him—not thirty feet tall on a movie screen, but the real thing, life-size, in the flesh—was in 1981, in northwest Arkansas, on the set of *The Blue and The Gray*. Filming on the ambitious mini-series was well underway. The First Battle of Bull Run, the Siege of Vicksburg and the Wilderness campaign had all been waged; John Brown had been tried and hanged. Yet on this gloomy October morning, as we stood huddled together in the bone-chilling mist of the Ozark Mountains, there was a renewed sense of event.

Gregory Peck was about to arrive.

"He's coming."

"There's the car."

"He's here!"

The hushed announcements were relayed through the set, with each transmitter—assistant director to director, director to producer, producer to executive producer—a study in calm, as if it would be unprofessional to betray a sense of excitement. But why not be excited? Weren't we all in the business of making movies? And hadn't

———

we all grown up paying admission to see *his* movies? Enduring movies, many of them, like *To Kill a Mockingbird, Roman Holiday* and *The Guns of Navarone*, that had passed the test of time to enter the fabric and fiber of our cinema-sated society. In an industry that operates from enthusiasm, why not be enthusiastic about the arrival of a film icon?

As the aptly named Lincoln Continental (Lincoln-Mercury was one of the show's sponsors) conveying Abraham Lincoln crunched to a stop on the gravel road that led to our remote location, the constant cacophony that attends every film set abated. For just a moment, the grips stopped gripping and the best boys stopped besting. In that standstill hush, ever so slowly, Gregory Peck, clad in full makeup as America's sixteenth president, emerged from the right rear seat.

He had to know that everyone was staring at him; there had never been a time since he became a movie star in 1944 that people hadn't stared. But what he could not know was what each individual was thinking. Stardom, I would later learn as we traveled America together, is created by the alchemy of an accumulation of intensely personal moments, and no two fans' accumulations are precisely the same.

Even as I watched him extricate himself from that Lincoln ten feet away, in an instant I remembered, as a boy in St. Louis, being taken by my grandmother to see him crash through a stained-glass window in *The World in His Arms*. (How else could he save Ann Blyth from a forced marriage?) In another instant, I was scuffing through fallen leaves as I walked from junior high school to see *The Big Country* the October afternoon it opened—a rarity, for I never went to movies on school days, but for some young, irrational reason, I needed to be the first to see *The Big Country*. In a third instant, I recalled the tense, electrifying silence in the cavernous Fox Theater after Bob Ewell spit in Atticus Finch's face in *To Kill a Mockingbird*—and the audience held its collective breath as we waited to see how Atticus would respond.

All this in an unexpected rush during those few seconds it took Gregory Peck to exit a black sedan and enter our lives. While at the same time, a hundred others—grips and greensmen and wranglers and costars—surely were reliving their own equally vivid memories.

Abraham Lincoln appeared in only six scenes in the eight-hour mini-series, but Peck immersed himself in the role. The next day I stood in a farmer's field and listened to him recite the Gettysburg Address over and over and over. With each repetition those familiar words assumed a new freshness and immediacy, and I began to hear them as if for the first time. (Ten years later I wrote a television movie about Lincoln at Gettysburg, which aired on ABC; the seed to write *The Perfect Tribute* was planted while listening to Gregory Peck.)

Today a mini-series will be rushed to broadcast mere weeks after it has been filmed. But in 1981 *The Blue and The Gray* was CBS's entry into the long-form sweepstakes back in those post-*Roots* days when mini-series still were deemed "event programming." We were given eleven months to publicize our product. I spent those months observing Gregory Peck.

For starters, he was one of the most articulate people I'd ever met. His effortless command of language dazzled me. He rarely reached for a thought, never stumbled over a phrase, yet his words were always wise and probing. I began to keep a notepad by the telephone. When he called, I wanted to capture his comments accurately so that I could record them in my daily journal.

I learned that he was a perfectionist, an attribute that caused seemingly needless *Angst* whenever he saw a moment in the film he thought he could have done better.

But here was my biggest surprise: I discovered that (when he wasn't berating himself) he could be very, very funny. Humor is not a part of his screen image. But in person, he is a natural wit.

After the mini-series aired in 1982, to my immense satisfaction, Peck elected to continue our association. Not aggressively, though we'd get together every couple of years. And he was assiduous about returning phone calls.

Then in February 1994 (by which time I had moved to Los Angeles), he invited me over for Irish tea and Moravian ginger cookies. "They come from North Carolina," he boasted, as proud as if he'd baked this batch himself. "We discovered them through Ava Gardner, who was from North Carolina." Of Peck's numerous beauteous costars, Ava, I would learn, was the woman of whom he was fondest—which probably means, with whom he could laugh the heartiest. As his steady hand poured the tea, the cuff of his Irish cardigan sweater brushed a spoon onto the carpet. When Peck leaned over to pick it up, one of the late afternoon's dying sunbeams passed through the large living room window and glanced across the thick white hairs of his temple. For a fleeting moment, the still-imposing profile took my breath away. The years had been kind to him.

Now he revealed the reason for our meeting. Although his film career was pretty much played out, he had no intention of wasting away behind the iron gates of his three-acre estate. He was considering a return to the stage in *A Conversation with Gregory Peck*, an informal program of anecdotes followed by an exchange of questions and answers with the audience. Would I, he asked, assist him in assembling a reel of film clips to open the evening?

You bet I would.

So began the year of my own private conversations with Gregory Peck.

Peck envisioned a clip reel that would show "variety and surprising juxtapositions." The more I perused his fifty-six movies, the more variety I found. From the bashful Captain Horatio Hornblower to the possessed Captain Ahab, from psalm-writing King David to evil-incarnate Dr. Josef Mengele, I detected how throughout his career Peck had consciously sought to avoid portraying the same persona ad infinitum. Spencer Tracy, when accused of having done precisely that, is said to have replied, "Who should I play? James Cagney?" But Peck's weary Jimmy Ringo in *The Gunfighter* is a far cry from his rapscallion Lewt McCanless in *Duel in the Sun*. His martinet General Frank Armstrong in *Twelve O'Clock High* bears no resemblance to his egoistic General Douglas MacArthur. And, despite his image as one of Hollywood's heartthrobs, I came to realize that many of his most satisfying films—*The Keys of the Kingdom, The Yearling, Twelve O'Clock High, The Gunfighter, Moby Dick, Pork Chop Hill, The Guns of Navarone, To Kill a Mockingbird, MacArthur, The Boys from Brazil*—have no romance at all.

Another discovery: Gregory Peck never allowed himself to get too far ahead of his audience. In 1947, for instance, he starred as a big-game hunter in *The Macomber Affair*. Although it is still regarded as one of the most faithful adaptations of an Ernest Hemingway story ever filmed, it didn't register at the box office. So five years later Peck returned to Hemingway and big-game hunting in *The Snows of Kilimanjaro*, which wasn't nearly so true to the novel, but was one of the year's most popular movies. Another example: *Pork Chop Hill* (1959), an account of one of the final battles of the Korean War, was as uncommercial as it was uncompromising. Yet Peck's next war film, the undemanding *The Guns of Navarone*, was the highest-grossing movie of 1961.

"I suppose there's a certain truth to what you say," the actor acknowledged when I shared my observation. "*Pork Chop Hill* is very nearly a documentary depiction of combat. We didn't make too many concessions to what you might call *entertainment*. We told it very straight, with integrity and without sentimentality. No talk about

Mom's apple pie. No girlfriends. Just men doing a terrible, bloody job. And in the end, it's totally futile. The heroism, bravery, courage under terrible firepower, all wasted. That's a picture I feel good about. Even if it wasn't a box-office bonanza, I don't think I'd change anything in it. *Navarone*, on the other hand, is a steeplechase, a hazard course. We didn't think for a moment we were making a serious war picture."

But when our clip reel was finally assembled, it was the more successful *Guns of Navarone*—not the more serious *Pork Chop Hill*—that we included. Film stars, after all, are the creations of their public. Ask a playwright which is his favorite work, and inevitably he'll choose the play that flopped on Broadway. Ask a movie star which is his favorite picture; just as inevitably, he'll choose his biggest hit.

Another movie that didn't make our final cut was the landmark *Gentleman's Agreement* (1947), with Peck as a crusading journalist who pretends to be Jewish in order to expose anti-Semitism. Because it was his only film to win the Academy Award as Best Picture, I had assumed we would feature it. But when I showed Peck what I thought to be a powerful scene in which his secretary, played by June Havoc, discovers that her boss is not Jewish, the actor vetoed the clip—and the picture.

"Look at my performance," he complained. "It's too serious, too earnest, too humorless. The truth is, I was a bit of an in-and-outer when I first came to Hollywood. I did some good work early on, and I did some work that was not so good. Maybe in some ways I've always been an in-and-outer. But especially in those early years, working with Hitchcock, working with Elia Kazan in *Gentleman's Agreement*, I was somehow unsure of myself and a bit ill at ease." Returning his attention to the confrontation with June Havoc, he posed, "Just imagine how Spencer Tracy would have played that scene." He then engaged in an imaginary conversation with himself: " 'Do you want a retake?' '*Yes!*' "

Peck may have been ill at ease with Hitchcock and Kazan, but in *Twelve O'Clock High* (1949) he found an ideal partner in veteran director Henry King. Our clip reel featured a lengthy excerpt from *The Gunfighter*, the second of their six collaborations, and Peck's favorite of his eleven Westerns. "Everything works in that picture," he said. "It's wound as tightly as a Swiss watch."

I'm not as familiar with Henry King as I am with some of your other directors, I had to admit.

"He wasn't a genre director like Hitchcock," Peck said. "He was a director who would take on whatever the studio assigned him. He directed everything from *State Fair* with Will Rogers to *The Song of Bernadette* with Jennifer [Jones]. From the minute I met him, I loved Henry King, and I loved seeing the world through his eyes. We were somewhere between father and son, big brother and little brother. We never seemed to run out of things to talk about, though that doesn't mean we needed to talk a lot on the set. With Henry it really was a matter of directing by osmosis. Somehow we both wanted the scene to come out in the same way, and it wasn't necessary to do a lot of talking about it. I trusted him completely."

When I suggested that *Beloved Infidel* was the least of their six joint efforts, Peck did not disagree, but he didn't blame Henry King. Rather, he attributed the film's failure to its source material, Sheilah Graham's memoir about her love affair with F. Scott Fitzgerald. "Fitzgerald's life story was charged with drama," Peck defended. "But the Graham book was banal: Can a girl from the slums of East London rise to the heights of being a Hollywood gossip columnist?

"Sure, if two men make six films together, the odds are they're not all going to be hits. But sometimes even in the movies that don't work, there's a moment you can point to. Henry and I made a Western which I was not altogether fond of called *The Bravados*. It was a story where I was pursuing four desperadoes who had raped and killed my wife. I killed three of them in revenge. Then at the end of the film, I discover that I had killed the wrong guys. I think my realization of the enormity of what I had done, three or four minutes on the screen, was as good work as I've ever achieved. The picture wasn't very successful, and it's certainly not seen today. But an actor does have little ornaments hanging on the tree here and there, work that he's proud of that maybe no one really noticed."

Other films you don't *want* anyone to notice. In addition to assembling the clip reel, I helped Peck compile a video library of his movies. The most difficult picture to locate was the deservedly obscure 1971 Western *Shoot Out*. After I finally found it, and watched it, Peck, with a twinkle in his eye, asked what I thought of it.

It has to be the worst movie you ever made.

He laughed at my lack of diplomacy, then laughed again as he recalled how the film's director, Henry Hathaway, strove to duplicate his success with *True Grit*, even to the point of trying to persuade Peck to walk the same way John Wayne had walked as Rooster Cogburn.

"No," Peck disagreed, "my worst movie was *Only the Valiant*."

Only the Valiant. What a dog! It was one of only two pictures (*Beloved Infidel* was the other) that Peck was compelled to make against his will. He was pressed into that 1951 cavalry-versus-Indians cheapie when producer David O. Selznick, in need of fast cash, sold his remaining commitment on Peck's contract to Warner Bros. Once we took to the road, a frequent audience query was, "Did you ever make a movie you wished you hadn't?" Peck usually tried to sidestep the question. But the few times when he did mention *Only the Valiant*, he nigh apologized, "I shouldn't have done it, and I'm sorry that I did it." Always, though, Peck shouldered the blame himself; he never explained that he was forced into making the picture.

No one ever asked about *Shoot Out*, nor were there many questions about *The Gunfighter*. If audience curiosity is an accurate gauge, then Peck's most popular Western is *The Big Country*.

"*The Big Country* came about because Willy Wyler and I wanted to work together again after our happy collaboration on *Roman Holiday*," Peck told me as we viewed the scene where he is thrown off the bucking bronco time and time again. (Some of those shots on Old Thunder are really Peck.) "This time the collaboration turned out to be not so happy. I think the real problem with the picture, aside from the fact that it's too long, was that we didn't have a good enough ending. We should have persisted longer and excavated the material deeper and come up with a more satisfying ending."

Is it true that Wyler would repeatedly shoot the same scene without offering any direction?

"Oh, yes. I remember the day we filmed the scene where Charlie Bickford welcomes me to his ranch. Willy, without uttering a word of direction all day, had Bickford redo the scene over and over and over, until finally Charlie exploded, 'What the blankety-blank do you want!?'

"Wyler stared him down and said, 'I want it better.'

"And Bickford stomped off the set and locked himself in his Winnebago. Wyler sat by the camera, waiting. Every now and then he'd send the first assistant director over to rap on Charlie's door. Finally the first AD came back and said, 'Charlie's in there drinking a bottle of Jack Daniel's.'

"So Wyler said, 'Well tell him we don't have the scene yet, and if he doesn't come back soon, I'll call the Screen Actors Guild and say that he's in violation of his contract.'

"Eventually Charlie came back, red faced, surly and sweating, and proceeded to deliver the exact same line readings as he'd been giving before. Wyler did a few more takes, just to prove that he was in charge, then called it a day."

Didn't you also have a falling-out with Wyler? I asked gingerly, already knowing the answer. But Peck only chuckled at the unfortunate incident.

"Yes, over a close-up, of all things. Stupid of me. I wanted to reshoot it. When Willy refused, I too walked off the set, the only time I ever did that in my entire career; only I went much further than my Winnebago. I got into my car and drove from the Mojave Desert back to Los Angeles. After that, Willy and I didn't talk for a couple years. Then we wiped that disagreement off the slate and became as good friends as we ever were. But at least we didn't fall out over the way he worked. I loved the way Willy worked. I would do 194 takes if I thought we could get one extra subtlety, one moment better than we had done it before. Repetition never bothered me.

"I know that some people can't work that way. When we were in London doing interiors for *The Guns of Navarone* at Shepperton Studios, I went over to another sound stage to visit Cary Grant, who was making *The Grass Is Greener*. He was filming a scene with Bob Mitchum and Deborah Kerr. The camera was turning, and I watched Cary, just before he made his entrance, scan down the page and learn his lines for the first time. He put the script down, walked through the door, and it was an absolute perfect Cary Grant performance.

"Well, that's one way to do it, and you can't find fault with Cary Grant. There's been no one like him. But I have to work a little harder, dig a little deeper. I have to learn the whole script before the first day of filming. I have to immerse myself in it. Sometimes I'll sit down with a yellow legal pad and write my lines over and over and over, and try to live through them as I write."

(In 1997 I witnessed Peck do precisely that as he prepared to play Father Mapple in the television remake of *Moby Dick*. Although Peck worked on the film for only one day, he spent weeks immersing himself in the part. He completely rewrote his role, which was a six-minute sermon about Jonah and the whale. While retaining some of the original script, Peck painstakingly studied both Herman Melville's novel and the Book of Jonah, then incorporated key elements of both into his sermon. It was a laborious act of immersion, but the payoff came when Peck's day of filming went off without a hitch.

(Eighteen months later, he won a Golden Globe Award for his performance. When he accepted the award and told the star-studded assemblage of his peers, "I only worked one day," I knew better.)

"But the process of acting is not something I'm comfortable talking about," he continued back in '94, as we watched him take yet another tumble off of Old Thunder. "My approach to acting is parallel to that of Spencer Tracy. He once shared a house out at Malibu with Ruth Gordon and Gar Kanin, who had written one of those comedies he was filming at the time with Katharine Hepburn. They told me they would hear Spencer in his room until four or five o'clock in the morning, running his lines over and over and over again. Then two or three hours later, he'd walk onto the film set and blithely ask, 'Well, fellas, what are we doing today?' He was a closet rehearser. I think that's the best way to be."

Peck insisted that we include a scene from the gaudy *Duel in the Sun.* "Women respond to that performance," he confided about his role as Lewt, who rapes and brutalizes Jennifer Jones. I inquired about the film's celebrated producer, David O. Selznick. "We made *Duel in the Sun* seven years after David had produced *Gone With the Wind,*" Peck recalled, "but he still talked about it all the time. He couldn't get it out of his system. That's why *Duel in the Sun* had to be the biggest Western ever made, because David felt that's what people expected of him. He even repeated some of the *Gone With the Wind* camera setups in *Duel in the Sun.*"

Help me to understand Selznick's charm, I asked. He was a gambler, a womanizer, yet lots of people said they loved being around him.

"Oh, a lot of gamblers and womanizers are charming," Peck replied. "David was charming, but his was not what you think of as sophisticated charm, certainly not Continental charm. His greatest quality was exuberance. Appetite for socializing, appetite for life. Above all, appetite for moviemaking. He was consumed with the love of making movies, and he was excited about it, and he never tired of it. His charm was a little bit overwhelming, because he wanted excitement all the time.

"When we were in Tucson with *Duel in the Sun,* we were filming long days out on location, from dawn until nightfall. But then David was always ready for a big evening. He'd gather a dozen people for dinner. And if he learned there was a bootleg casino on the edge of town, which he did, he'd drag everybody out there to play roulette. The actors would start creeping away at midnight, because we had to get up at 5:00, but David would often stay until 2:00 or 3:00 A.M. Then he'd show up early the next morning. He didn't seem to need more than three hours' sleep. He had more than his share of adrenaline or whatever it is that fires people up and keeps them going at full speed night and day. He had this excess of zeal that made him *more enthusiastic* and *more excited* than anybody else around."

Selznick was known for his constant, and often intrusive, script rewrites. Did you experience that?

"Less so on *Duel in the Sun*. There, the script had been so honed and polished, for what it was, that there was not too much rewriting. But on the two Alfred Hitchcock films, *Spellbound* and *The Paradine Case*, David rewrote the dialogue *every* night, and he'd come on the set the next morning. They'd hand us the new pages when we were in makeup, and we'd have to start learning new dialogue.

"As a writer, David tried to make everything more obvious. It wasn't his nature to give the audience credit for picking up on subtlety. His whole tendency in writing was, state it plain and simple so they won't miss anything. Hit it on the nose. And that drove Hitchcock out of his mind. Two or three times I thought he'd explode like a big balloon, but he never said anything, never raised his voice. But I knew that it was driving Hitch mad every time he saw ten brand-new pages, which invariably would be a rehash of what had already been written, only more obvious, more simplistic, exactly the opposite of how Hitchcock would write it."

One day, when we were screening *MacArthur*, I declared that Peck's performance as the legendary general was the best of his career.

"I thought I got pretty close to him," the actor allowed. "There are occasional moments where I think I hit him dead on. The problem . . ." He paused, reluctant to dwell on a negative. Then he succumbed, explaining, "I wanted *MacArthur* to be a great film, but the studio, Universal, didn't comprehend what they had. They did not allow us to realize the full potential of what I saw as a chronicle play, particularly the dispute between President Truman and General MacArthur during the Korean War. I very much wanted that enormous conflict of personality to emerge as *the* climax of the picture. Instead we refought World War II, and everyone already knew how that came out.

"We should have been telling the story of these two great patriots who were unable to form a bond and instead became two ships that passed in the night. MacArthur was an inspired commander, a brilliant scholar, a master of rolling Victorian prose, a great administrator of Japan after the war. He personally wrote the new Japanese Constitution; he emancipated Japanese women. But he brought his downfall on himself. If only he hadn't been so cocky, imperious and arrogant, he might have made a friend of President Truman. Had they enjoyed a meeting of minds, America could have retaken all of Korea without kicking off World War III.

"I know this is true, if I can believe something that Henry Kissinger told me. He said that Chou En-lai told him that in no way was China prepared to trigger World War III. Had we sent in the troops and the reinforcements that MacArthur wanted, no way would China have engaged in a major land war with the United States. But the British were terrified that if a major war ensued as the result of our trying to retake North Korea, they would lose Hong Kong. They put great pressure on Truman not to risk all-out war. So it ended up in a stalemate, and we're still paying for it today. North Korea is now *the* renegade, dyed-in-the-wool Communist country, threatening the world with nuclear capability.

"To me, the relationship between those two men is the essence of drama. That is a story worth telling. But Universal didn't see it that way. After I signed on to the project, they cut the budget from twelve million dollars down to seven million. They did the picture on the cheap. It lost its sweep and size, and I do blame them for it. Even after all these years, I still hold them accountable." He paused again, deciding he'd said enough. "Let's just call it a lost opportunity."

Back in the early 1980s Peck had sought to initiate a new screen version of the Sinclair Lewis novel *Dodsworth* (which William Wyler had directed in 1936). Long after our conversation about *MacArthur*, when I asked if his failure to get *Dodsworth* to the screen was Peck's biggest career disappointment, he brushed my question aside: "Not at all. After working on *Dodsworth* for a couple years, I was well out of it. I sold the script to Warner Bros. and retrieved my investment. My biggest disappointment . . ." I could see another internal debate being waged. How much to reveal? Then: "I try not to think about disappointments. But if I really wanted to narrow it down, my biggest career disappointment could be that we didn't come off with a great film with *MacArthur*."

It took us nearly a year to assemble the clip reel. Not that we worked every week, or even every month. But when we did work, they were fun sessions, and always informative. Unlike other actors I've known who detest watching themselves on the screen, Peck enjoyed viewing his old films. Only *Roman Holiday* elicited a twinge of sadness. "Look at that face," he sighed, as the camera panned in on Audrey Hepburn's elfin smile. Then, more to himself than to me, he whispered, "I can't believe she's gone."

As the reel began to take shape, it inevitably featured the costars we knew the fans would want to see: Audrey and Ava and Sophia. It's a shame, I suggested, that we can't also include that earlier generation of greats you worked with, like Walter Huston and Charles Laughton and Ethel and Lionel Barrymore.

Peck nodded in agreement, then said, "You can't not learn from old pros like those. By nature I'm somewhat withdrawn, somewhat of an introvert. Those fellows taught me to come on strong, take center stage, carry the scene, carry the picture if you have to. That's your responsibility as a star.

"I remember back in 1944 working with Lionel Barrymore on my third film, *The Valley of Decision*. By that point in his life, Lionel was confined to a wheelchair. At the climax of the story he delivered a tirade to striking steel-mill workers. The minute we started filming that scene at 8:30 in the morning, Barrymore gave it everything he had. He was going all out in the long shots, and in the crowd-reaction shots when the camera wasn't even on him. Finally the director, Tay Garnett, said, 'Lionel, I may not get to your close-ups till late this afternoon. Take it easy. You'll give yourself a heart attack.' And Barrymore looked up from his wheelchair and snarled back at him, 'Well, who gives a goddamn?' Because he was loving going all out. He was loving giving a bravura performance. Nothing could hold him back."

Peck was right: He is withdrawn and introverted, private and compartmentalized. So for me that year was a rare opportunity to look past the master shot and observe him in close-up. He is a man, like all men, with flaws. For one thing, he's been famous for so long, that the fact of his fame sometimes renders him inflexible. Why do we have to do such-and-such *that* way? I might ask. "Because I said so," he would reply, his voice stiffening. "I've been doing things my way for a long time now, and it's worked out pretty well." Whenever he would resort to such a specious rationale, I'd mutter to myself that he was being *star-stubborn*. But he is a good man, a decent man, worthy of the stature that so many have bestowed on him.

And in a curious way, our renewed association bestowed stature on me. At a party I happened to meet Alan Pakula, who produced *To Kill a Mockingbird*. When he heard I was working with Peck, he welcomed me as a colleague. "Gregory Peck is the truest, noblest film star I've ever known," Pakula averred, his eyes aglow with resonance. On another occasion, when Charlton Heston learned I was associated with his longtime friend and political nemesis, his voice actually softened as he confided, "I think I respect Greg more than any man in this business."

By early 1995 the clip reel was assembled; my job was done. But Peck suggested that I go along on his first three-city swing to Miami, Gainesville and Jacksonville to help ensure that things ran smoothly. I had no background in stage management. But if that's what he wanted . . .

I preceded him to Miami by a day to check out the theater, then met Mr. and Mrs. Peck at the airport. Beneath his bluff smile, I could discern the nervousness any professional experiences on the eve of ascending to a new challenge. As we left the airport, he queried, "How are the tickets selling?"

I hadn't thought to ask.

He pondered what must have sounded like an evasive answer, then reassured himself: "Well, we'll be there."

We weren't alone. Our 4:30 P.M. curtain had to be delayed twenty-five minutes due to a rush at the box office. After the clip reel debuted to a demonstrative response, twelve hundred whistling, stomping fans cheered Peck's entrance. "I thank you so much for coming here this afternoon," he began after they finally resumed their seats. Then, playing off his own insecurity, he self-effacingly joked, "You never know." The audience rewarded him with the first laugh of his new career.

An old icon had found a new venue.

So began our journey through America. Things didn't always go smoothly, but it took more than missed connecting flights or lost luggage to ruffle GP (as I began to address him in memos and faxes). At the Detroit airport an imperious staffer, upon discovering that Mr. and Mrs. Peck were traveling with their two tiny Maltese dogs, barred the Pecks from the VIP club. I found them unceremoniously seated at the entrance to the cloakroom. "We've been relegated to the leper colony," GP quipped, in unperturbed good humor.

Onstage in Dallas, as the stage lights dimmed for the showing of a *MacArthur* outtake, GP got whacked on the head by a descending curtain pipe.

But these were minor mishaps, outweighed by the dividends of seeing America. Regardless of whether we were flying or driving,

Peck's face was always pressed to the window, absorbing the view. In Mobile I found him perched in the window of his hotel suite, rapt as he observed the Intracoastal Waterway river traffic that passed twenty-eight floors below, bemoaning the fact that he didn't have a pair of binoculars. On the drive from Albany to Boston, as we left the interstate highway and entered Stockbridge, Massachusetts, for lunch at the Red Lion Inn, GP looked like a wide-eyed kid peering through a candy-store window as he savored the gray, gabled salt-box houses that lined the road. He literally shook his drowsy wife into alertness: "You have to look at this! You *must* look at this!"

At other times, the view was a panorama only he could see. In Memphis GP and I toured the National Civil Rights Museum, which has been built around the Lorraine Motel, where Martin Luther King, Jr., was assassinated. As we stood gazing into King's final motel room, I overheard a deeply stirred Peck muse to himself, "Hatred. How are we ever going to get rid of hatred?"

When we checked into the funky old La Posada hotel in Albuquerque, GP was charmed by the lobby's musty ambience. "This place reminds me of a hotel in Tucson," he said. "When we were making *Duel in the Sun*, I rode a horse through the hotel lobby and into the ballroom and performed tricks for the crowd." Reacting to my disbelieving stare, he added, "That was another Gregory Peck."

The longer we were together, the more I learned about that other Gregory Peck.

Occasionally our travels assumed the aura of a personal farewell tour, as GP encountered scenes from his earlier incarnation. They were brief encounters, and Peck tended to make light of his reminiscences. But doubtless our journeys flushed them out—as in St. Louis, when he paused to admire the towering cathedral where his parents were married in 1915.

Gregory Peck is the grandson of Irish immigrants who made their way past Ellis Island to upper New York state, then across America to the sleepy seaside hamlet of La Jolla, California. (If my biggest discovery about Peck was how funny he is, my second-biggest discovery was how Irish he is. He often lapses into the brogue and delights in reciting William Butler Yeats' poetry from memory. "The older I get, the more Irish I become," he remarked one day; it was another way of saying that he is still his father's son.)

A lack of money prevented his father, Gregory "Doc" Peck, from pursuing the education that would have allowed him to become a physician. Instead he obtained a degree as a pharmaceutical chemist. Doc was running the local La Jolla drugstore when he met and fell in love with vacationing Bernice Ayres. They were married the following year at the St. Louis Cathedral in her hometown. Ten months later, on April 5, 1916, their only child was born in La Jolla. "My mother wanted me to have an unusual name," Peck explained. "She found *Eldred* in the phone book, and I was named Eldred Gregory Peck. I bore the brunt of that first name for twenty-one years."

The marriage barely lasted twenty-one months. "I cannot remember ever having lived with my mother and father together," Peck told me. "They split up when I was about three. After that I have the vaguest recollection of living briefly with my mother in a run-down boardinghouse back in St. Louis that was straight out of Tennessee Williams. My strongest memory is of a Filipino who also lived there who I thought was going to kill me with a knife. From St. Louis, my mother and I went to San Francisco, where we moved in with one of her brothers, who did not want us. My mother didn't know what to do with herself, I guess. Eventually she remarried, this time to a traveling salesman. I received postcards from Ithaca, New York, and Mobile, Alabama."

By the time Eldred was eight, his father's drugstore had failed and Doc was working an all-night job at a San Diego pharmacy. "That's when my parents decided to park me with my grandmother in a modest little bungalow in La Jolla," Peck said. "Those next two years are my best memories of childhood. I bicycled to school every morning. Every afternoon, like clockwork, my dog would show up at the bicycle rack just as school was letting out, and off we'd go." What Peck describes as his "Booth Tarkington days" came to an abrupt end when he was enrolled in a Los Angeles military academy for four years. Then, reunited with his father back in San Diego, but shy and aimless, he frittered away his high school years. It was only after he was out of high school and (like the father he always sought to emulate) working an all-night job as a watchman that young Eldred finally, belatedly, began to appreciate the value of education. He decided to seek admission to the University of California at Berkeley.

When seventy-nine-year-old film star Gregory Peck appeared before an SRO crowd at his alma mater, a woman in the audience asked, "Could you tell us why you chose Berkeley over the myriad of other schools that were available to you?"

"I don't think that a myriad of other schools were interested," Peck wryly replied.

After the laughter subsided, his tone changed as he elaborated, "I felt very lucky to come to Berkeley. My high school grades were not great, and I spent a year and a half at San Diego State studying in order to bring my grade point average up to where I could be admitted here. Berkeley became a great revelation and discovery in my life—the cosmopolitan nature of the place, the erudite faculty members. It was an awakening. It woke me up from my long adolescent sleep, and I'm very grateful for that."

Although at Berkeley he originally intended to realize his father's thwarted dream of becoming a doctor, Peck soon realized he was not cut out for a medical career, so he switched to English. "As an English major, I was inundated with great literature," he continued, "Balzac and Dickens and Thomas Hardy and Mark Twain, which became very, very important to my life. I so loved my reading that I considered becoming a teacher and remaining at Berkeley. I fancied myself as the cliché English professor in tweeds, walking around the campus with a pipe, and living in one of those quaint hillside bungalows."

All that was forgotten when, during his senior year, he was invited to act in a production of scenes from *Moby Dick*. Captain Ahab was already cast with a short actor, and the director wanted someone tall for Starbuck. He spotted six-foot-three-inch Eldred Peck walking across the campus. So quickly can a life be transformed.

"I wasn't a very good actor," Peck admitted, "but I loved doing it." Because he knew that he wanted to continue doing it, now he had to learn *how* to do it. In May 1939, at the end of his senior year, the novice actor didn't wait for graduation exercises; the university could mail him his certificate. As soon as he took his last final exam, he was off to New York City. The first thing he did on that cross-country train trip was to rid himself of his despised first name. He may have boarded as Eldred Peck, but he disembarked at Grand Central Station as Gregory Peck.

On the tour, Peck's return to Berkeley was especially edifying, but GP loved all the college dates. One bright autumn morning at the University of Iowa we took a stroll in search of a Sunday *New York Times*. As we wandered along a teeming outdoor pedestrian mall, he was fascinated by the young balladeers, musicians and chess players. "Do these kids realize how lucky they are?" Peck asked. "A protected environment with thirty thousand of their own kind, the best instructors, clean air to breathe." I could only wonder if the gay panoply along the mall bore any similarity to the fairway at the 1939 New York World's Fair.

Having moved to New York in May, Peck planned to seek a scholarship to study acting at the Neighborhood Playhouse. But the new term didn't begin until September. He needed a summer job. Soon enough he had one, as a talker on the fairway at the World's Fair. "I wasn't even a barker," Peck clarified. "There's an arcane distinction, I quickly learned, between being a *talker* and a *barker*. A barker was considered to be more skillful.

"The Meteor Speedway was a huge wooden bowl. It had a kind of caterpillar car on an arm that held twelve people. And it started whirling, and eventually these twelve people were riding in the thing upside down and screaming their heads off, held in by 'centrif-you-gal' force. I loved that phrase, and I incorporated it into my spiel: 'A mile a minute! A thrill a second! Held in by centrif*you*gal force.' They put me in white coveralls, helmet and goggles. And I was up on a platform haranguing people with my spiel, a half hour on and a half hour off from noon to midnight.

"During my half hour off, I walked around the fairgrounds and got acquainted with the Lindy hoppers and the people from *Mike Todd's Hot Mikado* and Ripley's Believe It or Not!, the midgets and so on. It was a raffish new world for me, the outer fringes, the bottom rung of show business. I only had that job for six weeks, but six weeks was long enough to develop a lot of empathy for people who work away at that. Circus people, for example, acrobats and clowns who dress up in costumes and put paint on their faces. I've been there. Briefly, briefly. So I have an empathy. I feel a little bit sorry for them, but I like their bravery. I feel we're distant cousins."

His comments reminded me of a statement he made at a press conference in Arkansas when we were filming *The Blue and The Gray*. In response to a query about his decision to become an actor, Peck concluded by declaring, "And I've never been sorry. I treasure the associations. I love the people I work with. I like actors. I think they're good, fine, intelligent, openhearted, generous souls, every last one of them." As we walked along the Iowa City mall, I reminded him of his words. He pondered them, as is his ruminant wont, then said, "The only adjective I left out is *courageous*. It's courageous to try to become someone else."

By now he had located his Sunday *Times*. As we returned to the hotel, a stylish woman approached Peck and asked, "Where'd you find the paper?" Suddenly recognizing him, her jaw dropped. She pointed at his cardigan sweater and stammered, "I thought you were a professor."

Thirty minutes later I was passing through the hotel lobby when I heard her talking into the pay phone: "Yes, Mother, it was really him. It was! I don't know what he's doing in Iowa City." I intruded myself long enough to confirm the Peck sighting for Mom. After the woman hung up, she identified herself as the wife of an associate justice on the Michigan Supreme Court. They were in town for a weekend conference. Then she said, "I want to tell you something I was too nervous to tell Mr. Peck. I grew up in a small backwater town in Michigan. I needed to begin my life, but I lacked the strength to break those family bonds and move on. Then one day—this was thirty-five years ago—I passed by our local movie theater, and the marquee read:

GREGORY PORK IN
PECK CHOP HILL

and I knew it was time to get out of that town. So in an indirect way he could never imagine, Gregory Peck directly influenced my life."

And who influenced Gregory Peck's life? So many people. His beloved father, of course, and father-figure Henry King. Acting teacher Sanford Meisner, stage director Guthrie McClintic, agents Leland Hayward and George Chasin. But one of the most influential was choreographer Martha Graham. In February 1996, five years after her death, we played an unusual date in Phoenix at which the Martha Graham Dance Company opened the evening.

When did you first meet Martha Graham? I asked GP as he surveyed the purple mountains outside his Arizona Biltmore hotel suite.

"At the Neighborhood Playhouse."

In September 1939 Peck received his Neighborhood Playhouse scholarship, just as he had planned. For the next two years he hurled himself into this brave new East Coast world. "Those were wonderful, wonderful impecunious days," he recalled. "New York became my turf. I roamed all over that city. We'd think nothing of sleeping in Central Park if we were low on money. You'd store your belongings in a locker at Grand Central and move into the Park. On those few occasions when I did have some money, I usually spent it on jazz. Any time I could afford to go to the Hickory House on East Fifty-second Street to hear Red Nichols and His Five Pennies, or to see Benny Goodman at a movie theater, I was there."

In addition to daily classes at the Neighborhood Playhouse with Sanford Meisner, where the students studied the Stanislavsky system of acting, three times a week Martha Graham conducted movement classes. "She was already a legend," Peck said, "a priestess of the modern dance, and we got a lot of benefit from her instruction. But what I got," he added, ruefully recalling the distant memory, "was a ruptured disk. We did an exercise where we sat on the floor, put our heads between our knees and tried to bend over. A lot of the girls could do it without even trying. But men are not so flexible. And Martha came along and said, 'You can do better than that, kid,' and she stuck her knee in my back and snapped a disk in my lower back. It was what they called in those days a ruptured disk. Nowadays they call it a herniated disk. Whatever you call it, it ended my career as a Martha Graham dancer."

When World War II began two years later, that ruptured disk would make Peck ineligible for military service, and it would continue to plague him throughout his reign as a romantic lead. (He was not so adept at hoisting Ava Gardner as the movies would have you believe.) Darryl Zanuck decreed the reason for Peck's 4-F status—an injury in a dance class—unmanly, so he had the Twentieth Century-Fox publicity department fabricate a story that Peck had been injured while rowing crew at Berkeley.

But Hollywood was still five years into the future. . . .

During our travels we saw whales in Alaska, a not-to-be-forgotten big-sky rainbow in Colorado, cornfields in Iowa that seemed to stretch to eternity. But I rarely saw GP more relaxed than in Maine, when we strolled along the Atlantic Ocean beach below our seaside inn. "The smell of the ocean," he exclaimed, inhaling the salt air, "the seaweed on the sand. It takes me back to my days in Dennis, Massachusetts, when I was a young actor learning my lines on the beach."

During the summers of 1940 and '41, between terms at the Neighborhood Playhouse, Peck was one of the anonymous acting multitudes in search of work. He found employment in summer-stock productions on Cape Cod, at the Barter Theater in Virginia, and in Suffern and White Plains, New York. ("I was making twenty-five dollars a week playing support to Diana Barrymore in *Captain Jinks of the Horse Marines* and glad to get it.")

Did you have any favorite roles? I made the mistake of asking.

"Favorite—?" Peck gagged, as if he'd choked on seaweed. "I was just damn glad to have a job! I was too young to be thinking of favorite roles. I was thinking, damn glad to be here, to be on the inside instead of on the outside. That's what you think about when you're twenty-three and think maybe it would have been better to stay home in California instead of embarking on such a tricky and haphazard career, which so many people think is a waste of time, and I wasn't so sure yet but that they weren't right. So just to get cast in a play, any play, was what was on your mind. You weren't thinking of favorite roles to play. My favorite role would have to wait until I got to Broadway. Broadway—that was when I crossed the River Styx."

After Peck was graduated from the Neighborhood Playhouse in 1941, producer- director Guthrie McClintic offered the fledgling actor a bit part in a tour of George Bernard Shaw's *The Doctor's Dilemma* starring McClintic's wife, the legendary Katharine Cornell. Many a theater luminary (led by Alfred Lunt and Lynn Fontanne) trained down to Philadelphia for the gala opening-night performance, which coincided with Cornell and McClintic's twenty-fifth wedding anniversary. Late in the play, Cornell made an entrance—and promptly forgot her lines. Peck, who was onstage, discreetly cued the star, and the action resumed. Cornell's appreciative husband did not forget.

One year later, in September 1942, Guthrie McClintic cast twenty-six-year-old Gregory Peck in his first Broadway role. Theater critic Brooks Atkinson, writing in *The New York Times*, didn't much care for *The Morning Star*, Emlyn Williams' drama about life in London during the recent air blitz, but he saw promise in the new leading man. "As the wayward son," Atkinson wrote, "Gregory Peck plays with considerable skill—avoiding in his acting the romantic tosh of the writing." Added John Mason Brown in the *New York World-Telegram*, "Especial praise must go to Gregory Peck, a remarkable young actor . . . sensitive, intelligent, expert and an uncommon type . . . who promises to go far."

"*The Morning Star* gave me the hope that maybe I had a chance of making a career," Peck said. "To walk out in front of all the critics, and get away with it, that changes your insides around. You're no longer one of thousands of hopefuls. You're no longer going to drama school and eating the Nedick's nine-cents breakfast. When you make the leap from obscurity to Broadway, you're crossing a much greater chasm than when you move from Broadway to Hollywood, because once you believe in yourself, you're no longer making leaps. You're taking incremental steps."

But *The Morning Star* closed in three weeks. On the day after the closing, a Sunday, Broadway's newest unemployed actor attended game four of the World Series (the St. Louis Cardinals beat the New York Yankees, 9-6), then went directly from Yankee Stadium to a Lutheran church on Fifth Avenue, where he married Greta Konen, Katharine Cornell's hairdresser.

There was no money for a honeymoon—and no time either, for Peck was soon cast opposite Martha Scott in John Patrick's first Broadway play, *The Willow and I*, which opened two months later. The *Rip Van Winkle*-ish tale of a woman who emerges from a coma after thirty years was not well received. One critic dismissed it as an entry in "the what-not school of playwriting," while another termed it "a psychopathic melodrama." But once again Peck, in dual roles as both a doctor and his son, received the kind of reviews that launch careers.

Although *The Willow and I* lasted only four weeks, the momentum was with him. Four months later, as the star of Irwin Shaw's highly anticipated *Sons and Soldiers*, he earned his best notices to date:

> Ward Morehouse, *New York Sun*: "Gregory Peck, making his third Broadway appearance of the season, is proving himself quite a fellow to have around."

> Burton Rascoe, *New York World-Telegram*: "Mr. Peck grows in stature with each new role."

> Burns Mantle, *Daily News*: "Gregory Peck happens to be one of the most genuinely promising young leading men of his time."

> John Anderson, *New York Journal American*: "Gregory Peck gives an admirable account of himself and still deserves the sort of play he is entitled to and never gets."

Despite a virtuoso director (Max Reinhardt) and a talented cast (Stella Adler, Geraldine Fitzgerald, Karl Malden, Millard Mitchell, Kenneth Tobey, Jesse White), *Sons and Soldiers* closed after twenty-two performances. So when a movie offer came Peck's way, the young actor listened.

"I took *Days of Glory* for the money," Peck admitted. "A thousand dollars a week for ten weeks. I was in debt. I owed fourteen hundred dollars to an interesting dentist named Julius Y. Pokress, who was famous for being a softy with actors. He'd allow you to run up a big dental bill and not press you for payment. I wanted to pay him off, and *Days of Glory* allowed me to do that."

The low-budget tale of Russian partisans fighting the Nazis was hardly a star-making vehicle, and Peck might happily have returned to the stage—were it not for the fact that World War II was into its third year. With stars like Clark Gable, Tyrone Power, Henry Fonda and Jimmy Stewart away at war, the film studios were strapped for virile leading men. Peck's powerhouse agent, Leland Hayward, parlayed his client's return to California into a feeding frenzy that resulted in contracts for sixteen pictures divided among four competing studios—all before anyone had seen this new actor onscreen! There's never been a deal quite like it in the annals of Hollywood.

Peck would have enjoyed at least one long run on Broadway, but he never acted there again. No longer could he afford to gamble on what might prove to be another four-week flop. After a lifetime of hand-to-mouth, finally he was a sought-after, saleable commodity. Henceforth his live-theater appearances would be pretty much limited to the stage at La Jolla High School. That's where, in 1947, together with Dorothy McGuire and Mel Ferrer, he cofounded the La Jolla Playhouse, a summer-stock haven for film stars who still had a yen to tread the boards.

Peck's transfer of allegiance from stage to screen occurred during the making of his second picture, *The Keys of the Kingdom*. Although today he looks back on his portrayal of Father Chisholm as not so good ("I put all the sincerity I had into it, and not much else"), nevertheless the novice film actor realized that he had been seduced: He loved the meticulous process of making movies.

And movie audiences loved Gregory Peck. During his first five years in Hollywood, Peck was nominated for the Academy Award four times (*The Keys of the Kingdom*, *The Yearling*, *Gentleman's Agreement*, *Twelve O'Clock High*). As America's first post–World War II film star, he was at the top of a sober new class that included Robert Mitchum (whose first important role was in 1944), Kirk Douglas and Burt Lancaster (who made their screen debuts in 1946), Richard Widmark (1947), Montgomery Clift and Rock Hudson (1948).

Talent aside, much of Peck's early success was due to his lean, chiseled good looks, which made him a rival for Tyrone Power and all those other celluloid gods whose careers were sustained by sighing women in dark movie theaters. His position as a screen idol was validated in the 1950 Academy Award winner *All About Eve*. When Bette Davis (as Margo Channing) reminds her beau that he's no great romantic catch ("You're conceited and thoughtless and messy"), Gary Merrill replies, "Everybody can't be Gregory Peck."

Alas, and typical of Hollywood's illusory facades, all was not bliss for America's new heartthrob. By 1952 his marriage to Greta—despite the births of their three sons—had deteriorated beyond repair.

"During the seven months that I was in Italy working on *Roman Holiday*, my wife and I separated," Peck said. "It was a difficult time in my life. When the production ended, I put my wife and the Nanny and the secretary and the three kids on the *Ile de France* at Le Havre. For tax reasons, I had been persuaded to remain in Europe and make three pictures. But we had decided we couldn't go on, so I . . ." He paused, searching for the precise words. "It just about broke my heart to put those three little boys on a ship for America. I remember driving from Le Havre back to Paris. Very down. Very, very down, and went to my hotel, which was the Lancaster. And I went into a depression. I didn't see anybody for two weeks. There are so many things I'd hoped would not happen in my life. But I especially hoped that I would not divorce, and that my kids would not grow up, as I did, in a broken home. So I was quite depressed. After a while I began to go out walking at night. I would walk four or five hours, till I'd exhausted myself. Then I'd walk back to my hotel and sleep half the day. After two weeks of that I got stir-crazy and needed company."

Peck sought comfort and reassurance from Veronique Passinet, whom he had met in Paris while en route to Rome. She was an ambitious young journalist who had grown up poor in France; he was a glamorous film star who had grown up poor in America. They were married on New Year's Eve, 1955. They are still deeply in love.

None of the three pictures Peck remained in Europe to make (*Night People, Man with a Million, The Purple Plain*) has withstood the test of time—although *The Purple Plain*, a survival story about fliers who have crashed in Burma, is, like *The Macomber Affair*, a sturdy, mature film that happens to be uncommercial.

But then he was persuaded to stay on and make a fourth film. *Moby Dick* (1956) became Peck's great white reel, a motion picture that inflicted scars that have never healed—primarily because the movie never goes away. When we began to assemble our clip reel for the tour, Peck made it clear that *Moby Dick* was not to be included. Over the years I tried to change his mind, but he remained adamant in his opposition.

When Turner Classic Movies aired the 1930 film version with John Barrymore as Captain Ahab, for a lark I taped the decrepit old movie and took it to GP. After watching for a few minutes, he turned it off. "Barrymore's no good as Ahab," he scowled, "and neither was I."

What do you mean, your Captain Ahab was no good?

His reply was laced with the pain of a keening moan: "One of the reviewers described my performance as feckless!"

I was amazed by his admission, amazed to learn that, more than forty years later, he could still be hurt by one review.

"Not one review," he countered. "There were plenty of bad ones. Reading some of those reviews made me feel as if I'd been kicked in the stomach by a mule."

It was pointless to remind him of the many insightful and laudatory notices. Gregory Peck was living proof of the axiom that actors never believe the good reviews and never forget the bad ones. Nor was he swayed by praise from the film's director. In his 1980 memoir, *An Open Book*, John Huston wrote, "Peck brought a superb dignity to the role. . . . The picture is now truly coming into its own, and Greg Peck is getting the applause he always deserved."

The fact is that Gregory Peck simply doesn't talk about John Huston. During our years together, I brought up Huston's name repeatedly. Only rarely would Peck swallow the bait. Finally one day he did reveal, "I thought I was used on *Moby Dick*. Two years after we made the film, I learned that Huston had really wanted another actor for Ahab—first, his father; then after Walter died, Fredric March or Orson Welles—but the studio would not finance the picture with those actors. So he came to me, and led me to believe that I was his choice. I thought I was too young for such an obvious character role. I thought I'd be miscast, and I told him so. But he did a tremendous sales job. So I signed on, Huston got his picture, and I did my utmost to bring crazy old Ahab off.

"That was a big stretch for me, and I needed direction. One day when we were filming a particularly challenging scene I went to John for help. He looked at the script, and he pondered for a moment. Then he said, 'Just give it all you got, kid.' Lord-a-Mighty! What kind of direction is that?

"I once read a magazine interview in which a very good friend of mine, a director, made the comment that 'Greg wants to be loved,' and only rarely did I show a dark side. That may be true. That may go back to my roots, to my broken childhood. And that desire to be loved *may* have led me in the direction of playing heroes, of people on the side of the angels, people who wanted to put things right, who wanted to make the world a better place. That could be. And it also could be the reason why, if I felt someone has lied to me, or betrayed me, or told me something that wasn't true, that deceit may have struck deep down and reminded me of a time when I felt abandoned in my early life, or at least without stability. So if I feel someone has been false, or has attempted to use me for their own gain, my tendency is simply to separate myself from them.

"I'm quite often surprised by young people who have seen *Moby Dick*, and as far as they're concerned, it's a great picture. The flaws, and the dissatisfaction that I might have felt with it, all that goes right by them. They don't know how I saw it in my head, what I was striving for. They only know what they see on the screen, and they're raving about *Moby Dick*. What's the phrase that's applicable here? 'Time cures all ills'?"

Not all ills.

Our audiences asked about *Moby Dick* at almost every performance. GP would respond with a whimsical account of how he nearly drowned after being tossed off the rubber whale into the Irish Sea. But he would not talk about John Huston. "A colorful character," Peck acknowledged in Memphis when someone pressed him about the craggy director. "I have so many stories about Huston. I don't think I'll go into them now."

But I eventually came to realize that you could take *Moby Dick* and *Roman Holiday* and *The Guns of Navarone* and *Spellbound* and toss them all into the Irish Sea. If Gregory Peck had not made *To Kill a Mockingbird*, there would have been no conversation with . . .

A Conversation with Gregory Peck always begins with an introduction by a local dignitary. Governors, senators, university presidents all welcomed the opportunity to be a part of the program. In Clearwater, Florida, George Steinbrenner ad-libbed an amazing, if hyperbolic, encomium in which he described Peck as *great* fifteen times in four minutes! But because not everyone is as facile as Steinbrenner, early on (without Peck's knowledge) I wrote a brief introduction, which was made available to each theater. The text suggested that, although audiences may have come to see a movie star, they would leave the theater having made a new friend. But I was wrong about that, for what I came to appreciate was that he was *already* their friend.

He was Atticus Finch.

In a curious way, our audiences knew Peck better than he knew himself. Although GP took pride in his career-long refusal to repeat characters, the public had him pegged. His heroic persona—an amalgam of humility, integrity and intelligence—was established in 1944 with his valiant Father Chisholm in *The Keys of the Kingdom*, took root with devoted father Penny Baxter in *The Yearling*, then blossomed with caring journalist Phil Green in *Gentleman's Agreement. To Kill a Mockingbird* was more than merely another in a continuing list of sensitive characters; it was a coronation, an immersion wherein actor and role fused into the ultimate hero.

"Which role was most like yourself?" became one of the questions most frequently asked of Peck, as if audience members wanted to believe, *needed* to believe, that an actor *is* the character he portrays.

An Iowa City man asked Peck how he got along with Skip Homeier, who played the young punk who kills him at the end of *The Gunfighter*. "Fine," Peck replied, unable to stifle a laugh. "It's only acting, you know. It's all pretend."

Yet he sat before his faithful fans, life-size, yet somehow larger than life, as living proof that behind the pretend, not all heroes have feet of that moldy, ugly clay that is compounded of hypocrisy, egocentricity and megalomania. With Gregory Peck, you could believe the truth of what film critic Judith Crist once wrote: "Somewhere within that man we know is the best of us, in fact or aspiration."

Which role was most like yourself?

Peck's audiences knew the answer before they asked: Atticus Finch, of course.

Intriguingly, Harper Lee's Pulitzer Prize-winning 1960 novel about prejudice and fear in a small Alabama town avoids a specific physical description of the admirable Atticus. Instead, early on daughter-narrator Scout Finch repeatedly establishes him simply as "my father." Although there is an occasional reference to Atticus' "graying black hair and square-cut features," the most telling description comes from neighbor Miss Maudie Atkinson, who explains to Scout and her brother, Jem, "If your father's anything, he's civilized in his heart."

No wonder Gregory Peck was offered the role. It was, as they say, typecasting.

On April 8, 1963, three days after his forty-seventh birthday, Peck strode onto the stage of the Santa Monica Civic Auditorium and accepted the Academy Award as Best Actor . . . and not a moment too soon. Seven months later President Kennedy would be assassinated, and a national cynicism would begin to fester. Ten months later the irreverent Beatles would spearhead the largest British invasion of American soil since the War of 1812. Within two years of Peck's Oscar win, four of the five nominees for Best Actor would be British.

With his Academy Award finally in hand, Peck's career should have been at its apex. Instead, he soon found the ground slipping beneath his feet. As the Vietnam War escalated, and protesting Americans began to reject their former heroes, Peck's career went into premature eclipse. *Mackenna's Gold, The Chairman, Marooned, I Walk the Line, Shoot Out, Billy Two Hats*—these are the irrelevant films he made during the turbulent late 1960s and early '70s when moviegoers were responding to such once unlikely protagonists as Bonnie and Clyde, Joe Buck and Ratso Rizzo, Cool Hand Luke and Don Corleone. The times, they are a-changin', Bob Dylan (a big Peck fan) wailed; and they were. Now, the only actor to enjoy success playing conventional heroes was Sidney Poitier. (Poitier, by the way, drove down from New York to see our show in Princeton, New Jersey. After the performance, he was nigh speechless. Time and again he tried to articulate his feelings, failed, and instead resorted to "wonderful." I was stirred by his inarticulate fervor. I sensed that what he was striving to convey was simply this: *A Conversation with Gregory Peck* made Sidney Poitier proud to be an actor.)

Ironically, during those same mid-1960s and early '70s, when Peck's film career was treading water, offscreen his stature continued to grow. He evolved into a moral leader. After the Watts riots in Los Angeles, Peck donated one hundred thousand dollars to help create the interracial Inner City Cultural Center. He was twice appointed to the National Council on the Arts, served two terms as president of the Academy of Motion Picture Arts and Sciences, served one year as national chairman of the American Cancer Society (during which the charity raised fifty million dollars), and was founding chairman of the American Film Institute. During those years, countless lives were affected by his tireless activities—and at least one life was saved.

"In 1969 we were making *I Walk the Line* in Gatlinburg, Tennessee," Charles Durning recalled. "In the picture, Peck is the sheriff and I'm his unscrupulous deputy. I get murdered, and Peck has to dump my body into a lake. John Frankenheimer directed the movie. Now, John is not a mean man, and he's a very good director. But he's abstract. When he's finished with one scene, he's on to the next one. So they had just dumped me into the water, tied up in chains. I'm a strong swimmer, and I wasn't a hundred feet from shore; but when you're tied up with sixty pounds of chains, they're going to drag you under. John's onshore saying, 'All right, the next setup will be—' and he starts moving on. And I'm floundering in the water, calling, 'Fellas—' But they're all leaving, and nobody hears me except Gregory. He swam out and pulled me to shore. There was a publicist on the picture who wanted to put out a release. Peck said, 'No, no, print nothing.' But he saved my life."

With his career stalled, Peck considered retiring from acting and becoming a producer instead. In 1972 he produced the anti-Vietnam War polemic *The Trial of the Catonsville Nine*, which helped to land him on President Nixon's infamous "enemies list." Then in 1974 he produced what he hoped would be a more commercial entry, *The Dove*, based on the true story of a teenager who set out to sail solo around the world. "I hired a director who at the time was receiving a lot of publicity for directing a musical version of *Lost Horizon*," Peck said. "But it hadn't come out yet, and I fell into the trap of buying into the hype. It turned out he wasn't a very good director. But then," GP added, between self-deprecating laughs, "I wasn't a very good producer."

Suddenly (with a change of agents) Peck's acting career enjoyed an infusion: *The Omen* (1976), his biggest box-office success ever; *MacArthur* (1977), his most underrated performance; *The Boys from Brazil* (1978), a venture into character work. Another lull, and then *Old Gringo* (1989) revealed the seventy-three-year-old actor at the peak of his powers. Had the picture been successful, surely Gregory Peck would have been nominated for a sixth Academy Award. Even so, the roles were fewer and farther between.

But one role—*that* role—never went away.

In 1991 the Library of Congress and the Book-of-the-Month Club asked people to name the book that had the greatest impact on their lives. Not surprisingly, the most influential tome was the Bible. The second most influential? *To Kill a Mockingbird*. Doubtless, novel and film had symbiotically sustained each other through the decades. For countless readers, and viewers, Atticus Finch/Gregory Peck had personified stability and solidity during unsettled, uncertain times.

He had become an integral part of their lives, a friend. Now, when Atticus Finch came to their towns visiting, they turned out:

• In Springfield, Missouri, there were so many questions about the film that Peck actually encouraged the audience to broach other subjects: "I don't want to make *To Kill a Mockingbird* our exclusive topic here tonight."

• A woman in Iowa City who had viewed the film more than a hundred times ("no movie has made such a great impact on my life") delivered an emotional recitation of the picture's final speech.

• In Portland, Maine, a girl whose father had died when she was a child echoed the sentiments of many when she spoke about how both Atticus and Peck were surrogate father figures. "That's a scary movie for a kid," she continued. "That was scary." Her voice trembled with fear and urgency.

Across America, attorneys told GP about how the film had inspired them to take up the law, and English teachers asked him questions on behalf of their students:

• In New Brunswick, New Jersey, a teacher said, "Ninety-five percent of my kids wanted to know why you didn't punch Bob Ewell when he spit on you."

• In Green Bay, Wisconsin, a teacher asked, "One of my students wondered if you felt that a hero like Atticus Finch could exist in today's society." "Yes," Peck answered, "I think that there are quiet heroes who are truthful, dependable, trustworthy and honest. Yeah, I think that the country's filled with them, but they don't get much publicity."

• Another Green Bay teacher read a statement from one of her twelve-year-old students: *That Atticus would face these men in the defense of the defenseless strikes me as absolutely remarkable. I only hope that I can achieve a portion of his nobility in my life.* "It gives you a tiny idea of the impact you've had on generations of young people," the teacher continued.

"Thank you, thank you," Peck acknowledged. "Thank you for saying that." Time and again this usually eloquent man had no reply for the onslaught of affection other than a simple "thank you."

He was, however, quick with a retort when humor was involved. In Hartford when a wag wisecracked, "In *Mockingbird* I thought the rabid dog stole the scene from you," GP agreeably conceded, "A rabid dog will steal a scene every time."

As Atticus, Peck had to contend with scene-stealing dogs and children. In Austin a woman wanted to know how Mary Badham and Phillip Alford, who played Scout and Jem, delivered such natural performances.

Peck explained that director Robert Mulligan initially rehearsed the kids without a camera in sight, "just playing make-believe in the yard, the way kids do." When, finally, Mulligan added the camera, he kept it far away. "Eventually we began to move the camera up closer. By that time, the kids didn't pay any attention. Regardless of how close the camera came, they remained completely unselfconscious."

But Peck's number-one, most frequently asked question was this: *Are you still in touch with the two young actors who played Scout and Jem?* You could almost feel a catharsis-like relief ripple through the theater every time he affirmed that he is.

In Louisville and Winston-Salem, Peck created a sensation when he introduced Mary Badham in the audience, then invited the grown-up Scout to join him onstage. "It is so touching to see the two of you together," a Louisville woman called out from the balcony. "This is really quite an evening for all of us who grew as human beings from having seen that film." Then she asked, "Mary, is he in any way Atticus to you?"

"He is totally Atticus Finch," Mary Badham replied. "People often ask me, 'What do you call him?' And I say, 'I call him Atticus.' He always has been and he always will be my Atticus."

It is good to be loved; it is even better to know you are loved. Gregory Peck is loved, and if he ever doubted it, those doubts were quelled after touring with *A Conversation*: He knows it now.

But all that love can also take a toll.

In August 1997 Peck was offered a juicy leading role opposite Bruce Willis in a film adaptation of Kurt Vonnegut's anarchic novel *Breakfast of Champions*. His eyes sparkled at the prospect of playing a scrofulous character with the unlikely name of Kilgore Trout. He seriously considered the offer and even asked me to read the screenplay. I could easily hear Peck delivering the edgy, satirical dialogue.

But when he had to make a final decision, Peck wavered: "I'm not sure I'm right for this part. They should get someone crustier, like Harry Dean Stanton or Rip Torn."

I reminded him that his hero Laurence Olivier once reenergized his stage career by playing against type and performing John Osborne's *The Entertainer* at the antiestablishment Royal Court Theatre.

"I get your point," Peck replied, his voice beginning to stiffen, my first clue that he already had decided to reject the role. He recited a list of reasons. When I countered that none of the reasons was very convincing, he suddenly implored, "But what about them?"

Who?

"*Them!*" he repeated. "The people who come to the show. I'll be disappointing them if I say some of these off-color words."

So there it was. Once again a choice had been made, and a price had been paid: the sacrifice of an actor in the perpetuation of a hero.

Maybe it was a fair tradeoff: There are, after all, lots of actors, not so many heroes.

Or maybe it was a choice beyond Peck's control, a choice that had been made for him by those countless fans who need to believe. His effect on them had affected him too. *A Conversation with Gregory Peck* had become *Gregory Peck's Conversation with America*, and he had heard their voices.

Maybe it was no big deal; after all, every star turns down roles. After Peck made *The Gunfighter*, he turned down *High Noon*. (That was a now-lamented error.) And after *To Kill a Mockingbird*, he turned down *Shenandoah*, another homespun story about a concerned and caring Southern father who stood for righteousness. In both instances Peck acted out of "a natural instinct to avoid what I thought would be a direct repeat. I thought that to take those roles would be a kind of cheat." But prior to *A Conversation with Gregory Peck*, the star would have hotly denied that he ever allowed the aura of his fame to affect his work.

That time has passed.

But here's what saddened me the most about Peck's decision *not* to act. The week he turned down *Breakfast of Champions* was the same week he traveled to Australia for his cameo role in the television remake of *Moby Dick*. Two months later, when I watched the dailies of Peck's six-minute sermon, I saw an eighty-one-year-old actor who was *still* at the peak of his powers, so authentic that he might have stepped from Melville's pages. I saw an actor who didn't blow one take, didn't muff one syllable. Peck was eager to add some of that scene to our *Conversation* clip reel. He wanted his audiences to know that "the old boy can still do it."

That's what saddened me, the knowledge that the fire still burns within him, that he still relishes his craft . . . but it is not to be.

Now, since it's unlikely there will be any more starring roles to add to our clip reel, I have begun instead to assemble a clip-reel-of-the-mind, a mosaic of memories from our time together on the road. Many of these moments involve choices too:

• After the Albuquerque performance, the stage manager—after alerting me that the limousine was surrounded by a throng of waiting autograph seekers—showed me how the car could be driven into the secure privacy of the theater loading dock, thus avoiding the crowd. When I presented Peck with this second option, he scoffed, "You mean take the cowardly way out?" (I knew he wouldn't let me down.)

• In Minneapolis a grade school student naively asked if any of the words in Atticus Finch's summation to the jury had been written by Peck.

"No, my dear," he replied. After the audience's knowing laughter ebbed, he continued, "No, they were written, in the novel by Harper Lee, and then adapted for the screen by Horton Foote. I said it letter for letter, word for word, and very, very glad to have such a wonderful speech to deliver."

At that point, he might have moved on to the next question. But he didn't. Something troubled him. I think his acute sensitivity told him that the young girl might have been hurt by the laughter, might have thought the audience was laughing at her. So in a split second, as quickly as a mockingbird might flutter its wings, he chose to bestow on that child the gifts of time and seriousness. He chose to continue talking to her. He spoke about why it is sometimes necessary for actors to improvise, and how they go about doing that. What he said isn't really important; *why* he said it was deeply moving.

• In Atlanta several actors (including Angela Bassett, Al Freeman, Jr., Samuel L. Jackson, Phylicia Rashad and Joan Van Ark) joined Peck in his dressing room for a post-performance photo. The diminutive Emmanuelle Lewis was the last of the invited actors to arrive. When Lewis entered the dressing room, Peck welcomed his pint-sized guest with such sweetness and benevolence that I wondered if this wasn't how Abraham Lincoln's eyes might have looked as he greeted tiny Tom Thumb at the White House in 1864. . . .

Even a clip reel can run too long. Originally, I was only going to join GP on that initial three-city swing. Came the day, after four years and fifty-two performances, when I knew it was time to withdraw from *A Conversation with Gregory Peck* and move on with my life.

"I suspect this has been rather a diversion for you," Peck acknowledged when I told him I was leaving. Indeed, it had been. But I moved on with the reward of having come full circle, from that misty morning in 1981 when Abraham Lincoln arrived on the set of *The Blue and The Gray*, to a friendship with a man who, behind his civilized image, is truly civilized in his heart. I moved on with the reward of having come to know a man who, even after his flaws are weighed on the scale of judgment, still personifies the best of us.

He is not Abraham Lincoln, of course; he is not even Atticus Finch. He is only Gregory Peck.

But that's enough.

SIDES:
GETTING STARTED

"I watched Lloyd Nolan every night for hundreds of performances, and he never let down."
—JAMES GARNER

"You can't ever forget about acting if you've been bitten by it."
—SAM NEILL

"It's not easy to live in New York City on forty-five dollars a week."
—LOUIS GOSSETT, JR.

Every actor has a story about his or her beginnings. They're always good stories because they're always original. No two actors ever traveled the same route to success or had precisely the same experiences along the way. This next trio includes memories of those early journeys . . . unlikely, unexpected, unpredictable.

As the first draftee from Oklahoma during the Korean War, **James Garner** (actually, he was still Jim Bumgarner back then) hailed from a family without any show-business background. After the war he tried lots of jobs ("about seventy, and I didn't like any of them") before he latched onto acting. In 1953 *Maverick* was still four years into the future when a friend offered him a nonspeaking role in the Broadway-bound production of *The Caine Mutiny Court-Martial*:

"The production was directed by Charles Laughton; it had three big film stars—Henry Fonda, Lloyd Nolan and John Hodiak—and we put the whole thing together in Los Angeles. I was cast as one of the judges on the court of inquiry. No lines. My main job was to understudy John Hodiak, who played Lieutenant Maryk. But my first job was to cue Lloyd Nolan for the role of Captain Queeg. Long before rehearsals began, I would go over to Lloyd's house every day for anywhere from two to four hours to cue him on that role.

103

"At the first day of rehearsals, all the actors were sitting around the table reading the script. Comes the middle of Act Two, and they finally got to Queeg, and Lloyd never opened his script. He knew the entire part letter-perfect. When he delivered that long, tour-de-force speech about the stolen strawberries without ever opening his script, Fonda's eyes bugged out of his head. He went to Lloyd afterward and said, 'How the hell did you do that?' Lloyd told him that I'd been cuing him. So Henry came to me and wanted to know if I would cue him too, and I said yes. So first I got to know Lloyd, and then I got to know Henry very well. And of course, because I understudied John Hodiak and functioned as his valet, I got to know John very well.

"We opened that play in Santa Barbara, California, and then we toured it for three months before opening on Broadway in January of '54. I was a handyman and a friend and a bodyguard for all three of those guys. Practically everywhere they went, I went. But that's not where I learned from them. I learned from them in the theater, by sitting there on the bench night after night after night with nothing to do except watch them work. I learned about phrasing, and I learned about concentration. I began to be able to dissect their performances. It was a slow, gradual kind of, 'Oh yeah, I see what he's doing there.'

"I have to tell you. I watched Lloyd Nolan every night for hundreds of performances, and he never let down. He gave a totally solid performance every night.

The same was true of Fonda, although he left before the run was over. Barry Sullivan replaced him. He had his good moments and his bad moments, his good nights and his bad nights. But Henry and Lloyd were good every single night! Their ability to concentrate was amazing.

"So I learned a lot from *The Caine Mutiny Court-Martial*. But most of all, what I learned was how to be a professional."

James Garner got that first job thanks to a friend. But on the rarest of occasions, you don't even know who your friends are. **Sam Neill** likely never would have starred in *Reilly, Ace of Spies* or *Jurassic Park* or *The Piano* had it not been for . . . no, we'll let him tell it:

"I was born in a very small, sleepy mountain town in Northern Ireland. That was in the days when Ireland was still a peaceful place. Nowadays, sadly, the town is filled with a lot of barbed wire and bombed-out buildings.

"My family returned to New Zealand when I was eight. Eventually I began to act onstage, only to discover that I'm not actually a theater person. I do enjoy the business of rehearsals, and I like audiences. But I don't enjoy stage fright, which I got very badly. Nor did I like working at night, and having a miserable day, feeling sort of sick because I knew I had to go to the theater to work that night. So I stopped acting, and I began to make film documentaries. I made quite a good one about skiing. I made another one about wind surfing that turned out all right, though it's a pretty boring sport. I made two films about architecture, which were a mistake. Never make a film about things that don't move; this is the lesson to be learned from that.

"But I hadn't really forgotten about acting. You can't ever forget about acting if you've been bitten by it. Then around 1976 a friend of mine named Roger Donaldson rang up and asked me to play the lead in a feature film, which surprised me, because no one had made a feature film in New Zealand in about fifteen years. We made a film called *Sleeping Dogs*, which was a sort of adventure-political story.

"When *Sleeping Dogs* was released in Australia, they sent me across to publicize it in Melbourne. They had a press conference. Only one reporter came. He was from the sports page, and he'd made a mistake. But as a result of that film, Gillian Armstrong spotted me. They'd been looking for someone to play the part in *My Brilliant Career*, and I was cast in that.

"Then a rather amazing thing happened. James Mason and his wife, Clarissa, saw *My Brilliant Career*, admired my performance, and took an interest in my career. I had never met these people. Nevertheless, and quite unbeknownst to me, James called my agent and arranged to buy me a plane ticket to England. As a result of their generosity, I started working in films. But I might never have left New Zealand and Australia if this hadn't happened. He was a nice man, James, and also, of course, one of the great screen actors. I miss him."

In his amusing theater memoir *It Would Be So Nice If You Weren't Here*, Charles Grodin recalls the excitement of his first résumé-worthy role (an appearance on *Armstrong Circle Theater*), then puts that big break into perspective by quoting Walter Matthau: "All you need are fifty good breaks." For most young actors, how you survive while you're getting started . . . there's the rub.

Long before his Emmy Award-winning performance in *Roots* and his Academy Award-winning role in *An Officer and a Gentleman*,

Louis Gossett, Jr., had to struggle to make ends meet. "Back around 1959, 1960," he recalled, "after I'd done *A Raisin in the Sun* on Broadway, it felt as if the New York theater was shut down to American actors, and the British took over. There was Laurence Olivier in *Becket* and Richard Burton in *Camelot*. There was Paul Scofield in *A Man for All Seasons* and Joan Plowright in *A Taste of Honey* and Harold Pinter plays everywhere. So I had to go Off-Broadway. I did *The Blacks*. In this one production, you had Roscoe Lee Browne and James Earl Jones and Cicely Tyson and Godfrey Cambridge and Maya Angelou. *The Blacks* was a hit, but *The Blacks* only paid forty-five dollars a week. It's not easy to live in New York City on forty-five dollars a week.

"Downstairs from where we rehearsed was a coffeehouse called the Cafe Wha? where they put on the hootenannies. This was the first year of the hootenanny fad. Through those doors came such unknowns as Bob Dylan and the Mamas and the Papas and Jimi Hendrix and Richard Pryor. And I went down there, and I saw somebody singing spirituals. I knew spirituals from church, so I started singing them too. Then they passed a straw basket among the crowd, and they collected five hundred dollars! So I started to sing folk music every night after *The Blacks*. That was the summer of my folksinging.

"As the years went by, I continued to sing. When the Vietnam War started I even wrote an antiwar protest song called 'Handsome Johnny.' It only took me about twenty-five minutes, because it's a formula song. But I used to sing it, and everybody loved it.

"Now we're up to 1970, and I get a job as an actor. I put the guitar away, and I come out to California to do a TV series called *The Young Rebels*. It didn't last too long, but I stayed out there trying to get other jobs. In 1971 there weren't many jobs in television for a young African-American actor, and I started to run out of money. I couldn't even pay the rent. I BS'd the landlord for as long as I could. Then one day he showed up with a truck and started putting my furniture out in the street. That very day, *that very day*, the mailman, another out-of-work black actor, arrived with a bunch of letters that had been following me from address to address. The first envelope I opened had a check for $11,552.73. Richie Havens had sung 'Handsome Johnny' at Woodstock, as well as on an album. This was the residual check that had been following me all around the country.

"I paid off the landlord, and I was back in business."

CHAPTER FOUR

WAND'RIN' STAR

*"Few things on this earth are as pathetic as an
actor out of control."*
—STERLING HAYDEN

After he succumbed in his two-year bout with prostate cancer
in 1986, the headline of his *New York Times* obituary read:

Sterling Hayden Dead at 70;
An Actor, Writer and Sailor

It is true those were his vocations. Combined, they comprised
the substance of his life. But the word order, the sequence, which
would have been so important to Hayden, a man who revered words,
was out of joint. He was a writer first, and proud of it; a sailor second; and then, ever so begrudgingly, an actor.

In 1981 Hayden, like Gregory Peck, was cast in *The Blue and
The Gray*. Peck of course was Abraham Lincoln, our nation's most
dedicated citizen-servant. Sterling Hayden portrayed mad-as-a-hat-
ter abolitionist John Brown.

The dignified Peck and the iconoclastic Hayden were born ten
days apart in 1916. Both boys were subjected to keen family upheaval.
Both boys, introverted and shy, felt an affinity for the sea. Peck grew
up within reach of the Pacific; Hayden, within sight of the Atlantic.
Both boys grew up to be tall and handsome, and both married their

first wives at age twenty-six in 1942, by which time both aspired to the acting trade.

Now the contrasts begin, for Hayden seems as relaxed and assured in his first film (*Virginia* [1941]) as Peck appears earnestly rigid in his (*Days of Glory* [1944]). But Peck was seduced by the camera; he was eager to master his craft. Hayden spurned, and feared, his new endeavor. If Peck became an honored leader of the Hollywood establishment, an activist-celebrity, Hayden veered into eccentricity. He became a professional outsider. He evolved into the dark side of Gregory Peck.

Even as a boy in St. Louis, I could sense the difference between Gregory Peck and Sterling Hayden. Going to a Peck film was an event that entailed getting into the car and driving downtown to the majestic movie palaces. Sterling Hayden's movies played on Saturday afternoons at the local Bijou; I could ride my bicycle to see him.

I also sensed he was not competing with Peck for roles. Hayden was akin to Richard Carlson and Marshall Thompson, actors who seemed doomed to the bottom of the heap. I liked those actors and often felt sorry for them. But I never felt sorry for Sterling Hayden, because he refused pity. In most of his movies, there emanates from him an arrogant contempt for the words he was spewing out. No one else acted with such disdain, at least not until Tommy Lee Jones appeared in the late '70s. Tommy Lee Jones was the Sterling Hayden of the 1980s. In mediocre movies, Hayden and Jones manifest a judgmental attitude that scoffs, "Sure, I'll take your money, but I esteem myself too highly to feign enjoyment."

Because the John Brown scenes were the first to be filmed, Hayden was already gone before I arrived on the *Blue and The Gray* set. So in June 1982, seven months after the film wrapped, I flew to San Francisco to meet with him at his loft apartment across the Golden Gate Bridge in South Sausalito. During the cross-country flight, I reread portions of his memoir, *Wanderer*. In a profession that strives for air-brushed perfection, Hayden had laid bare his pock-marked, conflicted soul in a testament that enters the reader's nervous system like a tapeworm. Once read, it is not forgotten, so hauntingly written is it, and so unsparing in its condemnation of a life defined by compromise.

Wanderer lays out the arc of his life in broad, bold strokes. He was born Sterling Relyea Walter in Upper Montclair, New Jersey, a New York City commuter suburb. His father died before the son was ten. After his mother was remarried to a smooth-talking charlatan named James Hayden, the family began to move about New England, usually a quick step ahead of unpaid landlords.

One such move, to Boothbay Harbor, Maine, introduced the boy to his calling. While still a teenager, he ran off to sea. He grew into manhood (six feet, five inches tall; a lean 220 pounds) sailing on schooners. By age twenty-one, he had received his master's license; by twenty-four, he'd sailed around the world four times, garnering the kind of education you don't learn from textbooks. One of the things Hayden learned was that he had found the sea too late. The Schooner Age was already an anachronism; *he* was an anachronism. There was no future to be found on the wave-tossed decks of a windjammer.

Hayden wasn't much of a moviegoer (there aren't many theaters out in the Pacific), but he had eyes. He could scan movie magazines and see the photos of the reigning stars. He could also look in the mirror and immodestly know that he was as manly as anything Hollywood was selling. So at age twenty-four he actively pursued a screen test, which led to a contract with Paramount, which led to his first film, *Virginia,* in which he received third-star billing after Madeleine Carroll and Fred MacMurray. In the thankless, throwaway role of a rich New York socialite, Hayden came off looking like a Viking god. The studio publicity department labeled him "The Most Beautiful Man in the Movies."

The memoir chronicles his marriage to leading-lady Carroll, his discontent in Hollywood, his request—after two films—to be released from his contract, his hair-raising experiences with the Office of Strategic Services (OSS) during World War II, the end of the war in 1945, the end of the marriage in '46 and the resumption of his self-induced Hollywood nightmare in '47.

John Huston, a kindred spirit, was the sole director to sense Hayden's emerging darkness. "Only seldom do you find a face like Huston's in an office," the actor writes in *Wanderer.* "It's one that belongs on the road, in a boxcar doorway, in a mine, or in a Left Bank garret." In 1950, Huston—despite the protests of MGM executives—cast Hayden in the top-billed role of luckless hooligan Dix Handley in *The Asphalt Jungle.* In his memoir Hayden relates how, during his screen test, "slowly my joints unlock, I shiver a little, and for the first time I begin to act." It is not a process with which he's comfortable, or even one over which he has much control, but for the first time the movie star begins to appreciate the craft that is paying his way through life.

Huston, master of the visual, filmed *The Asphalt Jungle* in shadows and artificial light. No natural daylight was allowed to infiltrate the gritty story until the final scene, when a dying Dix returns to his family farm and keels over into the Kentucky bluegrass, his lifeless body protected by an honor guard of three inquisitive thoroughbreds. Throughout the film Huston kept Hayden as immobile as possible. The man's *presence* was the core of his performance.

Wanderer recounts Hayden's brief flirtation with the Communist Party and his name-naming appearance before the House Un-American Activities Committee in 1951. His punishment for the betrayal of his friends was exile to a movie purgatory of role after forgettable role. Between 1952 and 1955 he starred in twenty-one movies, of which maybe three (*The Star*, opposite Bette Davis; *Johnny Guitar*, opposite Joan Crawford; and *Suddenly*, opposite Frank Sinatra) are worthy of mention.

"Bastards, most of them," Hayden sneers, "conceived in contempt of life and spewn out into screens across the world with noxious ballyhoo; saying nothing, contemptuous of truth, sullen and lecherous. . . . Small wonder I dumped the money they paid me. Money earned like that doesn't deserve to be saved."

In the late 1950s a new generation of talented young directors began to tune into Hayden. Twenty-eight-year-old Stanley Kubrick starred him in *The Killing*, and twenty-eight-year-old John Frankenheimer drew a powerful performance from him in Horton Foote's *Playhouse 90* adaptation of William Faulkner's short story "Old Man." But it was too late. By then, Hayden's life was so wretched that he could not continue with his career. In 1959 he defied a court order and took his four children, remnants of his crumbling second marriage, to Tahiti on the schooner *Wanderer*. The story behind that journey is also related in his memoir. After its 1963 publication, Hayden settled into a temporary truce with himself that saw him through his remaining years. By the sheer act of facing down his demons, he had unintentionally elevated himself to a height just below the timberline. As John Huston wrote in his autobiography *An Open Book*: "Sterling Hayden is one of the few actors I know who continued to grow over the years. . . . There is a kingliness about Sterling now."

After a six-year absence from the screen, and with the memoir finally behind him, in 1964 Hayden returned to acting as the crazed General Jack Ripper, protector of Americans' bodily fluids, in Stanley Kubrick's *Dr. Strangelove, or: How I Learned to Stop Worrying and*

Love the Bomb. That performance led to his being sought out by Francis Ford Coppola for *The Godfather*, by Robert Altman for *The Long Goodbye* and by Bernardo Bertolucci for *1900*.

In Richard Nixon's war-torn early 1970s, when some Americans found anarchy an attractive option, Hayden was viewed as a stoned-out sage. He grew a flowing beard worthy of an Old Testament prophet and refused any role that required him to shave it. (Robert Shaw became a wealthy actor by snatching the starring roles in *Jaws* and *The Sting* that Hayden rejected.) He bought an 1890 railroad car in Illinois, had it towed to Sausalito, and lived in it for several years. His third wife, Kitty, bore him two sons. Mother and sons lived in Wilton, Connecticut; but by 1982, Dad mostly divided his time between a European river canal barge and a room with a view in South Sausalito.

From the street, the modest brown-shingled two-family apartment building at 213 Third Street in South Sausalito is undistinguished. But enter its lair, and with a gasp the visitor discovers that the view is all. The San Francisco skyline, Alcatraz, the encompassing bay, all lie in splendor before you.

The front door was open when I arrived. I rang the bell and was greeted by an orotund blast. If a bull elephant could speak, surely this would be its thundering voice. A moment later, the entire doorway was filled with Hayden's massive frame. He wore a collarless, buttonless blouse. A green-and-white-pattern silk scarf hung loosely around his thick neck. Another scarf belted his waist. His ruddy, sun-stained face was offset by the full white beard, which seemed to defy gravity and grow out perpendicular to his chin. His once-thick, wavy blonde hair, now thinning, had curled itself into tight locks appropriate to a Roman emperor.

Hayden prefaced our time together by explaining that he was on a "near fast." "I'm off the booze now," he explained, "and I have the grass under control. But I have nothing to offer you except tea and cigarettes." During the next three hours, he would rely relentlessly on both. We conducted our business first. I needed his comments for the mini-series press kit.

"A couple times I was asked to play John Brown in one picture or another," Hayden began. "I always said I wouldn't have the temerity to undertake to play a man like Brown. I had the same reaction when somebody contacted me in France last year about this one. Then I thought about it. This script was not Brown's entire life. Not even the raid at Harper's Ferry. Just the trial and the hanging. Yet I approached it with a good deal of temerity still. Hell, it put me on the wagon for about three weeks before I did it, because you need strength to carry off a character like Brown. He was, as the Wobblies used to say, a blowed-in-the-glass fanatic.

"But it felt good the day I did it. I know that. It felt good."

I made the innocent observation that John Brown originally hailed from Connecticut, the same state where Hayden's wife and two youngest sons lived. He cut me off fast. "The part of Connecticut where my wife is living is not Connecticut anymore," he bellowed. "It's suburbia. Suburbia is national shit."

Hayden's language often was spiced with profanities, but in his mouth the words never sounded vulgar. They were appropriate to a man of his size, a man of the sea. They weren't obscene; they were salty.

After the obligatory publicity questions were out of the way, I thought he might dismiss me so that he could return to his work. But no, he was happy to talk.

"I was watching television last night," he said, "and I saw part of a Woody Allen picture that had to do with the blacklist. It took me back to that bloodbath thing with the House committee."

That bloodbath thing . . .

He was, of course, referring to Martin Ritt's film *The Front*. Six years earlier, when the film was released, Hayden had told a reporter he refused to see *The Front* for fear it would rekindle dreaded memories.

For six months in 1946, twenty-nine-year-old movie star Sterling Hayden was a member of the Communist Party. He joined at a time when World War II still haunted him, a time when he felt that he "wanted to do something for a better world." But he bristled when Party members tried to tell him how to behave and what to think. Hayden was too much his own man to take orders from anyone, so in December 1946 he resigned. Chapter closed. Except that this chapter would never be closed. This chapter would continue to be written and rewritten until the day Hayden died.

In 1950 when war broke out in Korea, Hayden instructed his attorney to send a letter to J. Edgar Hoover at the FBI. The letter, which did not identify Hayden by name, referred instead to an anonymous client who, "in a moment of emotional disturbance, became a bona fide member of the Communist Party in the State of California" and who now was seeking government clearance should he be recalled to service. Hoover could not provide the requested clearance. Instead, on April 10, 1951, the actor found himself in Washington, D.C., testifying before the House Committee on Un-American Activities (HUAC).

Formed in 1938, for the first decade of its existence the HUAC was something of an embarrassment, the committee to which congressmen least wanted to be assigned. But in 1947, after President Harry Truman embarked on the Cold War, the committee found a new reason to justify its existence: It would weed out Communists who might pose a danger to the American way of life. The HUAC began by searching for reds within the federal government. But when that pursuit upset the Washington establishment, the committee retargeted and set its sights as far away from the Capitol as possible. Thus began the probes for those in Hollywood who might be insinuating Communist propaganda into movies.

The Hollywood Ten, as that group of accused writers, producers and directors came to be known, did their best to show up the HUAC for the sham they believed it to be, and went to prison for their efforts. After that fiasco, the committee steered clear of the movie industry. But three years later, with the onset of the Korean War, the HUAC once again decided to ferret out reds in Hollywood. This time the congressmen knew better than to harass those faceless craftsmen behind the cameras. To assure maximum publicity, they went after the stars themselves. Sterling Hayden was made to order.

"I went into the thing voluntarily," he told the committee. "Certainly I think it was the stupidest, most ignorant thing I have ever done." Ignorant, to the extent that Hayden literally did not know what Communism was. "I was constantly told, if I would read forty pages of *Dialectical and Historical Materialism* [by Joseph Stalin], I would understand Communism. I never got beyond page eight, and I tried several times." He described how the Party assigned him to persuade other members of the Screen Actors Guild to support a strike of artisans. Hayden made no headway with this effort, because at the time SAG was being run by Ronald W. Reagan, "a one-man battalion against anything Communistic."

But Reagan's wasn't the only name Hayden mentioned. He recalled having attended Party meetings with actor Howard da Silva, still other meetings at a house owned by Morris Carnovsky. Mostly he spoke about Captain Warwick Tompkins, "an open and avowed Communist," but also, and more important, a sea captain Hayden had revered since he was fourteen. During the 1940s, Tompkins lived in San Francisco Bay on a schooner named *Wander Bird*; in 1958, seven years after the detested HUAC hearing, Hayden would emulate Tompkins by buying an old schooner, the *Gracie S.*, and renaming her *Wanderer*.

But in 1951, under oath and with God as his witness, Hayden was reduced to the humiliation of having to distance himself from his mentor, of having to describe him as "this man Tompkins." When Hayden completed his testimony, the Committee praised the former World War II hero as "an intensely loyal citizen." His career was secure.

That was the *bloodbath thing*.

Didn't you refuse to view *The Front*? I asked.

"That may have been true once," Hayden acknowledged. "But I watched some of it last night, and I didn't leave it. I enjoyed it, because it was so goddamn good. It was funny as hell. I suppose everything, if it marinates long enough in us, the brutality of the thing, the importance is lost. That fucking, awful day that I testified, it's still the only day in my life I'm ashamed of. But things have happened. I remember sitting over in Belvedere in 1965. Harry Bridges, the old longshore leader, was there. We were at the house of a man named Vincent Hallinan, who ran for president of the United States on the Progressive Party ticket. . . ."

Some background:

• Belvedere is a San Francisco Bay town near Sausalito.

• Harry Bridges, the longtime president of the West Coast longshoremen's union, was constantly the target of U.S. Immigration Department efforts to have him deported back to his native Australia.

• Vincent Hallinan was the prominent San Francisco attorney who defended Bridges against one of these purges, in a trial that dragged on for five months in 1949-50. Bridges remained a free man, but Hallinan was sent to prison on contempt charges. He ran his 1952 campaign for the presidency of the United States from his cell.

"So I was talking about that awful day, and Harry Bridges—who was a great old scrapper and a real radical, who during his years as a labor leader was jailed, was beaten, was slugged with every damn thing—Harry said to me, 'Sterling, don't be so hard on yourself.' He says, 'We all make mistakes.' This was coming from a man whom I reverenced very much. He said, 'Now you've got one big problem. You're a loner. When I get clipped on the jaw, I go down for the count. But my boys, my longshoremen, they put their hands under my shoulders and throw me back in the ring. When you get clipped, you're alone. You go down.'

"Well, that was very generous. And I guess one figures, it's done, and a guy can't make amends—though I tried to in *Wanderer* by castigating myself pretty heavily."

His comments called to mind a quote from his memoir: "Make no mistake about it. Escape has nothing to do with plunging toward far horizons. Escape is taking the easy way out."

"I was ahead of myself on that one," Hayden said when reminded of his words, "because that's pretty good. I'm glad I said that. Do you know Ernest Becker's book, *The Denial of Death*? I think if I had to go to prison tomorrow"—curious that he would use the analogy of prison rather than a desert island—"and they said I could take along one book, it would be *The Denial of Death*. I had never heard of it when I wrote *Wanderer*, but Becker says the same sort of thing. He says he used to wonder how a man could work in a restaurant or on an assembly line, till he realized that the man with a specific job at least has the security of knowing where he's going to work and what he's going to be paid. I've thought about that a lot in recent years. Being an outsider ain't as easy as it looks. So to me, escape is a commuter train going into New York or that ferry out there, going across the bay. Which is not to knock it."

Hayden knew he was in no position to criticize anyone else's career. "I've often said to my kids, 'I never worked a day in my life until I got to Hollywood.' You know what I mean by that. If you like a thing well enough, it doesn't matter what the hell it is. Not that there's anything wrong with acting, not if you know what you're doing. But I never knew what the hell I was doing, and that is a very uncomfortable feeling, to not know your trade, your craft."

I interrupted to tell him I knew where he was headed. He was about to give me his stock interview palaver about how viewers think he gave a great performance in *Dr. Strangelove* without realizing he agonized through thirty-seven takes of the same scene (or forty-eight takes, or whatever astronomical figure he arbitrarily tossed out from interview to interview).

"That story has become a constant in my repertoire," he conceded. "But it's also unassailable. Because what turned out to be Jack Ripper's performance, particularly in that long scene with Peter Sellers off-camera, was an actor fighting to survive. And I just got worse and worse and worse, which is what inspired Stanley Kubrick to say that beautiful thing to me: 'The terror in your eyes may be the quality that one wants in Ripper.' But I would suggest to you that few things on this earth are as pathetic as an actor out of control, which I was. An actor who can't even do pickups. This means one thing: You're lost. You're mush. And I tell you, it's a terrible thing to see. I saw it happen to old H. B. Warner. I don't even remember the movie we were making [it was *Journey into Light*, whose filming was interrupted by the HUAC hearing], but I'll never forget the agony of watching this man. You just wanted to look away.

"I'll tell you what turned me around. Fourteen years ago I started smoking grass. Only then did I begin to learn how actors feel. It was 1968, my next picture after *Dr. Strangelove*, and I was working for the first time in Spain, some movie with James Coburn [*Hard Contract*]. My first day on the set was the usual first day: can't remember dialogue, nervous, awkward. I had just started smoking two months earlier here in Sausalito. So in Spain, out of despair, I thought, maybe a toke or two. Next day on the set, it went beautifully. I went backwards and forwards with the dialogue. For the first time in my life, I said to myself, 'I have confidence in what I'm doing. This is how an actor is supposed to feel.' Since then, I've enjoyed acting immensely."

Is it true that you turned down the starring role in *Jaws*?

He shrugged, took a long drag on his cigarette, exhaled, watched the smoke float to the ceiling. Then he said, without regret, "The government would have put a lien on my salary anyway. I wouldn't have seen anything out of it." He sipped his tea, then added, "The government and I have always been at odds over money."

But Hayden didn't really want to talk about his movies, or his run-ins with the government. He wanted to talk about his writing. It was not going well.

"Right after the war," he prefaced, "I rented a house down there in Hollywood, and I put in a desk and a typewriter. But I couldn't write. Even then I was fighting something I'm still fighting, something called a depression, stress, alcoholism. Obviously I'm an alcoholic. At that time I didn't know it, but I couldn't figure out why I couldn't harness myself and function. I seem to have functioned well in ships. Why couldn't one write?

"Going to Tahiti triggered writing. The trip itself wasn't that big a deal, but the newspapers made it look like a big deal. I suppose the gesture of defying the court gave the trip more wallop than it deserved . . ."

Wasn't that big a deal? More wallop than it deserved? Perhaps, once again, in Hayden's mind the importance of the event was lost.

Here's what happened. By 1958, in a bitter court battle with his second wife (they had met and married after his divorce from Madeleine Carroll), Hayden was awarded custody of their four children, Christian, Dana, Matthew and Gretchen, who ranged in age from seven to eleven. In making the decision, Los Angeles Superior Court Judge Emil F. Gumpert stated, "In forty-three years at the bar and at the bench, the author of this opinion has never heard a more forthright witness than the plaintiff, nor one who indicated a more zealous desire to be completely honest, truthful and factual . . . The uncontradicted evidence . . . impels the court to express the wish that all children might be blessed with a love and devotion, a concern and a care, equal to that which this father has bestowed on his offspring."

But there was a catch. By now Hayden had purchased the 1893 schooner, renamed *Wanderer*, on which he planned to sail his kids to Copenhagen. But Judge Gumpert forbade any long journeys, deeming the sixty-five-year-old vessel unseaworthy. Hayden feigned compliance. As an act of acquiescence, he even accepted a role in the film *A Summer Place*. (He would be replaced by Arthur Kennedy.) All the while, "like an arrow in a drawn bow," he was poised for a grander scheme.

On January 24, 1959, one week after the court ordered him to stay put, Hayden defiantly set sail with his children from Sausalito on a voyage "across the broad plains of the Pacific," bound, not for Denmark, but for Tahiti. He left behind a letter, saying he had "sold out for years" while filming "pathetic trash." The letter continued: "I am a decent enough man, not too bright perhaps, but impelled by some ideals as to conviction and principle. I was sustained by my inner determination to break out . . . and now is the time to go." His angry, humiliated agent could only announce to the press, "This man was born in the wrong century. He should have been a sea captain in the 1800s."

Hayden and his kids remained in Tahiti for seven months. There in the South Seas, at age forty-three, he finally began to write. Letters first. Long letters, letters that loosened his joints as he approached this newest challenge.

". . . *more wallop than it deserved*," Hayden was saying. "But the great thing about Tahiti for me was that it triggered writing."

When the family returned in November 1959 ("After running away comes the time to run back home"), Hayden had his day of reckoning with the legal system—and with the very same judge—he had so brazenly snubbed. On January 7, 1960, Judge Gumpert solemnly pronounced his decision: "It is the ruling of this court that Hayden be sentenced to a fine of five hundred dollars and serve five days in jail." He paused, to allow the leniency of the sentence to sink in, then shed even that light penance. "The sentence is suspended." ("I later had a drink with that good judge," Hayden confided. "He told me he didn't want to give me any sentence, not even a suspended one. But he had to do it as a sop to motherhood.")

Now he buckled down to work. He set out to write, not merely another celebrity memoir, but rather "a book people won't forget." When *Wanderer* was published three years later, critics hailed Hayden as an authentic writer in the tradition of Joseph Conrad and Herman Melville. Indeed, his descriptions of a life aloft ("The ship rolled down to leeward, scooped up a ton or two from the sea, then forced herself back on her feet, the water cascading riotously over the deck") resound with eloquent authority; his account of life on land ("Hayden the cowboy, tall in the rented saddle, king of the nonfrontier . . . big houses big salaries big fuss when you walk down a street big fuss as you check into hotels—big big big") is scathing in its self-denunciation.

Hayden dedicated *Wanderer* to his third wife, Kitty, and to Warwick M. Tompkins and Rockwell Kent (SAILORMEN ARTISTS RADICALS). It was part of his atonement for having abandoned his mentor at the HUAC hearing. Though Hayden eventually returned to acting, he also continued to write. *Voyage* was published in 1976, thirteen years after *Wanderer*. This seven-hundred-page novel about a sea journey in 1896 was chosen as a main selection by the Book-of-the-Month Club.

"But I'm not working now the way I used to," Hayden complained to me (and to the unseen writing gods who shared his Third Street abode). "And I ask myself, 'Why do I still have to fight so hard to write?' I think one reason is because I've got the alcohol well under control. Now there are days when I just can't seem to suck it out of myself. Draw. Roll. Work. Secure in the knowledge that one can peel off all these pages out of the typewriter and throw 'em away if you want to at the end of the day. I often say to myself, 'Look, you asshole, go ahead, write it!' Instead, what do you do? You hem and haw around. You chain-smoke. You stare out the window. You do this; you do that. My God, my God, my God."

His sentences rolled, pitched and tossed like a great schooner fighting the tide. Mine, by contrast, sounded like a leaky dinghy as I suggested that all writers know the frustration of sitting for two, three hours at a time and not finding that lead sentence. I added that I found it difficult to write more than four hours a day.

"If you can write four hours a day, you're home free," Hayden exclaimed, his voice back to full organ. "Suppose you can't even write one page a day? When I wrote the two books, I'd sit down at 6:30 in the morning and write for four hours, five hours, six. I haven't had that rhythm going in ten years, and I don't know why. This problem is like nothing else that I know of.

"A few years ago they brought out a second edition of *Wanderer*. They asked me to write a foreword. I went something like six or seven months, couldn't write a goddamn foreword to my own book. And here's the clincher. The foreword is shit. I did it because I had to do it, and it's no good. So we're not entirely bullshitting ourselves, are we? I said, 'Fuck, it's no good.' I knew it was no good. Finally I was doing the best I could, and I did have a deadline, and I did want to see the book come out again. Sure. New publisher. Pictures this time. And it wasn't any good. The foreword was nothing like the original book."

But when it was good for Sterling Hayden—and it was very good in *Wanderer* and *Voyage*—he knew an exhilaration he'd never before experienced: "Shakespeare said of the actor, 'Not a word hast thou spoken but was put in thy mouth by others.' Well, this is the glory of writing, isn't it? Nobody around.

"You know the greatest thing I ever heard about writing? Years ago here in San Francisco, the paper ran a book review of a biography of Stephen Crane. The reviewer quoted a line from the book, and it said this: 'A writer and nothing else. A man alone in a room with the English language trying to get human feelings right.' Isn't that beautiful? Goddamn it!"

He walked to the open door leading to the sun deck and surveyed the bay where two decades before his anachronistic schooner had proudly preened. Now *Wanderer* was a distant memory; she had been sold long ago. On this brilliantly sunny morning, the placid blue bay was studded with the white canvases of Saturday sailors.

Wouldn't you like to be out on one of those sailboats right now? I asked. Or better yet, on another schooner?

"No," came the stern reply. "No, I would not. Yesterday afternoon I was watching them sail out here about six o'clock. And it was cold. I was chilly. And I thought, Jesus, no, it's too cold out there. I've had that. No, I think the things that are magical to us at one time, they don't endure forever, do they?"

His voice softened a bit as he mused, "In recent years I've thought that I'd like to make one more long haul in a schooner and smoke a little grass. Because I never drank at sea, and I never allowed it in any ship I had. But that's just a thought. The truth is that, as years have caught up with me—actually, I don't feel they're catching up, I just feel the progression of time—you don't have the strength; you don't have the ability to take hold; you don't want to go running around up in the rigging. Everything I used to love. To hell with that. I've had that. Fortunately, I've found a fascination on the rivers that matches the sea, matches the sea. It's different, of course."

How did it happen, the transference of your affection from open water to water with land on either side of it?

"It was the charm," he said. "The charm of barges. When you get into the canals, you're moving right through the heart of the land. I can show you pictures of the small canals, and the trees and the willows and the reeds and the birds. Through this you move very slowly, so slowly that you actually have to have an acute sense of what's going on. You can't relax the way you can on a schooner at sea, where you've got the whole world around you. But the river life is just as fascinating as the schooner life was when I was a kid. 'The mystery of ships,' as Longfellow said. The mystery! What is it? The mystery. Well, barges have that mystery. So I was totally swept in.

"Another part of the charm is that the barges are beautiful. Beautiful! And with infinite variety. Unlike on the Mississippi River, or on any other American river, where all barges are pretty much the same, in Europe they have every size and shape, and are beautifully painted. To me it was like paradise."

How does someone go about buying a barge?

"You'll recall I said I made a movie in Spain in nineteen hundred and sixty-eight. When I finished, I took the money, went up into France, went on up into Holland, and spent a weekend with a writer named Jan de Hartog [the author of the play The Fourposter] outside Rotterdam. And he said, 'Sterling, I can't help you in your quest, because you don't know what you want yourself. But twelve miles from here there's a town named Dordrecht, and in this town is a hotel named Bellevue, and it may be the most magical hotel in all the world for people who love ships, because three rivers meet in front of the hotel, and between eight and nine hundred working barges go by five days a week.'

"So I went to Dordrecht, and I checked into this hotel. You know how you gotta keep moving through a hotel till you get the right room? I always walk around outside a hotel now and look at the windows, and pick out the room I want, and then go for that. Fuck the desk. They don't know what I want.

"So I finally got a room up in the corner, and it had five cots in it for a barge crew. I folded four of the cots up against the wall, piled the mattresses right up even with the windows. I looked out, and here was a 1620 custom house with three helmeted Dutch ladies looking down out of granite onto the river. And out here—" Hayden's voice softened to a reverential hush "—a barge rolled by!" His voice resumed its rusty timbre. "All the time. My God. And there I was! So I sat there and lived and studied the river and watched the ships. I knew the size I was looking for, around one hundred fifty tons, and I began to chase 'em up and down the river. I finally bought one in Rotterdam after six months of looking.

"The thing I love most about the canal barges is the people you meet. To my surprise, I've turned out to be quite gregarious. Endless, endless conversations with people, and the opportunity to invite people aboard, let's say, in the middle of Paris, and talk and laugh and drink and smoke and play music." A pause. "But even then, one feels alone, you know."

One thing about Sterling Hayden: He was a straight shooter. "That I can say," he concurred. "Early on I developed the theory: If nothing else, kid, be honest." With his children, for instance. "I didn't play the father role very much. I always figured, let my life be an example, either for good or bad."

By way of illustration, he recalled a winter evening in New York City when he was out with his teenaged son Andrew. As he spoke, Hayden became the storyteller, layering his tale in rhythms that never could be captured on paper:

"We'd been on Staten Island. We come back on the ferry. Now we're going up to South Street, and I look across and there's a place I remember from my past. I said to Andrew, 'It used to be called the Paris Cafe. I knew it when I was fifteen.' I headed across the street, and I looked in the window. Jesus Christ, it's going wide open. So I go through the double doors, and Andrew is with me, and the bartender's name is Mike.

" 'Hey.' He gives me the big hello, and he says, 'What are you drinking?'

"I said, 'Double gin.' Double gin. Straight. Double gin.

"Andrew had a beer.

"I buy Mike a drink. Mike buys me a drink.

"All the longshoremen are there, keeping warm on oatmeal. Big fires in the oil drums outside. Pretty soon Andrew said, 'Well, Dad, I think I'll have a drink with you.'

"I said, 'OK. You want a double?' Because I figure if he wants a single, he can say single.

"He said, 'Double.'

"We had three doubles. And by this time I'm in pretty loose shape.

"We walked across the Brooklyn Bridge, came back, jumped in a taxi, went up to the Grand Central Station, got out on Forty-second Street. A big traffic jam, so I bailed out first, and I see a new hotel I've never heard of called the Harley. Big limousines outside.

" 'Hey, Andrew, let's take a look.'

"So I led the way into the Harley through the revolving door, and on into the bar. And I guess my hair was blowing around. I had a big, heavy, old coat on, boots on. And the little guy tending bar steps up to me. He says, 'Sir, we can't serve you.' Just like that.

"And I'd been smoking some grass too, and when I'm smoking I'm very mellow. I'm a mellow guy.

"And I said, 'Would you mind telling me why?'

"And he said, 'Well, I'm sorry, sir, but we just can't serve you.'

"And I thought, well OK, I don't want any trouble, and we went back out onto Forty-second Street. We got about a block closer to Grand Central, and I stopped, and I said, 'Hey, Andrew. They refused to serve us, didn't they?'

"He says, 'Yeah.'

"I said, 'Should we go back?'

"He says, 'Yeah.'

"So we start back across the street, and I said, 'You know, I'm not a man goes looking for trouble.' Then I said, 'But I don't take no bullshit neither.' This is Daddy. Drunk.

"Now I come storming into the Harley, and the assistant manager, it's like he's expecting me. He steps right up. 'Mr. Hayden, there was a big mistake. We're very sorry, sir. Could we buy you a drink?'

"I said, 'You sure can.'

"We go back into the bar, and we had three more double gins. Holy shit.

"We get back to 'the Kitty's' house in Connecticut, and I kept on drinking. And I was drunk, and I knew it. And I said, 'Andrew, take a look at your old man.' I said, 'You know what I am now? I'm crippled, aren't I?'

"He said, 'Yeah.'

"And I thought to myself, maybe this is the way to get him off it."

I'm not a man goes looking for trouble, but I don't take no bullshit neither.

I would recall that sentence in 1986, five months after Hayden's death, when I spoke with D. Perry Moran, an executive with the Delta Queen Steamboat Company in New Orleans. During World War II, Moran served with Sterling Hayden's OSS squadron in Barletta, Italy, on the Adriatic coast. Their highly secret operation entailed delivering gold to Marshal Tito and his Communist partisans in Yugoslavia. The gold, Moran explained, was ransom money paid out in exchange for downed Fifteenth Air Force fliers who had been forced to ditch their planes over Yugoslavia and Albania en route back to Italy after bombing missions in Rumania. Once the partisans received the gold, the OSS teams then were allowed to "rescue" the fliers. These rescue operations were conducted in two stripped-down PT boats.

As life imitates art, so Moran described an exchange that might have been modeled after the Act Two scene in *Cyrano de Bergerac* when the cadets instruct Christian never to refer to Cyrano's nose. "When I arrived in Barletta," he recalled, "several of the guys took me aside and asked, 'Have you ever heard the name Sterling Hayden?'

"I said, 'Isn't he a movie actor?'

"And they said, 'Yeah, but he's no movie actor over here.'

"It turns out that after the war started, in an effort to get as far from Hollywood as possible, Hayden had changed his name to John Hamilton. These guys were warning me not to make the mistake of calling him by the wrong name. When we were with him, he was addressed as Commander Hamilton. But behind his back, when we talked about him, he was Sterling Hayden.

"He was built like a tree. He had these broad shoulders and thick arms. Then his torso tapered down to a thin waist. He had a passion for privacy. He was highly selective about who he chose to speak to and who he chose to drink with—till he got drunk. Then he'd drink with anyone.

"I never saw him in a full uniform. Always an open collar. He could be very casual about those kinds of regulations. But when it came to the boats, everything was by the book. He would end every briefing with the same statement: 'Protect the goddamn boat, and you're gonna protect your own ass.'

"When we were cruising through open water, he always had the binoculars up to his eyes. He could go hours at a time without speaking, but he was an incredible navigator. He knew how to look at a coast and find coves where we could hide out. He knew where we could slip in behind reefs, and where the water would be most calm. He could tell you what time it was by maneuvering the boat around and looking over the side at the shadows on the water. He was absolutely amazing."

Some of the experiences Hayden and Moran shared were also amazing.

"On this one run, we picked up four downed crewmen. Two of the fliers were critically wounded, and a third was slightly wounded. Coming back from Yugoslavia, we were spotted by two German Q-boats. They chased us, and our boat was pretty well shot up, and the least-wounded flier was shot again and now was bleeding severely.

"When we finally got back to Italy we fired off two flares, which was the signal that we had wounded onboard, so the army ambulance could be at the dock to take them to the hospital. As we approached the dock, the ambulance was there, but it was further away than it should have been. In its place was a Red Cross wagon. That didn't make any sense. We'd never seen Red Cross wagons in our area before. Anything the OSS did was done with tremendous security.

"Sterling Hayden started shouting to get that Red Cross wagon the blankety-blank out of there. By that time we'd tied up, and I noticed a woman standing next to the wagon in full Red Cross regalia. I didn't know who she was, but anyone could see she was extraordinarily pretty. Next to her stood the Fifteenth Air Force public information officer, a major.

"About that time, one of the other crew members came running over and said, 'Christ, that's Madeleine Carroll. Don't let the boss see her.'

"Suddenly the problem was crystal clear. Madeleine Carroll, Mrs. Sterling Hayden, had come to Italy with the USO. She'd met the commanding general of the Fifteenth Air Force and had immediately transferred from the USO to the Red Cross and was living in the general's villa. Rumors were rampant about whether or not our CO was being cuckolded.

"Captain Hayden was in a wretched mood due to this pickup run which had gone so badly. When he saw his wife, he started screaming, wanting to know who sent this cheap wharf-rat whore down to meet his boat. Then he opened up with profanity the likes of which I had never heard in my life, nor have I ever heard again since that day. Being in the army, I thought I'd heard it all, but not the language he used against her.

"This major, who looked as if he'd just stepped out of the store window at Brooks Brothers in New York, tried to interrupt. At first Hayden ignored him. He made sure that all the wounded were taken off the boat and put in ambulances. Then he inspected the boat to make sure she wasn't going to sink right there at the dock. When he finished with that, he proceeded to go over to the major. He grabbed this senior officer by the shirt and tossed him into the harbor. Then he turned on Madeleine Carroll, who by this time was in absolute fear. She went running up the dock.

"We pulled the major out of the water. He started ranting and raving something awful. We told security, 'We suggest you get this guy out of here before Captain Hayden kills him.' Later we learned that the whole thing was a setup to do a puff story on Madeleine Carroll's involvement with the Red Cross, in order to legitimize what she was doing in Italy. But it was a ridiculous premise, because nothing was ever reported in *Stars and Stripes* or *Yank* about OSS secret missions."

The time served under Hayden was always charged with such events, right through the final cruise before Moran was transferred. "You have to understand," he explained. "The Americans held the west coast of Italy, but the British held the east coast, where we were. So all our runs had to be coordinated through the British. The last mission I was on with Sterling Hayden, we were caught by two German Q-boats. We got shot up something terrible. We were screaming to the British for help. We even used open voice transmissions, which you weren't supposed to do unless absolutely necessary, identifying who we were and asking for a piece of their air cover. They responded, 'Negative, negative. Can't help you, old chap.'

"We finally got out of that scrape. But by that point Hayden had just had it with the British. He'd been on too many missions where the British were miserable to him. He raced our boat right up against the British MTB [Motor Torpedo Boat], and he was screaming his bloody head off to our gunner up front to turn his gun on the British! We were all afraid that either we were going to get thrown off the boat by Captain Hayden, who was in a tirade, or we were going to have to shoot up the British MTB. And a few of our machine-gun bullets did break the MTB windshield, although we weren't trying to hit it. We were actually trying to fire over the British boat, and they drove right into our spray.

"Next thing you knew, a British destroyer escort flagged us down and escorted us into our base. Then a voice on the DE's loudspeaker told us to remain at our vessel, that we were under arrest. Our radio had been shot up by the Germans, but Hayden was not about to be arrested by the British under *any* circumstances. So he told one of us to slip off the boat and get the MPs, which is what happened. The next thing you knew, the destroyer escort was surrounded by American soldiers armed with Thompson submachine guns, which was a ridiculous sort of standoff.

"To make a long story short, Hayden was brought up on charges. We were all interrogated, and we all denied having received any orders from Captain Hayden to fire on any kind of a British MTB. We denied everything. Because he was our captain. We weren't going to allow him to get into trouble any more than he would have allowed us to get into trouble. Eventually the entire matter was dropped."

When the war ended, Hayden was awarded the Silver Star.

There were other stories on that Sausalito Saturday in 1982. Always, Sterling Hayden's words conjured up the visual. He described being in the De Gaulle Airport in Paris with "all these escalators going up and down like mail chutes," and laughed as he recalled being in the Grand Hotel in Stockholm, where he and a friend ended up shattering the bedroom window. So he called down to room service, ordered a sumptuous meal, then added, "But what we really need up here is a little plywood." He talked more about his love for canals and urged me to read Robert Louis Stevenson's *An Inland Voyage*.

Then he said, "I'll tell you what you do. On the next street below here, there's a market with a little deli. Go get yourself a sandwich, some chips, something to drink. Bring it all back up here, and we'll make a day of it."

I wish I could, but I'm expected tonight in Santa Cruz.

"Fine, fine. You go on. It's a beautiful day. You'll have a good drive." But there was a tone of sadness behind his posturing, as if I'd let him down. Or maybe it had nothing to do with me. Maybe my presence simply helped to delay that dreaded moment when he'd once again be alone in his loft, under obligation to try to get human feelings right.

It was time to leave. But not without one last question. Fifty years from now, I proposed, some encyclopedia will need a one-paragraph description of Sterling Hayden. What should it say?

"I'd have to think." He walked out onto the sun deck and stared across the blue bay to Alcatraz. As I followed him outside, I noticed that the ship's bell from *Wanderer* was perched on the balcony ledge, a shiny remnant from his past. A moment later he answered, "Oh, something like this: He was a beautiful old fucked-up son of a bitch who loved touching strangers passing by."

I never saw Sterling Hayden again, but for the next several months we spoke by telephone on a regular basis. CBS held a huge publicity event for *The Blue and The Gray* in Washington, D.C., but he shunned it. Then, two weeks before the mini-series aired, he gave me the unlikeliest of gifts.

In the midst of a phone conversation, he said, "I've been thinking. You've worked hard on this show. I know it means a lot to you. How would it be if I went down to Los Angeles next week and did a couple days of publicity? Sort of a chaser to everything else that's gone down?" I was stunned. If Sterling Hayden disliked anything more than publicity, it was Hollywood. Yet he made the offer, and he followed through. To my knowledge, that was the last time he met with the press.

After the mini-series aired, the spaces between our phone calls grew wider. Eventually they ceased. Then, the surprise of his death in May 1986. Somehow, Sterling Hayden had seemed too tough to die.

In 1994, twelve years after our morning together, I returned to South Sausalito. This time I went to the market and ordered a sandwich and chips. I asked the butcher if he happened to remember a fellow named Sterling Hayden, who used to live on the next block. "Do I remember Sterling Hayden?" the butcher repeated, as if I were a fool for even having asked. "I used to go up to his place all the time and hang out. We were best friends. Do I remember Sterling Hayden?! No one who knew him will ever forget him."

SIDES:
Being There

---

*"Throughout rehearsals, Kazan had sat on Lee Cobb
until there was not one ounce of self-pity in his
performance. And it paid off on opening night."*
—CAMERON MITCHELL

*"By opening night, I think everybody in the company
truly detested that play."*
—BERT CONVY

*"John Dexter had driven us to a peak for that one
moment, opening night."*
—ROBERTA MAXWELL

I always envy people who can say, "I saw the original Broadway production of *Death of a Salesman*." Or *Carousel*. Or *The Glass Menagerie*. Even more do I revere those who can say, "I *was in* the original production of . . ." Here are three accounts of the making of memorable theater and of working with memorable directors.

Cameron Mitchell was a disgruntled camper in December 1985 when he arrived in Virginia to act in a mini-series . . . and his luggage did not. Outside, the temperature was a brisk fourteen degrees. But inside his tiny cubicle of a dressing room, the luggage and the weather were promptly forgotten when I asked him to recall the historic original production of Arthur Miller's *Death of a Salesman*.

"In 1949," he enthused, "I was a thousand miles from nowhere in Saskatchewan when I got a phone call from my agent in New York telling me he's sending me a great new play. I read it. I cried seven times in the first thirty pages. I phoned my agent. I said, 'I have to play Happy! Get me this play!'

"They got me an appointment with the director, Elia Kazan. Everybody called him 'Gadge.' I pay for my own airline ticket. I fly across Canada through blizzards and snowstorms—I remember, the plane lost a motor—and I arrive in New York on Saturday morning. I'm supposed to meet Kazan that very morning, and he's not there. I call my agent: 'Kazan is waiting for you in New Haven.' He was directing a Kurt Weill-Alan Jay Lerner musical called *Love Life*.

"I was dead tired. But I caught the train, got to New Haven, went to the Taft Hotel, called Kazan. He said, 'Look around the lobby for a tall guy who looks like a young, Jewish Abraham Lincoln. That'll be Artie Miller.' I looked around, found Artie Miller. Kazan came down. The three of us walk out of the hotel, into that little park across the way, just chatting. By the time we reached the end of the park, Kazan says, 'Artie, he's our boy, isn't he?' I still hadn't read a line.

"Kazan had to attend a matinee. He said, 'You and Artie go play tennis.' He took me aside and said, 'Let him beat you.' So we played tennis. Between the matinee and evening performance we go up to Gadge's room. He threw me the script. He said, 'Read it.' I read Willy; I read Linda; I read everybody's part, including stage directions, from page one through to the end. The first time *Death of a Salesman* was ever read aloud in the history of man, I read it, in the Taft Hotel. And Artie and Gadge just sat there and beamed at each other, because they knew it was a great play.

"Their first choice for Willy Loman was Paul Muni, but his wife, Bella, botched that up. She wouldn't allow Kazan to meet with her husband until after the contracts were signed. In 1949 Gadge was the number-one director in America. You didn't say that to Kazan. Then Freddy March read it and turned it down. Walter Huston read it and said it was the greatest part he'd ever read, but that if he played it he'd be dead inside two months. Ironically, he died the next year, anyway. Lee Cobb was almost the bottom of the totem pole. And Mildred Dunnock, who played Linda, almost didn't get to read. They wanted a physically larger woman. But she begged them. Finally, out of desperation, they let her read, and the rest is history.

"I played Happy, and we filled out the family with Arthur Kennedy as my big brother, Biff. He didn't want any part of it. Gadge flew out to Los Angeles, found him in the middle of a tennis game, and pleaded with him for thirty minutes to do the play. I think Kennedy only relented so he could finish his tennis match.

"We rehearsed on top of the New Amsterdam Theater building on Forty-second Street. Throughout rehearsals, nothing was changed. The script I read aloud in New Haven was the final script. There was no need for changes. We all knew it was good. Everybody except

Arthur Kennedy. Every night after rehearsal, he and I would walk up to our hotel on Fifty-eighth Street. I would be so exhilarated, and he'd start complaining: 'This fucking play. We'll be lucky if we get to opening night.' I'd come back at him: 'You're wrong, Johnny'—his real name was John Arthur Kennedy—'Thirty, forty years from now, kids in drama school will be acting our bedroom scene.' But by the time we reached the hotel, he'd have me so depressed I'd want to jump out the window.

"We opened in Philadelphia, at the Locust Street Theater, on a Saturday night. So many of the regular first-nighters didn't attend. Honest to God, they thought it was a murder mystery. There were no stars. Who was Lee J. Cobb? Well, the next morning the *Philadelphia Bulletin* ran its review on the front page, and Lee became the biggest star in the American theater. Throughout rehearsals, Kazan had sat on Lee Cobb until there was not one ounce of self-pity in his performance. And it paid off on opening night. Lee was a mountain, a monument.

"That first Philadelphia audience was so great, I cannot tell you. When I combed my hair and said, 'I'm gonna get married, Mom,' they loved Happy. But later, in the scene where I deny my father—'That ain't my old man. Are you kidding, honey? Come on, we'll paint the town'—a woman in the audience threw her purse at me.

"I swear, the audience that night stayed till 3:30 in the morning. They would not leave. And of course, once the reviews came out, we were the toast of Philadelphia. Henry Fonda brought the whole company of *Mister Roberts* down from New York to see a matinee. Kirk Douglas, Van Johnson, local Mafia gangsters. I remember them all backstage crying their hearts out, because every one of them had a problem with his father. Danny Thomas was playing at Palumbo's, the local nightclub. He invited us all to come as his guests. He told the audience, 'Beg, borrow, steal. You've got to see this play.'

"I spent the next two years on Broadway, playing Arthur Kennedy's brother. Twenty-five years later, I bumped into him in Albuquerque. I hadn't seen him in a lifetime. He threw his arms around me. He said, 'By God, you were right about one thing.'

"I said, 'What's that, John?'

"He said, 'They *are* doing our bedroom scene in drama schools.' Of course they are, and they always will. It's a universal play, a timeless play. Let's face it. Even today, we all try to sell ourselves. We're all salesmen. Everybody."

———

By the time I spoke with **Bert Convy** in 1975, he had departed the theater for the more lucrative world of TV game-show hosting. Nevertheless, he was proud of his Broadway roots, proud of having created the role of Cliff in *Cabaret* and of having costarred with Robert Ryan in the hit 1969 revival of *The Front Page.* But perhaps he was proudest of having survived the Broadway tryout of *Fiddler on the Roof.*

"Jerome Robbins was our director-choreographer. Jerry is a genius, but he is also a killer. Offstage he is the nicest man in the world. Onstage he is an enormously creative and gifted monster. In rehearsals he gives you a note for every line, and then he rips you to shreds.

"We opened in Detroit in July '64. The first review said *Fiddler* was an ordinary show about an ordinary subject. After that, the tension became something awful. We were the last show to go out of town without a day off. The company would arrive at the Fisher Theater at ten in the morning and rehearse all day in intense heat. The actors were dropping like flies. We worked long and hard, under duress.

"It was while we were in Detroit that Zero Mostel first began to cut up. I was playing Perchik, the revolutionary. One night, during the scene where I ask for Tevye's daughter's hand in marriage, Zero turned upstage and looked at us with a big red Life Saver stuck between his teeth. Julia Migenes and I stood there and shook with laughter, trying desperately not to break up. The next day at rehearsal Jerome Robbins tore into us. He told us to not ever allow that to happen again. 'Zero has so much energy,' he said, 'he can carry it off. You can't.'

"We moved on to Washington, D.C. In Washington Jerry asked me why my performance had become so lifeless. I told him it was because I was playing from note to note, that it was no longer my performance. I'm still amazed I had the courage to say that to him. But it freed me, and he allowed me to go back to what I had been doing.

"The turning point for *Fiddler* came in Washington when Jerry added the bottle dance to the wedding scene. That number was pure genius. When we heard the audience response to the bottle dance, we realized *Fiddler on the Roof* had evolved into something special. Even so, the show didn't really come together until the previews in New York. At the final preview before opening night, we received our first standing ovation.

"But by opening night, I think everybody in the company truly detested that play. Being on the road with *Fiddler* was like being in prison."

Peter Shaffer's *Equus* likely will not endure with the same popularity as have *Death of a Salesman* and *Fiddler on the Roof*. But in this era of dwindling Broadway drama, its 1,209-performance run in the mid-1970s now seems miraculous. *Equus* concerns a psychiatrist's tormented journey as he works with a deeply disturbed young patient who has blinded six horses. Shaffer stunned his '70s audiences by employing total male and female nudity. It was riveting, yet unsensational. How better to show man at his most vulnerable?

Anthony Hopkins' psychiatrist was supported by a strong cast that included Peter Firth, Marian Seldes, Frances Sternhagen, Michael Higgins and, as the stable girl, **Roberta Maxwell**. By the time she appeared in *Equus*, Maxwell, a product of Stratford, Ontario, and Minnesota's Tyrone Guthrie Theater, had already played most of the major classic roles. But because for five minutes a night she was highly visible on Broadway, she was being approached by strangers in sleek limousines who wanted to whisk her away to South American plantations. We spoke in her dressing room at the Plymouth Theater.

"Our director, John Dexter, can be a very difficult man," she said with a laugh. "He's one of Guthrie's boys, a pint-sized Guthrie, a real weaselly version of Dr. Guthrie." Then serious: "There's one thing on his mind at all times, and that is the work. The work is everything. He instilled in us that we must not be complacent, that you are only as good as the ground you stand on, and that everything else except the work is absolutely irrelevant to an artist.

"First he broke us down physically. We did rigorous physical exercises for half an hour before every rehearsal. Then when we were literally prone and exhausted on the floor, lying on our stomachs gasping for air, one of us would get up and read his or her favorite poem. Through those poems, we found out a lot about each other. Within two days we were a functioning company, all working for the same thing, which was the play.

"The boy, Peter Firth, was eventually let off because he was the only actor who had done the play before at the National Theatre in London. Dexter thought he was too far ahead, that he was holding his performance, that we weren't interacting properly with him. So he was sent home to lie in front of the television and eat junk food and be Americanized, and the understudy rehearsed for a week.

Amazing: that Dexter should have that confidence in his play and in his own work that he would be able to let the leading actor off. Not making the other actors reach for him, but letting it take shape.

"As the opening came closer and closer, Dexter protected us completely from the outside. He would not allow Kermit Bloomgarden, our producer, into rehearsals. Would not allow photos. Would not allow interviews. No one even saw a runthrough. Dexter felt that the show was being oversold by word of mouth. He stressed the fact that it's just a play. If it succeeds, that's wonderful. If it doesn't, it's been an effort in our lives and we'll go on and do other things.

"During rehearsals I never took my clothes off. When the first preview came, Peter and I were scared, and the rest of the company was scared. Nobody had seen us without our clothes. At that first preview, at the end of the first act, the end of the boy's horse ride, there was a *stunning* silence, followed by tumultuous applause. It was very exciting. Then at the end of the play, when we took our clothes off for the first time, we could feel the tension from the rest of the company. When that moment happened, and when *we* realized what it was, it really was like the Garden of Eden."

Now her voice softened, and stillness settled on the dressing room. Time truly seemed to stop. No one in the hallway. No one on the stairs. We might have been the only two people in the theater. Long silences between each soft phrase. And the lightbulbs that surrounded her dressing-room table seemed to swell in intensity until we were in blinding light, vicariously reexperiencing that first performance.

"It was like a hot, hot day. Total purity. Completely naked. A real experience, not an acted experience. Not knowing what was going to happen. So open; so vulnerable. Everybody giving to that moment, hoping. And the stillness and the heat from the stage lights, like being in the desert. Dead quiet. When I put my arms around the boy, his body was running with sweat. Slipped off him. At the end of the play there was a sense of expansion, and the audience going crazy because they'd been at this event."

She stopped. In the silence we each found our breath, and the clock resumed ticking.

"After that first preview Dexter pulled us back. We were all on tenterhooks, and Dexter kept us like horses reined in. Never gave us anything. 'Well, darlings, now you've done that, you think you've accomplished something. Well, it's just not so. You've got a million miles to go.' So we were kept going and going right up to the last day.

"On the last day he did something incredible. He said, 'Right, darlings, you're all coming in in the afternoon. We're going to watch the understudies do the show.' Our hearts fell. Nobody wanted to do it. The understudies didn't want to do it. We all wanted to kill him. He said, 'And we'll have a little drink before they perform.'

"We came at twelve o'clock, and he had a sumptuous feast laid on in the downstairs foyer. Cold salmon, lox, French champagne. We all got quite merry. Then we went upstairs, and the understudies did the first act. During the break Dexter said, 'Now darlings, we don't want to see any more of that. Everybody go up onstage and you'll all do a poem for me.' So we did poems, and by that time we were no longer high. We all had headaches, but it was too late to go home and take a bath. So we went to our dressing rooms. We opened our packages and telegrams. We all loved each other. Such a unit. Such care. And it was him. Incredible man. Work, work. Beyond and above everything. Manipulative emotionally. John Dexter had driven us to a peak for that one moment, opening night. And then we came onstage and did the play.

"At the end, there was a tremendous ovation. And Peter Shaffer's face shone, because he'd been afraid. We were all afraid how the play would be perceived. Afterwards there was a huge party. Dexter wouldn't come. He was left on the corner with a torn paper bag trying to get a taxi. Looked miserable. His job was finished."

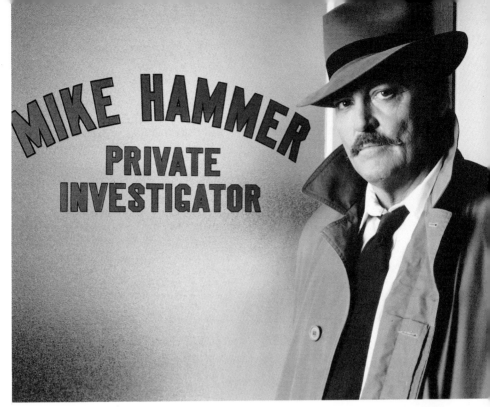

Stacy Keach as Mike Hammer

...and as Richard III

Credit: Joan Marcus

George Rose and Company in *Beacon Hill* (1975)

George Rose rehearses
Kismet in St. Louis

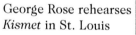

Credit: St. Louis Mercantile Library

Barry Bostwick, the original Danny Zuko in *Grease* (1972)

Bostwick sings like Dick Powell in *Movie Movie* (1978)

State Theater, Minneapolis, 1995

Gregory Peck in
*The Valley of
Decision* (1945)

Atticus, with Scout (Mary Badham) and Jem (Phillip Alford), in *To Kill a Mockingbird* ((1962)

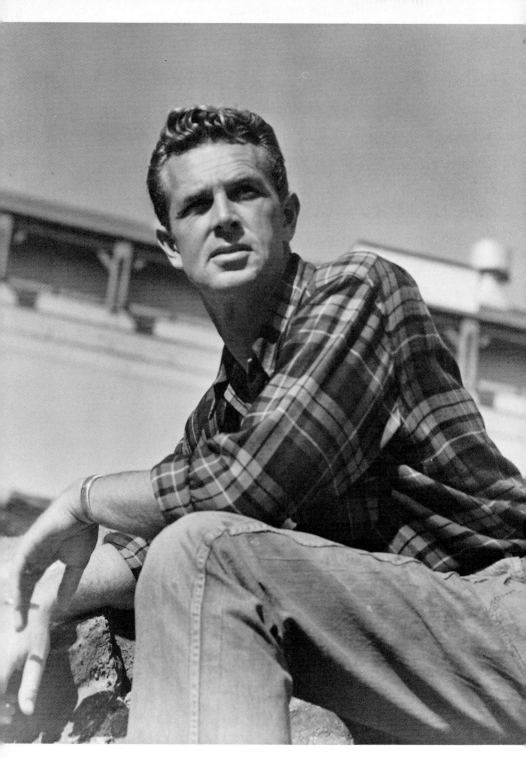

Sterling Hayden, "The Most Beautiful Man in the Movies"

Sterling Hayden as Gen. Jack Ripper in *Dr. Strangelove* (1964)

...and on his Sausalito balcony (1982)

Jeannie Carson, Igor Gavins (left) and William Biff McGuire in *Camelot* (1963)

Roberta Maxwell and Peter Firth in *Equus* (1974)

John Cullum (left) and Kevin Klein in *On the Twentieth Century* (1978)
Credit: Martha Swope

Frank Langella as Count Dracula   John Voight as *The Champ* (1979)

Lillian Gish in *Souls Triumphant* (1917)

Lillian Gish at age 90 (1984)

Clark Gable and Beulah Bondi in *Lone Star* (1951)

One of Bondi's many
mother roles in *Track
of the Cat* (1954)

Jessica Tandy in
Driving Miss Daisy
(1989)

Jessica Tandy and Hume Cronyn in *To Dance with the White Dog* (1993)

Danny Kaye in *Skokie* (1980)

Eli Wallach and Anne Jackson in *The Diary of Anne Frenk* (1978)
Credit: Elizabeth Wolynski

Paul Winfield in
Sounder (1972)

Paul Winfield and Cicely
Tyson in *King* (1978)

As Arthur Franz (center) and Herbert Anderson (far right) look on, José Ferrer douses Fred MacMurray with champagne in *The Caine Mutiny* (1954).

Ferrer with Julie Hagerty in *A Midsummer Night's Sex Comedy* (1982)

Cyrano

CHAPTER FIVE

ACTOR LADIES

*"Film is the most powerful and persuasive develop-
ment of this century, and America just treats it like
popcorn."*
—LILLIAN GISH

*"I'm sure I have never played two characters alike. If
you have a different mentality and really become that
person, you can't repeat yourself."*
—BEULAH BONDI

*"You cannot say to yourself, this character reminds
me of so-and-so in that other production, so I'll play it
that way. You must always begin anew."*
—JESSICA TANDY

"Not possible. Not possible." Not possible for shy, awkward young
girls to succeed in a profession that weighs so heavily on poise and
beauty? But acting is a vocation in which *miracle* is practically a
byword. Not possible? Consider.

My most enduring image of Lillian Gish: The actress is seated
on a sofa in her beige bathrobe, spoonfeeding lentil soup to an ailing wayfarer. As she gazes intently into his brown eyes, the tresses
of her waist-length ash-blonde hair gently brush across his wan, color-
drained face.

An indelible moment from *The Birth of a Nation*, you ask? Or *Way Down East*, or *Broken Blossoms,* or any of those other D. W. Griffith-directed silent films we all regard as classics, despite the fact that most of us haven't seen them?

No. This image does not appear in any Gish film. It occurred in 1980 on Seabrook Island, off the South Carolina coast. I was the pale wayfarer, and legendary Lillian Gish, "the first lady of the screen" before the movies had even learned to speak, was my nurse. It was a rare occasion when being ill seemed almost worthwhile.

To set the scene: In June 1980, while working as a publicist for CBS Entertainment, I was assigned to a television movie titled *Thin Ice*, to star Kate Jackson as a high school teacher who becomes entangled in a clandestine love affair with one of her students. Lillian Gish was cast as Kate Jackson's grandmother.

When I learned that I'd be working with Lillian Gish, I knew little about silent movies other than the celebrity names—Chaplin, Fairbanks, Gish, Keaton, Pickford, Valentino. If Gish was among the most prominent of those names, I assumed it was due as much to endurance as talent: She simply had outlived the others.

I had a lot to learn.

Lillian Diana Gish was born in Springfield, Ohio, forty miles west of Columbus. Despite her lifelong denials of vanity, she adamantly refused to disclose her true age to reporters. Not until after her death at age ninety-nine in 1993 did her longtime manager, James Frasher, reveal that Gish was born on October 14, 1893. By the time her sister, Dorothy, was born five years later, their parents' marriage was already unraveling. After James Gish deserted his family, Mary Robinson McConnell Gish—forced to provide for her daughters— became an "actor lady." Using the stage name *May Bernard*, she barnstormed the country in now-forgotten heart-on-your-sleeve melodramas that loved to place a child in distress. Mary ignored Noel Coward's still-to-be-written dictum, "Don't Put Your Daughter on the Stage," and did precisely that. She toured with wee Dorothy and farmed Lillian out to other actresses.

Lillian Gish made her stage debut at age nine in a melodrama that featured another up-and-comer, eighteen-year-old Walter Huston. "It all happened before my memory," Gish would tell *The New York Times* in 1960. The threadbare nights spent trying to sleep on freezing railway-station benches, the painful separations from mother and sister, were best unremembered. At least the family could reunite in the summers, when theaters closed due to the heat. In June, July and August, the family Gish would share a New York City apartment with another unemployed mother-daughter acting team. The daughter, Gladys Smith, was Lillian's age.

When the opportunity arose, Mary Gish retired from the stage and opened a confectionery next to a movie theater in East St. Louis, Illinois. Lillian attended Ursuline Academy at a convent across the Mississippi River in St. Louis. That one year of schooling was her single longest stretch of formal education. Alas, the year came to a fiery end when, in a blaze singed with prophetic irony, the East St. Louis movie theater burned down, taking the confectionery with it. The Gish women were forced to return to acting.

One afternoon while on tour, Lillian and Dorothy (teenagers now) returned from the picture show all abuzz, for they had spotted their young chum Gladys Smith in a movie. (Poor Gladys! Was she on such hard times that she was reduced to making movies?) When next the Gishes were in New York, they located their former roommate at the Biograph film studio on Fourteenth Street. There, they learned that Gladys Smith had changed her name to Mary Pickford. Mary, who was working for director David Wark Griffith, arranged for all three Gishes to appear in *An Unseen Enemy*.

Griffith was about to relocate his film company to sunny California. Mama Gish and Dorothy also made the move, but Lillian—who was cast in an elaborate David Belasco play starring Mary Pickford—had to remain in New York. Although *A Good Little Devil* was a success, Lillian—once again abandoned by her family—grew seriously ill with pernicious anemia. The sympathetic Belasco released Lillian from the Broadway production and even paid her way west.

Thus began the Griffith years. Don't think that D. W. Griffith was directing classic after film classic. More often than not, he churned out movies as fast as his assistants could load film into the camera: Westerns, thrillers, tales plucked out of that morning's newspaper headlines. But along the way, Griffith and his players, in learning how to tell stories on film, were creating and refining a new art. The first "flicker," devised in 1894 (when Lillian was only a year old), lasted sixteen seconds. Griffith's *The Birth of a Nation* in 1915 held viewers spellbound for 160 minutes.

It also made a star of its twenty-two-year-old ingenue, Lillian Gish.

No one was more surprised than Griffith when the public latched on to Lillian. But once they did, he spent the next six years directing films tailored to her strengths, nearly forty pictures in which her persona was as pure as the wind machine-driven snow. In movies like *Broken Blossoms*, where her portrayal of an abused twelve-year-old broke viewers' hearts, and *Way Down East*, where she was rescued from an ice floe as it drifted toward a waterfall on the Connecticut River—no stand-in there; that was really Gish floating through those bitter-cold rapids—Lillian Gish was the innocent embodiment of the American Virgin.

(So she would ever remain, the goodness of her life mirrored in her pristine complexion. In her final major starring role at age ninety-four, Gish played Bette Davis' sister in *The Whales of August* [1987]. When I saw the film, I was mesmerized by the sweet chasteness that still radiated from Gish's face. Davis' sere face, by contrast, was so furrowed it looked ripe for fall planting.)

During those dizzying, impressionable years with Griffith, Gish was shaped and molded by her father-figure director, nineteen years her senior. Griffith transformed this essentially illiterate young girl into an accomplished filmmaker. He taught her how to run a camera and how to edit film. Like Pygmalion's, so great was Griffith's confidence in his Galatea that in 1920 he even allowed Lillian to direct a film in which Dorothy starred.

As a neophyte in *An Unseen Enemy* in 1912, Gish was paid five dollars. Now, as America's favorite actress, she was raking in a thousand dollars a week—and there was still more money to be made. But Griffith, an independent producer, no longer could afford to pay the salary she commanded. So in 1922 he pushed his creation out of the nest.

Gish made the most of her newfound independence. In 1923, in the first American movie ever filmed in Italy, she starred in (and edited) *The White Sister*, in which she cast Ronald Colman in his first leading role. A year later she starred with Dorothy (and young William Powell) in *Romola*—though by now, Lillian's name was above the title, Dorothy's below. Both films were directed by Henry King, who later would direct Gregory Peck in six pictures.

When she signed with MGM in 1926, her contract (eight hundred thousand dollars to star in five films over two years) made her the highest-paid actress in the movies. But more important than the money—and what was to prove more threatening—was the unprecedented degree of artistic control that the contract bestowed upon her. This, from MGM, a film factory unaccustomed to signing away power.

Silent-screen actress Louise Brooks later theorized that MGM placed Gish under contract at such a spectacular salary "in order to methodically destroy her." As Brooks explains in her 1982 memoir, *Lulu in Hollywood*, "Marked first for destruction was Lillian Gish . . . Of all the stars who stood between the movie moguls and the full realization of their greed and self-aggrandizement, it was Lillian Gish who most painfully imposed her picture knowledge and business acumen upon the producers."

Gish's first movie for MGM, the lavish *La Bohème* with John Gilbert, fit neatly into the company mold. But her second picture, an adaptation of Nathaniel Hawthorne's *The Scarlet Letter*, was made against the company's wishes. The fact that *The Scarlet Letter* was an artistic and commercial success was lost on the MGM brass, who so intruded themselves on *The Wind* that Gish lost her enthusiasm for filmmaking. Seventy years later, *The Wind* now stands out as Gish's *Magnificent Ambersons*. Like Orson Welles' recut 1942 classic, *The Wind* triumphs despite corporate obstruction. It is Louise Brooks' theory that *The Wind* "was so loaded with sex and violence that MGM held up its release until the first Academy Award had been safely dealt to Janet Gaynor."

By now sound had arrived, and Gish could hear the writing on the wall. Disillusioned that Hollywood was turning its back on the silent art form she had helped to establish, she left MGM for United Artists. There, at the movie studio co-owned by Mary Pickford, she made her first talkie, *One Romantic Night* (1930). When it proved undistinguished, Gish pragmatically faced the fact that, after having appeared in seventy-one motion pictures, her reign as America's favorite film star had ended. She publicly declared that Hollywood was "an emotional Detroit" and returned to New York, determined to resurrect her stage career.

This resurrection was supervised by *New York Herald* theater critic George Jean Nathan, with whom Gish was having a discreet affair that would continue for more than a decade. Nathan provided her with an entrée to the Broadway elite who might otherwise have looked down their noses at a mere movie queen. Instead, Gish returned to the stage in august company. She starred with Walter Connolly and Osgood Perkins in *Uncle Vanya* and as Ophelia, to John Gielgud's Hamlet, in the acclaimed 1936 production directed by Guthrie McClintic.

Then in 1942, without any fanfare, Lillian Gish returned to films as a supporting actress in *The Commandos Strike at Dawn* starring

Paul Muni. Five years later she received her first (and only) Academy Award nomination as Gregory Peck's tearful mother in *Duel in the Sun*. (She received an honorary Oscar in 1970.) She continued to star on Broadway and on tour, wherever the work took her. When television became popular, she acted there too.

Crime and Punishment . . . The Curious Savage . . . The Trip to Bountiful . . . The Night of the Hunter . . . All the Way Home . . . I Never Sang for My Father. Each new performance, every passing year, added to the legend of Lillian.

D. W. Griffith died in 1948, alone, ignored and embittered, in a Hollywood hotel room. That same year Mother Gish also died. Her two daughters, now true orphans of the storm, continued to live lives that might have been defined by their unsullied early film roles. "Back in the 1950s," Eileen Heckart recalled, "when I was on Broadway doing *Picnic* and *The Bad Seed* and *The Dark at the Top of the Stairs*, Lillian and Dorothy came to every single one of my opening nights. Afterwards, I'd be desperate for a Scotch, and they would insist on taking me to Schrafft's for a hot-fudge sundae. Only after I went to Schrafft's with Lillian and Dorothy could I go on to the opening-night party and have a drink."

Dorothy Gish died in 1968. Now, deprived of immediate family, Lillian turned with a missionary's zeal to the task of rekindling an appreciation for silent films. "It was a new art form and it's lost," she told a reporter. But it wasn't going to stay lost, not if Lillian Gish had her way. Her crusade began in earnest in 1969 when she published her memoir, *The Movies, Mr. Griffith and Me*. Then, as she had as a child, she barnstormed the United States and Canada, this time in a one-woman show that included clips from silent films. Once her battle for silence was joined, no matter where Lillian Gish's career took her in the ensuing years, her mind was never far from those glory days.

We first met on a Friday afternoon prior to our departure for South Carolina. Her spacious thirteenth-floor Manhattan co-op on East Fifty-seventh Street was a hushed shrine to the past. Gish had once told a reporter, "The only luxury left in the world is privacy." Here was her private world, a virtuous domain composed of cut glass, Chinese porcelain vases and silver services. The walls were hung with Italian rococo mirrors and paintings (one by Noel Coward, another of Sarah Bernhardt). Ornately framed photos covered the end tables. Hovering over everything was a huge oil portrait of Mother Gish. A bronze cast of Mother's hands rested on a nearby table.

Now, Mother's indefatigable eighty-six-year-old daughter sat poised on a Louis XV chair whose spindly legs looked as if they would splinter if anyone heavier than the gossamer Gish sat on them. It seemed as though she could float about the room if she so chose. It wasn't simply that she was slight, and frail; there was something translucent about her.

Her first remarks were a tribute to the woman whose presence still permeated the surroundings. "We had such a mother that Dorothy and I both adored," she began. "She was one of those women who was born to be a mother. She didn't have any other interest. But whereas our mother taught us the importance of security, the example of our father taught us the value of insecurity."

The value of insecurity? I wondered to myself. What value is that? Before I was able to ask, she explained, "Even now I can't tell you which is the more important, but I do believe that what happens to a child between the ages of ten and eighteen is enormously influential. Insecurity develops a child's character, helps that child to confront the world head-on, helps to instill maturity at an early age. I don't think there's anything wrong with a child learning early on that you have to work to earn your living."

The actress was pleased that the *Thin Ice* producer had scheduled a week of rehearsal prior to the start of filming. "There isn't anything in the arts with more than one person that does not rehearse, except film," she bemoaned. "Musicians, if there are two, they must rehearse. If you're in the theater, you rehearse. Dancers prepare for a performance for months. Prizefighters, football, baseball, you name it. Even athletes have better sense than the people in the movies, who hardly ever rehearse.

"Griffith taught us that you must rehearse. This was imperative to him, because more often than not we had no money for retakes. My earliest films were shot in just one or two days, but they were carefully rehearsed first. That's why Mr. Griffith looked for actors who were theater trained and disciplined. Everything's changed now. Today movies cost millions of dollars, and they don't rehearse at all. I feel sorry for actors who sit around on film sets and wait to be called. Of course, we didn't have to be called, because we were already there. We didn't have stand-ins, you see. That was a luxury that came later. Nine years I spent with Griffith, talking my way through silent movies."

Talking? I ignorantly asked. I thought they were silent.

"Of course we spoke, but no one ever gave me a word to say. Whoever my character was, I found her words during rehearsal. At the end of rehearsals, the cutter would come in and write down what we were saying. Our words often became the subtitles, because our improvised dialogue was borne out of the action. But Griffith never told us who our characters were. He'd say, 'I've got the plot. It's up to you to find your character.'"

Even a silent-movie ninny like me knew enough to ask about the making of Griffith's 1915 epic *The Birth of a Nation*.

"We rehearsed *The Birth of a Nation* for months," she said. "Consequently, the film itself was made in only nine weeks. Everyone was sworn to secrecy, because movies were filmed so quickly in those days, if other directors got wind of what Griffith was up to, they would have tried to get the same story out ahead of him. Griffith advertised that *Birth of a Nation* had fifteen thousand men in the battle scenes. Nonsense. We did the entire Civil War, both sides, with three hundred men.

"Nine weeks was a long time to take with a movie. *Judith of Bethulia* [Griffith's first feature-length spectacle (1914)] took four weeks. We made *The Battle of the Sexes*, five reels, in five days and five nights. There were no unions then. But however hard we worked, Griffith worked that much harder. We all worked hard, and we *liked* it."

She still liked it, liked talking about it. "Griffith was the father of film," she continued. "He believed that silent films were going to become a universal language and that film could lead men to talk out their differences. 'You think about that the next time you face a camera,' he told us. We *did* think about it, and we took film seriously. There wasn't anybody but Griffith in those days. And not since, either. The only person who's advanced film technique since Mr. Griffith's day is Walt Disney. His animation added birds and animals to movies. His films have found appreciative audiences around the world, the same as silent films did. Disney understood how to break past language in order to communicate with audiences."

It infuriated this bantam missionary that a movie theater around the corner from her co-op was named the D. W. Griffith. "It's a tiny little place, not much wider than this room," she fumed. "It hurts your pride to go in there, especially when you think of the movie palaces that were built to play Griffith's films. They were cathedrals. Every country had them, and people came by the millions. *Birth of a Nation* played to three times the population of the cities and towns it went into. In many a town, it was the first movie the people had seen, other than newsreels. Of course, newsreels are more important than anything we did, because they capture our history. All the wars, all the peace treaties, all the history of our century is captured on newsreels, if only they won't disintegrate. Out in Hollywood they're not interested in newsreels. They're only interested in money. But then, I sometimes wonder if anyone in this country truly appreciates movies anymore. Film is the most powerful and persuasive development of this century, and America just treats it like popcorn."

In an effort to say something supportive about sound films, I mentioned that *The Night of the Hunter* (1955), in which she faced down the menacing Robert Mitchum, had begun to be regarded as a classic.

"Why not?" she indignantly replied. "It's good. Any film that's good, time makes better, because films are getting worse." She recalled how *The Night of the Hunter* was the only motion picture Charles Laughton directed: "We all wanted to help Charles so much, we kept making suggestions. But he was so insecure, he took our comments to be criticisms, so we all stopped."

We stopped too. As she escorted me to the door, we passed a wall of books. Gish noted that her personal library included the collected works of H. L. Mencken and George Jean Nathan. Five biographies had been written about Mencken, she added; none about Nathan. "People simply aren't interested in him," she remarked about her former beau.

Why not?

"Mencken, you see, never pretended to be anything other than himself, but Nathan spent his life striving to *not* be himself. His life was a lie, and people aren't very interested in liars."

As I was leaving, she mentioned that she planned to watch *Dallas* on television that evening. Lillian Gish an aficionado of J. R.? She must have read my thought, because she rushed on: "The people who produce that show know what Mr. Griffith knew. They cast the show with beautiful people, and then they rely on close-ups to convey what they want to say. And not just close-ups, but close-ups from eye level. Right now, as we speak, I'm looking in your eyes. I'm not looking under your chin, which is what so many other television series do. Some filmmakers like to place the camera low, so they can sit down, and the viewer sees angles up the nostrils. Well, I'm not interested in nostrils. I'm interested in the eyes. Griffith painted the face with lights. That's what *Dallas* does, and that's why it's a hit all over the world. Sometimes when I watch it, I don't even turn the sound on. I just look at the faces. They're clean; they're interesting; and you know what the people are saying without hearing the words."

(There's nary a film actor alive who doesn't have an opinion about close-ups. Three years after meeting Lillian Gish, I received a dissenting view from British film veteran James Mason [whose favorite American television series was *Sesame Street*]. "There's absolutely no need for an actor to demand close-ups in order to convey what he thinks is an important point," said the star of *Lolita, 20,000 Leagues Under the Sea* and *A Star Is Born*. "In most instances, if an actor is properly recording how his character is reacting to his circumstances, then you can capture that emotion from whatever angle the camera happens to shoot him at. I always feel that there should be a very close relationship in the thinking of a screen director to a Movietone News cameraman. Something is happening, and the circumstances dictate how the news cameraman is going to photograph it. Sometimes the newsman must film under extreme difficulty. But so long as the viewer can understand what is happening, then it doesn't matter what the angle of the camera is. The same is true with movies. If the actors are creating a true happening, then they can be photographed from every which angle.")

Two weeks later we convened in South Carolina for *Thin Ice*. My final day there, I awoke ill and remained bedridden. But that evening I forced myself to drive to the Seabrook Island condominium shared by Lillian Gish and her assistant, James Frasher. I needed to retrieve a book I had lent Frasher. The instant Gish saw me standing in the doorway, pale and sickly, she took charge. She led me to the sofa and fluffed the pillows. She instructed Frasher to prepare a bowl of lentil soup, which she then spoonfed me. Looking up into her chaste, unlined face, I could actually see the child of her former self.

As she sat beside me on the sofa, Gish began to chat about topics a proper gentleman wouldn't dare raise in a formal interview. She described how she used to faint frequently, and how she had a physical fitness mentor who was more "womanly" than she was. Two circular strokes of the soup spoon made it clear that Gish was referring to her petite chest. But, she continued, she had learned the importance of hygiene. "The next time you go to the theater and are sitting behind people," she instructed, "look at their hair. It's dead. All the life is burned out. My hair is long enough to sit on.

That's because I never allowed an iron to be put on my hair. Suppose I put an iron on my skin. What would it do? That's what heat does to your hair. Hair is a living thing. It's alive. We first learned that when Mother took us to Francis Fox, Scientific Care of the Scalp. They had mostly men. I sent Burgess Meredith there. He's still got good hair, if you notice. I only use a comb on my hair, never a brush. It actually takes me seven combs and brushes to stay clean. Seven brushes for teeth, face and body, and to stir up circulation. But the most important thing is to avoid cigarettes and drugs of any kind, including sleeping pills."

That waving soup spoon underscored her stern advice. She noticed the spoon suspended above my forehead, returned it to the soup bowl, smiled, and said, "Just listen to me. I must sound like the most vain woman in South Carolina. But it's true. When I first got into the movies, I was obsessed with learning how my face worked. Since then, I've spent my entire life believing there's no room for vanity in the movies. All you have to do is watch your performance on film, and you'll see a thousand flaws."

Nearly three years later, in May 1983, we crossed paths again, this time in New Orleans on the set of a television-movie adaptation of the British stage comedy *Hobson's Choice*. Richard Thomas portrayed a young cobbler attempting to establish his own business; Gish had a cameo role as a wealthy woman so impressed by his artisanship that she financed his venture.

Her first scene was to be filmed in one of New Orleans' creamy pink mansions on picturesque St. Charles Street. It was a bright, balmy Saturday morning; but when I walked into the foyer and saw how low the camera was poised, I felt storm clouds brewing. Sure enough, as soon as Gish arrived on the set, she admonished the director of photography to raise the elevation. "If God had intended us to be seen from that angle," she declared, "he would have put eyes in our belly buttons."

The camera was raised.

That night I took Gish and Frasher to dinner in the French Quarter. She was still flush with enthusiasm from the day's work, having thoroughly enjoyed her scene with "that darling actor," Richard Thomas. Frasher mentioned that the preceding Sunday he had watched Thomas on television in *All Quiet on the Western Front*. "I couldn't watch it," Gish injected. "You see, I was there. During World War I, Griffith brought Dorothy and me to France and took us to the front lines. We filmed scenes for three different movies. You wouldn't even see a trained nurse up where we were. All those rats. All that mud. The filth was much worse than any movie could show.

"Then back in London Griffith made us go to Waterloo Station and watch the soldiers arrive home with no arms, no legs, no faces. And their loved ones meeting them. Sometimes the loved ones were there to meet the dead, soldiers in wooden boxes. That's where we learned about emotion and suffering. Griffith told us, 'You know nothing about life. Now's your chance. God willing, you'll never have another.'

"Four years later when we made *Orphans of the Storm* about the French Revolution, Dorothy had scenes down in the cellar with rats running all over. Muddy, dirty, filthy rats. People asked how she could do that. I couldn't explain."

We shared our mutual disappointment in *Thin Ice*. (The producer and director had wasted what was intended as a week of rehearsal; instead they occupied their days by taking a lovely script and "improving" it to mediocrity.) What Gish remembered most about the experience was Kate Jackson's ears. "She has such beautiful ears," the actress remarked admiringly. She also recalled how unhappy Jackson was because of her crumbling marriage to Andrew Stevens. "You don't need a husband when you have a loving mother and sister," Gish professed with alarming sincerity. Then, the worn record: "My mother was perfect, the most perfect human being I ever knew. She told me that men and women aren't made to live together—"

A young fan approached the table and requested an autograph. As Gish signed her name on a napkin, the fellow told her how much more he had enjoyed her silent-screen version of *The Scarlet Letter* than a recent television mini-series adaptation. Gish thanked him with a noncommittal smile, but after he left she said, "I saw *The Scarlet Letter* on TV. They spent three million dollars on it, and it was just awful. Do you know how many movies we could have made for three million dollars?"

What was so awful about it?

"It had no sense of period. That was 1640!" she answered with fragile outrage. "The actresses had their hair bobbed and their eyebrows all plucked. They wore makeup. They had no understanding that people moved differently in the seventeenth century. They weren't telling Nathaniel Hawthorne's story."

I reminded her that MGM hadn't wanted Gish to tell Hawthorne's story either.

"That's true," she confirmed. "When I went to MGM, I told Mr. Mayer what films I wanted to make, and I included *The Scarlet Letter*. Mr. Mayer said, 'The churches and the women's groups will not allow you to do it.'

"And I said, 'That's no reason. It's an American classic. It's taught in the schools. The only reason I haven't done it up to now is because I haven't been able to find an actor to play the Reverend Dimmesdale.'

"Mr. Mayer said, 'Oh, I have the actor, a Swedish actor.' He took me in to see footage of Lars Hanson. He also allowed me a Swedish director, Victor Seastrom. I knew he would understand the material, because the Swedes, temperamentally, are nearer to our early Puritans. Sweden only has sunshine three months a year, so the Swedes understand a slower rhythm. Meanwhile, I wrote to the churches and the women's groups, and got their approval.

"Did we have the right makeup? The right costumes? I don't know. They didn't have photographs in those days. All I know is that we tried with all our hearts to do it right."

It was time to go. We stood outside the restaurant, breathing in the thick, licorice French Quarter air. As James Frasher darted down the street to hail a taxi, the eighty-nine-year-old actress said, "See that man? He keeps me going strong. Without him, I'd shrivel up and die."

It's a curious thing, I noted, none of your silent films has ever been successfully remade as a talkie. The remakes of *Way Down East* with Henry Fonda, of *The White Sister* with Clark Gable and Helen Hayes, of *Broken Blossoms*, all flopped. Why is that?

When she didn't reply, I looked to see if she had heard me. She had. Her eyes were lit by a coy smile that blamed all later failures on that one dreaded word: dialogue.

I had to concede that perhaps she was right. Three years earlier, I'd been smugly bemused by her suggestion that the producers of *Dallas* "know what Mr. Griffith knew." Now, after three years of having been exposed to this fervent missionary, I was increasingly cognizant of the connective between the movies, Mr. Griffith and me.

The evidence was everywhere: The thirty-minute sequence in *The Black Stallion* where a timid boy and a wild horse meet on a desert island and fall in love was bravura moviemaking—without a single word of dialogue. . . . The luminous final half hour of *Close Encounters of the Third Kind* reduced dialogue to irrelevancy. . . . Scene after scene in *Witness* (especially the barn raising) eschewed dialogue to propel the story visually . . .

Until I met Lillian Gish, I never would have thought to view these movies as the descendants of history, or to view their directors as the inheritors of tradition.

As I say, I had a lot to learn. Fortunately, I was blessed with a passionate teacher. I looked down at the diminutive legend standing at my side and said thank you. Silently, of course, but heartfelt nonetheless.

Beulah Bondi was never a legend. She rarely received star billing. Though she appeared in sixty-three movies, Bondi was a supporting player, a character actress—but a *real* character actress, the definitive character actress, who from one simple instrument was able to produce a veritable orchestra of performances, each one original and true. There have been other character actresses, lots of them, cantankerous women like Marjorie Main and Mary Wickes. But if you hired Marjorie Main or Mary Wickes, you knew what performance you'd get before they opened their mouths. That's *why* you hired them: reliability. Beulah Bondi, on the other hand, would do everything possible to submerge herself into the role. And when she did, through some indefinable actor's alchemy, a fresh creation would emerge. To my knowledge, she never repeated herself, never gave the same performance twice.

Illiterate mountain women, repressed intellectuals, lonely Gypsies, mentally unbalanced sanitarium inmates, taxi drivers, French duennas, heroic teachers, heads of orphanages all came to life in her petite being. She was Lionel Barrymore's wife twice, Charles Coburn's wife twice, aunt to both Dorothy McGuire and Loretta Young. But mostly she played mothers. Understanding mothers, cruel mothers, crazed mothers. She was Helen Hayes' mother in *Arrowsmith*, Bette Davis' mother in *The Sisters*, Fred MacMurray's mother in *Remember the Night*, Martha Scott's mother in *Our Town*, Rosalind Russell's mother in *Sister Kenny*, Robert Mitchum and Tab Hunter's mother in *Track of the Cat*—and Jimmy Stewart's mother seven times, including the Frank Capra classics *Mr. Smith Goes to Washington* and *It's a Wonderful Life*. And always different. Never predictable.

I first met Beulah Bondi in July 1978, during a brief visit to Los Angeles. I didn't know how to locate her, so I tried the obvious ploy: I looked her up in the phone book. Her number was listed. I called, introduced myself, and asked if I could come over.

The eighty-six-year-old actress lived alone in a large stucco house in the Los Feliz hills, just east of the Hollywood Bowl. When I arrived, she cautioned that she hadn't much time, for she was leaving in two days for her annual visit to a Colorado dude ranch. "I have too much to do and too active a life," she complained. But the visit lasted more than three hours.

After the amenities were concluded, I directly put the question to her: How did you do it? How were you always able to be so different?

"I don't think I ever have repeated a character," the actress confirmed with justifiable pride. "My feeling is, if you have a different mentality, then you will have a different physicality. In the movies, I never went out of my way to physically change my appearance. You don't have to when you're dealing with the mind and the heart. Those are the two things that dictate my character.

"As a rule, the character comes to me as a result of all her yesterdays. I take a character as the author gives her to me. Then I ask myself, 'Why is she who she is today?' It makes no difference whether she's kindly or loving or bitter or austere. I use my imagination to try to go back and find the root causes for who she is. The script will tell me who she is today, but it rarely tells me what caused it. The answer to that question can only be found in my imagination. Then, my goal is always to *be* rather than to *seem*. Don't seem loving; *be* loving. Don't seem austere; *be* austere.

"For me, the process of finding a character is usually very slow. But once it happens, I can feel within myself that the character is there. What occurs after that, I can't explain, other than to say that I'm really outside myself. I'm no longer in control of what comes out of me.

"I had a lovely experience doing a TV show four years ago called *Dirty Sally*. My role was a pathetic old blind woman who lived alone out in the desert. It occurred to me that in all these years of acting, I had never played a blind woman. So this was a completely new experience. I only had three or four days to find the character before we started. But when we shot it, I was blind as a bat. I really didn't see anything. As I say, I can't explain it. And when it comes, I have nothing to do with it. It's simply there. But this is why I'm sure I have never played two characters alike. If you have a different mentality and really become that person, you can't repeat yourself, because all individuals are different, even twins."

You worked with nearly every star in Hollywood. You must have been witness to some amazing displays of ego, I brashly suggested.

"That's not true," Bondi protested. "I have never met temperament. If there was temperament, it must have been in the dressing room, because it wasn't on the set. I won't say this about the theater, but it's true of my films: I never met a star who behaved like a *star*, in terms of making me feel as if I was less important than he or she was.

"Actually, now that I think about it, the closest I came to seeing temperament on a film set was on a movie called *Track of the Cat*. The director was a man named William Wellman, who was known as 'Wild Bill' Wellman. Everyone said to me, 'You're going to work with Bill Wellman? *That's* going to be an experience.' He evidently was a man with a reputation for using strong language. If he liked you, he was fine; and if he didn't like you, he was very difficult.

"My first day on the set, had just met him, we had talked about the character a little bit. Then—I think it was my first shot—he called in a loud voice, 'Get over there, Bondi! Get on your marks!'

"And I left the scene, and I walked up to him, and I said, 'Mr. Wellman, please don't ever shout at me. I'm very cooperative, and if you'll just tell me exactly what you want, I'll always try to do it.'

"Well, from then on, he was wonderful to me. There was never any more shouting. I won't say that his language didn't get a little strong from time to time. But he was a very forceful man who knew what he wanted, and I loved working with him. But this is true of almost everyone I've worked with. You're going to think I'm Pollyanna, but I've loved them all. I can't say that I got to know them very well, because once I get into a character, I can't sit on the set and play gin rummy and socialize. I have to go to my dressing room and be quiet and, as I say, *hang on*. So, while I worked with many gifted stars—and while there was never a moment when I didn't feel that they gave as much as I gave—we never became intimate friends."

Not even Jimmy Stewart?

"Not really. Of course I loved working with him. I think we worked together seven times over forty years. But I don't think we ever discussed our scenes. We enjoyed a natural relationship, which only grew as the years went by. The last time we worked together was five years ago when Jimmy had his own TV series. I was vacationing at the dude ranch when my agent phoned me in Colorado and said, 'He wants no one for his mother but you. Will you fly back?' I returned that very day."

Tell me this: We hear a lot about actors rewriting their dialogue on the set. How often did you resort to that practice?

"Never!" she bristled. "At no time. It's true, today you do hear about actors wanting to improvise or rewrite. I never saw that on any set. Oh, certainly, a star might suggest a better line now and then. But your job was to learn your dialogue. That's what you were trained to do. Today you'll meet young actors on a set who have made one movie, and they'll want to tell you how to act. But acting is a profession, the same as medicine and law are professions, and these professions require training."

For Beulah Bondi, that training (as it had for Lillian Gish) started early on indeed. She was born Beulah Bondy in Chicago in 1892. By the time she was three, the Bondy family had moved across the state line to the soybean-growing community of Valparaiso, Indiana, where Beulah's father had a real-estate agency.

Encouraged by her mother to act, Beulah (like Lillian Gish) made her stage debut at age nine, in the title role of a local production of *Little Lord Fauntleroy*. She continued to act during high school and college. Even then, she knew she would not be an ingenue. "I was a shy girl," Bondi said, "and I think I was always happiest when I was hiding my own personality behind greasepaint and wigs and funny clothes."

Her first professional experience came in the summer of 1919 as a member of the Stuart Walker Stock Company in Indianapolis. "In Indianapolis I never played a character under sixty," she said. "There was even an article in the newspaper asking if Stuart Walker's new character actress would be able to withstand the Indianapolis heat at her advanced age."

After two years in Indianapolis, she spent her next four years with stock companies in Cincinnati, Toledo, Dayton and Baltimore and at Denver's celebrated Elitch's Gardens, regularly playing women ready for the retirement home. It was during this period that her name was misspelled *Bondi* on a playbill. The local critic told her to keep it that way, and she heeded his advice.

By 1925 she felt she was ready for New York. The day she arrived there, she was emerging from a subway when she ran into one of her former directors. He was looking for an actress to play a seventy-year-old servant in a new comedy.

"Luck!" she emphasized. "It can play such an important role in an actor's career." Bondi won the part and made her Broadway debut on December 21, 1925, in the now-forgotten *One of the Family*. She proceeded to prosper on Broadway in play after negligible play. Then in 1929 she landed a plum role in *Street Scene*, Elmer Rice's slice-of-tenement-life drama about racism, adultery and murder. The crass Emma Jones was even close to Bondi's own age. Tugging at her bra strap and patting her derriere, Bondi portrayed the acid-tongued bigot for more than she was worth without ever succumbing to caricature.

When *Street Scene* was awarded the Pulitzer Prize, producer Samuel Goldwyn doled out one hundred fifty thousand dollars for the film rights. To help replicate the authenticity of the Broadway production, Goldwyn hired eight of the original New York actors.

"*Street Scene* was the ideal project for me to make the transition to films," Bondi said. "Out on the Hollywood sound stage, we rehearsed for a week, just as if we were performing the play. But because I already knew the role, I was able to concentrate on this new technique of acting for the camera. I would be standing off-camera, and I couldn't even hear the actors who were working. I didn't realize the power of the microphone. Then I had to learn the limitations that were imposed on me by the camera. But learning about the different lenses was fun. I loved the learning."

For Bondi, *Street Scene* was a one-shot deal. She fully intended to return to New York when production "wrapped." But then producer Goldwyn, in alliance with MGM production supervisor Irving Thalberg, offered her a seven-year movie contract.

"That happened at the wrap party," the actress recalled. "It was a wonderful dinner. Mary Pickford and Charles Chaplin and Norma Shearer and all the greats from the '30s were there. I was very honored when Mr. Goldwyn and Mr. Thalberg took me aside and told me I was their girl. I was the actress they'd been looking for. This was a Saturday night. I was told to go up on Monday morning and get my contract, which I did.

"It was a pamphlet about two inches thick. A charming gentleman in the office handed it to me with a pen and said, 'Sign right here.'

"And I said, 'Thank you, but I haven't read it.'

"And he said, 'It's just the standard contract that we give everybody, except you will come in as a character actress.'

"And I said, 'Thank you, but I'm leaving for New York this afternoon. I want my attorney to read it.'

"It turned out that my attorney and Mr. Goldwyn had been boys together on the streets of New York selling kid gloves. They had not heard from each other for many years. But they had a friendly telephone conversation. Then my attorney said, 'Well, Sam, if you think you have a prize in this girl, as you say, why don't you give her a decent contract?'

"Mr. Goldwyn didn't like that remark very well, and he rather brusquely replied, 'If she doesn't like the contract, tear it up.'

"My attorney turned to me and said, 'Beulah, can you live without this contract?'

"And I said, 'I've lived a long time before I met Mr. Goldwyn. Tear it up.'

"So the seven-year contract was torn up, and to this day I have never known whether or not I made the right choice. But there was no doubt in my mind when I did it. I knew that I didn't want to be confined. I had talked with actors who were under contract, and not many of them were very happy. They had to play roles they didn't want to do. In the theater I had always been very particular about what roles I played, and I knew that if I started making movies I would want to continue to be every bit as particular. Of course, the money was a temptation, as it always is to any actor who is out of work. But I remembered that old quotation, 'Don't sell your birthright for a mess of pottage.' Finally—and I hope this doesn't sound egotistical, because I was so grateful that Mr. Goldwyn and Mr. Thalberg recognized my work—but I think I believed that if I had the talent that they wanted, then I wasn't doing a very risky thing."

She wasn't. Sam Goldwyn promptly called her back to Los Angeles that same year to portray Helen Hayes' mother in *Arrowsmith*. During her prolific 1930s and '40s she appeared in fifty-one films, freelancing for Columbia, MGM, Paramount, RKO Radio, Twentieth Century-Fox, United Artists, Universal and Walt Disney, and working for such directors as Delmer Daves, Cecil B. de Mille, John Ford, Mitchell Leisen, Leo McCarey, Lewis Milestone, Jean Renoir and William Wyler. Henry Hathaway, knowing he'd get two completely different characters, cast her as old mountain women in both *Trail of the Lonesome Pine* and *Shepherd of the Hills*. Clarence Brown, Frank Capra, Anatole Litvak, George Stevens and Sam Wood also used her twice.

Not that there weren't disappointments along the way. In 1937 she did sign a one-year contract with Paramount, in order to star in what would become her most cherished role, the dependent mother in Leo McCarey's *Make Way for Tomorrow*. Despite unanimous critical acclaim, the film was a failure at the box office.

Three years later she tested for the role of Ma Joad in Twentieth Century-Fox's *The Grapes of Wrath*. So persuaded was Bondi that the role was hers, that she moved into an "Okie" camp near Bakersfield, California, to familiarize herself with the ways of the character. While there, she learned that Ma Joad would be played by one of the studio's contract players, Jane Darwell.

"We don't need to talk about that," Bondi replied when I asked about the incident. "That was all a long time ago. I'll only say this: Nothing good ever came of a lie."

When her feature-film work began to slow down, she returned to the stage. In 1950 she supported Jessica Tandy on Broadway in *Hilda Crane*. In 1953 she returned to Broadway for a revival of *On Borrowed Time*, reprising the role she had played opposite Lionel Barrymore on the screen. She also worked regularly on such television series as *Playhouse 90*, *Route 66* and *Climax*. She guest starred on *The Waltons* as Aunt Martha Corinne Walton. In 1976 she played Sarah Bush Lincoln, stepmother to America's future sixteenth president, opposite Hal Holbrook in *Sandburg's Lincoln*. When Holbrook won an Emmy Award, in his acceptance speech the actor paid special tribute to "the great Beulah Bondi."

In 1977 her second appearance on *The Waltons* resulted in an Emmy Award nomination. Awards hadn't much come Bondi's way. In all her career, she had only been nominated as Best Supporting Actress twice (first, in 1936 [the inaugural year for the "Best Supporting" categories] as Mrs. Andrew Jackson in *The Gorgeous Hussy*, then in 1938 as Jimmy Stewart's mother in *Of Human Hearts*). She didn't win either Oscar and didn't expect to win the Emmy either, especially not in 1977, with *Roots* dominating the proceedings—including her category. When Beulah Bondi's name was announced as the winner, the tumultuous standing ovation she received from her peers was the capstone of her sixty-year career.

Now, ten months later, as we sat in her living room, the eighty-six-year-old actress proclaimed, "I'm still available. The reason I'm not more active is because of the material that comes to me. It's not that I don't think other actors shouldn't do it. I think we each should do what appeals to us. But the scripts that have come to me have been either violent or filled with language I don't use. And I don't plan to start now.

"I don't understand the movies today. There was a time when audiences loved to be carried outside themselves, loved to take flights of fancy. Isn't this the reason why *It's a Wonderful Life* is still so popular? Excessive violence was never a part of our films. And the noise! I've actually had to walk out of movies because the volume hurt my ears. I can only hope it's a phase and that the pendulum will swing back."

We would meet again two years later in New York City, on the eve of another vacation. Bondi was scheduled to embark the next morning on a fifty-six-day freighter cruise to Australia. A mutual friend invited us to lunch, after which I escorted Bondi back to her hotel. Our taxi driver, full of snarl and rage, tried to involve us in his anger. But the only thing Beulah Bondi wanted to talk about was what a joyous world we live in. "I'm perplexed," she said, "when people get upset by adversity and setbacks. They don't realize, it's a lesson." She'd been seeing a lot of Margaret Hamilton during her New York visit. "I wish someone would write us a play," she said, her eyes aglow with yet another flight of fancy. "We could be two old eccentric ladies. My character would be a devotee of roller skating."

Nine months later, in January 1981, the great Beulah Bondi died at age eighty-eight. "Nothing good ever came of a lie," she had told me. Yet in a profession where fakery is the name of the game, she was the consummate liar, for in her artful hands and eyes and body, lies revealed truth. By 1981 most moviegoers didn't even know her name. But that was OK. After all, Beulah Bondi had devoted her life to transforming her remarkable gifts into a veritable vanishing act.

Americus, Georgia, in August is not the most glamorous of locations. But pecan trees grow there, so that's where, in 1993, Jessica Tandy was filming a television movie, *To Dance With the White Dog*, for the Hallmark Hall of Fame.

Tandy didn't have a large role. In Terry Lee's eloquent novel on which the film was based, her character is already dead before the story begins. No, Jessica Tandy was there primarily to support husband Hume Cronyn. Forewarned that the eighty-four-year-old actress had been battling cancer, I was amazed the first time I saw her. As I stood sweating in the capacious lobby of the stately old Windsor Hotel, this sprightly, graceful presence whizzed past me like Peter Pan. Jessica Tandy?!

Later that afternoon I caught up with her in her hotel suite. The age lines were there. But her radiant eyes would have blinded any but the most callous Peeping Tom to the tolls that life takes. As she chronicled the story of a young girl, born in London in 1909, who *had* to act, Tandy began by recalling her training as a teenager at the famed Ben Greet Academy.

"The curriculum back in the 1920s had a great deal to do with the classics," she said. "Shakespeare, particularly, although we also worked on modern plays. Shaw was quite 'modern' in those days. The Ben Greet Academy had a great deal to offer me about adherence to the meaning of the text, learning how to treat the verse, how to not 'versify' it. I learned how to just get on with it, because if you have to think about it, as so many American actors do now—" She slowed down her enunciation to emphasize every single word. "—think . . . so . . . hard . . . about . . . it . . . before . . . they . . . say . . . it. . . . Make . . . sure . . . that . . . what . . . they're . . . saying . . . you're . . . going . . . to . . . be . . . able . . . to . . . understand . . . because . . . this . . . is . . . difficult . . . Instead, if they just said it, said it, said it, audiences would understand the verse perfectly."

When Tandy was a student, acting the world over was being revolutionized by the 1924 publication of Konstantin Stanislavsky's *My Life in Art*. "I immediately bought it and read it," she said. "I found it fascinating. What I learned from it was that Stanislavsky had a company of very experienced actors, and what they did was to work together and then ask, 'What is it that we do? Let us put a name to what we do so that other actors can do the same thing.' I remember, years later, talking to John Gielgud about it. And I said, 'That's what we've been doing all this time, but we never called it *affective memory*.'"

Another notable event occurred in 1924. Fourteen-year-old Jessica Tandy attended the London production of George Bernard Shaw's newest play, *Saint Joan*, and saw a fourteen-year-old actor named Jack Hawkins playing the small role of Dunois' Page. The size of the role was insignificant. What mattered was that the boy was Tandy's age, and that he "was onstage doing what I was *dying* to do. I remember going to see the production two or three times. I was so jealous of that boy." Eight years later, in 1932, Jessica Tandy married that boy. By then she had been acting professionally for five years in London's West End, in British repertory companies, and, across the sea, on Broadway. So many of those plays, *The Manderson Girls*, *Alice Sit-by-the-Fire*, *The Man Who Pays the Piper*, are long forgotten. But they provided the young actress with the experience she so desperately sought—

"No, no, no!" Tandy laughingly disputed. "When you're a young actress, you don't say, 'I'm going to go out and get experience.' You don't say, 'I'm going to shape my career.' Because you can't. What I went out to do was to get a job! I trained with the Ben Greet Academy for three years, and then I had to find a job. And one job leads to another, leads to another, leads to another. You do whatever comes along, regardless of whether or not you think you're right for the part, or whether you like or hate the play. *You do it*. And every director you work with will teach you something good or bad. So do all the other actors you perform with. And out of all that comes your experience. Out of all that, you find whatever it is you have to contribute.

"In all my career, the most satisfying work has come in repertory, be it at Stratford, at the Guthrie Theater in Minneapolis, or at Cambridge in England. Repertory, where you go from one play to another, and every day you're working. This is not like Broadway, where you get up at nine o'clock in the morning and loll around reading the papers, gearing your energy to that evening's performance. Repertory is where you get up and go to the theater and rehearse the next play. Back in 1932 I did a season at the Festival Theatre in Cambridge, twelve plays, a new play every week, and I was in eleven of those plays. And you did it! Today I couldn't possibly do it. I couldn't learn the lines that fast. But back then it was the most wonderful training in the world, despite the fact that I'm sure the productions weren't terribly good. But you're expending your energy all day long. Very good for you.

"It's also an enriching time, because very often rehearsals are the most satisfying part of acting. I love going to that first rehearsal, starting again from square one with a whole different character, a new author. I believe that every time you begin to rehearse a new play, it is as if you had never performed in a play before. You cannot say to yourself, this character reminds me of so-and-so in that other production, so I'll play it that way. No, no. You must begin anew always. I love that about acting. I love the problem solving. Some actors, especially in movies, want to rewrite their parts to make them more comfortable, but I rarely do that. An actor shouldn't mess with authors. If you do Shakespeare, Molière, Ionesco, Chekhov, you don't say, 'This line isn't comfortable for me to speak.' You *do* it, and you figure out how you can make the line work."

And so she acted. Even when the odds seemed stacked against her, she acted. "I was considered to be very plain," Tandy said. "And it's true that I was an awkward child. My arms grew to their full length very early, so that they seemed too large for my body. And I had big red hands from having scrubbed the floors at home. As a child I was not a pretty sight. Yet I look at those old photographs now from my early stage roles, and I think, what were they talking about? Why did they say I was plain? I wasn't plain. But at the time I felt plain, because if people tell you you're plain, you learn to feel it.

"I remember reading a letter of introduction that some actor-manager had sent on my behalf to the head of another theater, and the letter said, 'Don't be put off by the way she looks. She looks fine onstage.' So what happened was that I was very often cast in the more interesting role, who was not the ingenue. Once I started working, I didn't stop. I didn't have a holiday for ten years. Then I had my appendix out, and that broke the spell."

Those years of constant work help to account for the failure of her marriage to Jack Hawkins. "It was nobody's fault," she said. "We were both very young and very ambitious, and we didn't really understand what a relationship means."

In his autobiography, *Anything for a Quiet Life*, published after his death in 1973, Hawkins corroborated Tandy's account. "Looking back," he reflected, "I don't think we were really in love, although we loved one another's company. . . . My private and personal life came a very poor second to my professional career. . . . Ambition came between us, and instead of being content to build a home life like so many other young couples of our age, we concentrated on building our careers."

"We were married for eight years, but we weren't happy for five of them," Tandy added. Happiness had to be found in her work. In April 1940 she played Cordelia to John Gielgud's King Lear at the Old Vic. Now, more than a half century later, the production was among her most treasured memories: "Harley Granville-Barker, the great Shakespeare director and scholar, came out of retirement to help direct it. This was quite a coup. First, John worked with him privately in Paris. Then he agreed to come to London for the last ten days of rehearsal. Those rehearsals were something I will never forget all my life. Those were rehearsals where you didn't return to your dressing room when you were off-stage. You didn't *move* from the stage while everyone else was working, because the dynamic between the director and the actors was something remarkable. At one point we were rehearsing the scene where Lear returns to Cordelia, and Barker said something to the effect of, 'I would walk on my knees to see this scene played properly.' He staged it with utter simplicity.

"We performed the play for three weeks, and out of that entire three weeks, there was one matinee when John and I both came off the stage after that scene, *and we knew* we'd gotten it. John said, 'That was it.' But only that one, where we just caught it."

Later that same year, 1940, Tandy returned to the United States to act in a Broadway play that promptly closed, leaving her stranded in New York City, unable to return to war-torn England. That's when Jessica Tandy met Hume Cronyn.

What qualities did Hume Cronyn possess that allowed him to capture the heart of a married woman with a child?

"He was persistent," Tandy said. "He was very persistent. He was a wonderful friend, and I—having been flung into this country with ten pounds in my pocket and no work—I needed a friend in those days."

Tandy and Hawkins were divorced in 1940; she married Hume Cronyn two years later. They had a son in 1943, a daughter in 1945. The family moved to Hollywood, where Cronyn was beginning to find work in such films as Alfred Hitchcock's *Shadow of a Doubt* and *Lifeboat*. For his performance in *The Seventh Cross* (1944), Cronyn was nominated for an Academy Award as Best Supporting Actor. Jessica Tandy also appeared in *The Seventh Cross*, as Cronyn's wife. It was the first time they acted together. That same year, she (briefly) stole Gregory Peck from Greer Garson in *The Valley of Decision*. In 1946 she played Cronyn's *daughter* in *The Green Years*. But Tandy had children to raise, and her film roles were sporadic.

Then in 1946 she took the family east, for she was cast as Blanche DuBois in Tennessee Williams' new Broadway play, *A Streetcar Named Desire*. No matter that Williams later told people he had written the play with Lillian Gish in mind (or that Gish had given him *Streetcar*'s most haunting line of dialogue, "I have always depended on the kindness of strangers"). Jessica Tandy was cast as Blanche, then Marlon Brando was cast as Stanley, and then the lore became legend.

Streetcar director Elia Kazan, from his 1988 memoir *A Life*: "The rehearsals of *Streetcar* were a joy—which wasn't what I expected. . . . I'd anticipated there might be tensions—particularly with Marlon. He had mannerisms that would have annoyed hell out of me if I'd been playing with him. He'd not respond directly when spoken to, make his own time lapses, sometimes leaving the other actors hung up. I believed this might drive Jessie up the wall, or send her running to me for help. But she never complained, even about his mumbling—which didn't mean she liked it; it means that she didn't complain."

A *Streetcar Named Desire* opened at the Ethel Barrymore Theater on December 3, 1947. Tandy and Brando were contracted to play the first two years. Kazan, again: "There was no use pretending; shows don't keep up in a long run, they deteriorate, even when the actors work hard to improve their performances. . . . This cast did better than any I've had, but soon its prime became a memory."

"Certainly Marlon didn't sustain the long run," Tandy replied, when I read the Kazan quote to her. "He would be *brilliant* one night, and the next night, if he was tired or bored, he would play tired or bored. He didn't have the discipline. I used to get very cross at him. Kazan is right: It's hard to do a long run. But Karl Malden was disciplined; Kim Hunter was disciplined; I was disciplined; and Marlon was not. It used to drive me mad that every time he slammed that telephone down, he would break it. And the prop man was going mad.

"Then there was the scene where we were sitting at the table having a meal, and he would *slam* down the cup! And always on the key word of what I was saying. Now, Marlon was not doing that on purpose. But I did at one point say, 'Look, if you're going to slam it down, *slam* it down. But not on my key word.' It was difficult enough to be heard in that theater anyway, because of the air-conditioning units that made such a noise in the balcony.

"Kazan bawled him out one day, because Kazan had called a rehearsal for the two of us, to take out some of the 'improvements,' I guess. The first time Kazan did that, Marlon came very late. The second time, he didn't show at all. He simply forgot. It's not as if Marlon was aiming to be spiteful or malicious, because there wasn't a mean bone in his body. But Kazan apparently bawled him out, and said, 'You better apologize to her.' So Marlon wrote me a letter of apology. And I cared enough about him to write one back in which I said that I thought he had the capacity to be to America what Olivier was in England, but that he wasn't helping himself.

"I really cared a lot about him. He was a brilliant stage actor. But after *Streetcar* he never returned to the stage. I don't think he liked acting. I remember, he told me he would never make the movie version of *Streetcar*. I'm telling you, Marlon actually said that to me. Of course, that was practically the first thing he did. And we can all be thankful for the many wonderful performances he's given since.

"But long runs are a challenge. Sustaining a performance is one of the most difficult things in the world for an actor to do. But it can be done if the play is so well rehearsed that you know exactly what you're doing at every second. Then when the run reaches the six-month level and beyond, you have that knowledge to return to and to pull back into your consciousness. I actually think it is possible, not only to sustain your performance in a long run, but also to improve it. You improve it, not by doing more, but by finding you can do less—if it's a good script.

"The great danger of a long run is that you can allow yourself to be led away from your performance by an audience. One night the audience will laugh at something, and another night they won't. You then ask yourself, 'What did I do wrong?' Now you try harder. An insecure actor will kill his performance, because he will try to repeat that result rather than to simply play the play. You must not worry about 'How am I doing?' That's the pitfall. Instead, you must sustain a performance by concentrating on the author's intention, the director's intention and your own knowledge of the part."

There were many long runs to come, several of them opposite Hume Cronyn. Their first joint triumph was *The Fourposter* in 1951.

"Hume doesn't like to let the grass grow under his feet," Tandy said. "He saw a squib in the *Hollywood Reporter* about a two-character play that had been done in the West End, so he sent for it. Once he read it, Hume saw the possibilities much more than I did. I didn't think anything more than, oh, OK, let's go do it for the summer. Let's give it a bash.

"We did it all ourselves, paid for it ourselves. It was very hard to book. In those days, two-character plays were highly uncommon. They were thought to be poison at the box office. But by our second engagement, we realized we had a tiger by the tail. Once it was decided that we should take the play to Broadway, we needed to get the author, a Dutchman named Jan de Hartog, to come look at it so we could hopefully get him to rewrite the final two scenes. But he lived on a canal barge in Holland and was hard to find.

"Finally we did persuade him to come to Maine, and Hume persuaded José Ferrer to take over the direction of the production. We all got to work on the play, and Hartog came up with a much-improved ending, and Joe did a wonderful job of directing. I think Hume and I already had about 80 percent of it. What Joe did was to supply that extra 20 percent, which made a big difference. Then we came into New York, and it was immediately a great success.

"After the opening-night performance, we were sitting at Sardi's. Jan was there with his wife of the time, and her father, the great playwright J. B. Priestley. I'll always remember Jan coming over to our table to tell us, 'Old J. B. just said the most wonderful thing.

He said, "All we writers need is a couple of actors stupid enough to actually believe what we write." And he gave this to us as a great compliment. Can you imagine?'"

Tandy and Cronyn continued to act together, on television, on tour, in summer stock, in regional theaters and on Broadway (*A Delicate Balance, Noel Coward in Two Keys, The Gin Game, Foxfire, The Petition*). When the rigors of acting onstage proved too arduous, Tandy turned full-time to the movies. In 1990, at age eighty, she received an Academy Award for her performance in *Driving Miss Daisy*, and her film career was resurrected. "That was just luck," she said. "Luck can be very important to an actor's career."

The day after our conversation, Jessica Tandy went to work. As she and Cronyn played a scene out in a grassy Georgia pecan grove, the sun was brutally oppressive, and the gnats were attacking in waves. No eighty-four-year-old woman should have been out in that ninety-four-degree heat. As I stood behind the camera, turning my head away every time she fumbled her lines (as if my not looking would make matters easier), my heart ached. Yet I knew this was precisely where Jessica Tandy wanted to be.

Ten months later, in June 1994, when she appeared on a Broadway stage for the final time, clinging to Hume Cronyn's iron arm as they accepted an honorary Tony Award, it was clear for all to see that the malevolent cancer had returned, and this time was not to be denied. Jessica Tandy was past acting, but a glow suffused her eyes. Standing on that stage, once again she was where she wanted to be.

When she died three months later, on the morning of the night Hume Cronyn would win an Emmy Award for his performance in *To Dance With the White Dog*, my thoughts harkened back to our afternoon in Americus.

"It's true; he was right," she had confirmed, when I quoted former *New York Times* theater critic Brooks Atkinson's remark that Hume Cronyn and Jessica Tandy have "an obsession with acting."

"I really love acting," she elaborated. "I feel better; I'm much more on the ball; I'm more vital when I'm working. But I must say: If I had known at the beginning of my life that this is where I would get to, I would have said, 'Not possible. Not possible.'"

Like Lillian Gish from Ohio and Beulah Bondi from Indiana, Jessica Tandy, the shy, awkward, plain little girl from England, personified the art of the possible.

SIDES:
CHILD ACTORS

"The director turned to his assistant and said to get the actors. The assistant said, 'Wheel in the meat.'"
—JACKIE COOPER

"Sidney Poitier was one of my acting teachers. . . . He gave me the feeling, as a minority, that there was . . . a place for me in America."
—BILLY DEE WILLIAMS

"Her sweet voice called up to me, 'Oh, my dear little one, do remember this. It isn't this way all the time.'"
—PATTY DUKE

Lillian Gish and Beulah Bondi, both born in the nineteenth century, began to act as children. Jessica Tandy, born in the first decade of the twentieth century, would have, had she been allowed. Now meet three more child actors, born in the 1920s, '30s and '40s.

Jackie Cooper was born in Los Angeles in 1922 to parents who hadn't bothered to marry. Eventually they did, but when the child was two, his father went out one night for a pack of cigarettes and never returned home. To help support the family, at age five young Master Cooper became a movie extra, then was promoted to *Our Gang* comedies. At age nine he starred in *Skippy*, for which he received an Academy Award nomination as Best Actor. *Skippy* was followed by the equally popular *The Champ*. Those two movies, both released in 1931, made Jackie Cooper "America's Boy." Yet, despite the fact that he was taking home a thirteen hundred-dollar weekly paycheck, it wasn't all that long before the youth knew he didn't want to spend the rest of his life reading lines in front of a camera:

"So many adults just don't take the time with kid actors. They don't realize that a lot of kids are very sensitive. A child actor doesn't want a pat on the head or an ice-cream cone. He wants to be treated with respect. Lionel Barrymore was one of the few adults I worked with who made me feel I was a worker on the set, the same as he was. During *Treasure Island* [1934], I loved to watch him act. He would throw himself into his work. He liked to rehearse, as did I, because a kid is always frightened of not being able to remember his lines, and of slowing down the adults. That's still another pressure child actors feel—that if they make a mistake, all these people will have to do it over again. A child doesn't think that maybe the adult will make a mistake. He only thinks, I'm the kid and I don't want to inconvenience everyone.

"I remember being on a set once. The cameraman told the director he had finished lighting, and the director turned to his assistant and said to get the actors. The assistant said, 'Wheel in the meat.' Later I told my mother what the assistant had said, and I asked her what he meant. She said, 'He's talking about the actors, and don't you ever forget it.' So early on I realized that the actor didn't have the first place of respect on a film set. And when the appropriate time came, I made the transition to directing.

"Even now, the one actor I don't like to direct is the child actor. It's simply because I've been there. I know that kids would rather be out playing than doing this. And I know that they *should* be, if not playing, then in school rather than on a film set, sitting off in a corner for five minutes between scenes trying to learn algebra. Kids tend to be distracted easily, and they don't enjoy being told they're not paying attention. If I have to direct kids, I'll do it. But given my choice, I'm a lot more comfortable asking an adult to dig a little deeper inside himself than asking a child."

Billy Dee Williams, the debonair star of *Brian's Song, Lady Sings the Blues* and *The Empire Strikes Back*, was born in New York City in 1937. By age eight he was working on Broadway:

"In 1945 I acted in a lavish Broadway musical, Kurt Weill's *The Firebrand of Florence*, with Earl Wrightson, Beverly Tyler and Melville Cooper. At a rehearsal during our out-of-town tryout in Boston, I was running around in the seats, and Humphrey Bogart, Lauren Bacall and Audrey Totter came in to watch. I was introduced to them. In 1945 Bogart was as famous as you could get. I can still remember how thrilled I was.

"As I grew older, like lots of child actors, I turned away from acting. I was only interested in painting. But in my last year of high school, a director named John Stix was looking for a boy to do the

Broadway play *Take a Giant Step*, which Lou Gossett ended up doing, by the way. But John happened to spot me. He worked with me for two weeks and tried to get me to do it. He told me I had talent and should study, which I did.

"Sidney Poitier was one of my acting teachers. I studied with him for maybe a month. I was only nineteen, and he was in his early thirties, still trying to make it in this business. I think the reason he didn't continue teaching was because things really started opening up for him right about that time.

"But the moments I had with Sidney were good moments because he gave me the feeling, as a minority, that there was an opportunity for me, that there was a place for me in America to make certain kinds of achievements. Most minorities really need to hear that, because they live in a society primarily based on European/Western values. If you don't spring from that, you're like an alien being. So it's necessary for someone to come along and somehow open up a feeling that you didn't know even existed. Sidney Poitier did that.

"Eventually I got back to Broadway. But before I did, in 1959 I was cast in *The Last Angry Man*. It was my first big movie, and it was Paul Muni's last film. Working with Old Man Muni was a never-to-be-forgotten experience, because he was an extraordinary man. He was sixty-three. Yet there were moments when he seemed to be ninety, and other moments when he seemed to be twenty. When he was twenty, it was always when he was recalling the early years at Warner Bros. and he was telling Jack Warner to go screw himself.

"When Muni was working, he lived his role. He was hardly a Method actor along the lines of Brando or James Dean. He was of another generation, yet Muni worked like a Method actor, which showed me that Method acting is simply what you arrive at on your own. It's your own personal way of approaching a situation.

"Muni seemed to endure a great deal of pain as an actor. We were filming on the Columbia Pictures lot. I remember one day, by sheer chance, I happened to overhear him berating himself, 'Why do I go on like this? Why do I drive myself like this? Why do I kill myself like this?' This seemed to be his way of arriving at wherever he had to be in order to find his character.

"He was the kind of actor who never knew when to stop, never knew when he had gotten the right take. So his wife, Bella, was always there on the set to tell him. They had a little signal between them, which I could never figure out. One day I even asked her what it was, but she wouldn't tell me. She actually chided me for having asked. It was their secret. I thought that was really beautiful. They were fine people."

In 1959, the same year *The Last Angry Man* was released, William Gibson's *The Miracle Worker* opened on Broadway and made a star of thirteen-year-old **Patty Duke**. Like many child actors, her youth was filled with confusion and fear. Unlike most child actors, however, she was able to transcend her pain. Four decades later, she remains an actress of startling gifts and range.

I first met Patty (Anna Marie, actually; that's the name her mother gave her) in 1983 on the set of the mini-series *George Washington,* where she endeared herself to the crew by learning all their first names. Most stars don't do that; Anna Marie did. Maybe it had something to do with the fact that for so many years even those who knew her best didn't know her by her real first name.

More than merely saying hello, Anna Marie had an amazing capacity—a need, even—for listening. I still remember the September morning in Alexandria, Virginia, when she got to chatting with a young police officer who was working as a security guard on the set. They spent ninety minutes walking around the restored town, the star and the stranger, deep in conversation. Later that day he gave her his most cherished possession, a small unicorn, explaining that it was time for the creature to have a new home. In a deeply felt note, he wrote, "You are a very special person, for you make others not as fortunate as yourself, feel just as special. Thank you for taking the time to make me feel that way. The feeling won't last long but the memory that I will have, will last forever." This, from a stranger she'd never seen before and would never see again.

The mini-series moved from Alexandria to Williamsburg, then on to Philadelphia, which is where *The Miracle Worker* had premiered twenty-four years before.

"We tried out at the Locust Theater, which is now a garage" she told me. "I walked by there yesterday to wax nostalgic. I really wanted to have a mystical experience, and I saw a bunch of Buicks. It just didn't work."

So she waxed nostalgic with me:

"At half-hour on opening night we only had half a house. Nobody'd ever heard of *The Miracle Worker*. Then, one of those rare miracles, the kind that can only happen in the theater, occurred. Another play was trying out in Philadelphia that week. It was called

The Gang's All Here, and it starred Melvyn Douglas. That night Melvyn Douglas took ill and they canceled the performance. But they offered the audience the choice of having their money back or attending the opening night of *The Miracle Worker*. Enough people chose to see our play to fill up the Locust Theater.

"The audience was rapturous, and we received eighteen curtain calls. This was all new to me. I had never been on the stage before in my life. All my acting had been in television. I'm not even sure I'd seen a play at that point. But it was thrilling. After the curtain came down for the last time, there was lots of hugging backstage, lots of crying. Finally I began to bound up these old iron stairs for my dressing room, eager to read my opening-night telegrams, which I hadn't been allowed to open before the performance, when, from two floors below me, I heard the voice of Kathleen Comegys, an old character actress who played Aunt Ev. She must have been at least seventy, an exquisite-looking woman. And her sweet voice called up to me, 'Oh, my dear little one, do remember this. It isn't this way all the time.'

"How right she was. We opened on Broadway a month later and only received thirteen curtain calls, my first delusion! My second Broadway play barely got one curtain call and closed in a week. So Philadelphia has a very dear spot in my heart."

CHAPTER SIX

——

BE A CLOWN

——

"All that matters is what you feel when you say the words."
—DANNY KAYE

Comedy is confidence. I'm not a comedian, but this I know.

Audiences don't laugh at lines so much as they laugh at attitude, demeanor, confidence.

So answer me this: How can some of our most successful comedians be so assured onstage, so lacking in confidence in life?

It is June 1985, on the New York City set of a CBS television movie called *Izzy and Moe*, which marks the first onscreen reunion between Jackie Gleason and Art Carney in eight years. This set should be a publicist's dream. (I'm the publicist.) The stories should write themselves: *Gleason and Carney—"The Honeymooners" Stars Together Again! How Sweet It Is!* But sweet it isn't, for this is an unhappy set. It's unhappy because Jackie Gleason is a miserable man, and he wants everyone around him to be miserable too. There's actually more of sadness than of meanness about him. Although he is accompanied everywhere by his devoted wife, Gleason seems to be profoundly alone.

Reporters want to eavesdrop on the banter and byplay between Gleason and Carney on the first day of shooting. But reporters aren't allowed—only me—and there isn't any banter to relay. Carney is pain-

——

fully shy, and Gleason, when not working, is nigh comatose. He sits
with the immovable stillness of a Buddah. Except when he's complaining, which on this day is frequently. Having finagled a contract
that releases him after an eight-hour day (most actors work twelve),
he insists that he's required to work only from 9:00 A.M. to 5:00 P.M.
So why, he demands to know, was he called for work this evening?
(Didn't he read the script? Doesn't he know how much night shooting this film entails? Don't ask.)

Every publicist's Catch-22 occurs when you have a closed set,
but you're filming in a public place. During the second week of production, a *Daily News* reporter observes a morning's work on the
Bowery, then files a story that describes the Great One as "a great
pain" (accurate) whose missed cues slowed filming (inaccurate).

My office phone rings. The rings have an almost staccato quality, like gunshots in a firing squad. They can only be announcing
one caller.

"Did you read that story?"

I did.

Gleason waits for me to continue speaking, as if I'm expected
to share his *Angst*, so I add: It's a shabby piece.

"It's not shabby, it's a lie! I never missed a cue in my life. I came
to the set when I was called. I didn't delay anyone."

As I describe a letter to the editor that is being prepared, Gleason
cuts me off: "That won't do any good. You've got to bring that reporter to me. I want to see him on the set. No, that's no good. You've
gotta get that guy!"

I've gotta *what*? Where I come from, *get that guy* means only
one thing. As I sit at my desk trying to figure out where I'm going
to locate a hit man (and how I'm going to justify him on my expense report), Gleason hangs up in a rage.

Forty-eight hours later, the incident is history. This, without benefit of thugs. Out on the set, it's "those things happen" and "call
me Jackie." Which is fine, except that I notice he can't look at me
when he's talking. Which is not to be taken personally, because he
doesn't look at anyone else either. (One year later, in *Nothing in
Common*, he has difficulty looking Tom Hanks and Eva Marie Saint
in the eyes, too. And that's only acting.)

The final day on the set, he says, "I hope we work together soon."
He's lying. The catch is, I don't know if he knows he's lying. His
agent takes me aside to say Jackie doesn't like the film—which tells
me that at least he has good taste, because the film is not very good.

But everything that's wrong with it is wrong because of Jackie Gleason.

Less than two years later he will be dead. One can only hope he has found some peace.

Which is all that need be said, except to consider that most-asked question: Did Gleason and Carney get along? (Somewhere along the way, rumors got started that they didn't.)

Sure they did. They got along because Art Carney saw to it that they got along. By 1985 Carney had earned seven Emmy Awards and an Oscar as Best Actor. He was well aware of his more-than-substantial contribution to the Gleason-Carney mix. After having been around Gleason off and on for thirty-four years, Carney could poke light fun at the Great One's expense. ("I'm not going to hang around waiting for King Farouk.") But as far as I could discern, Art Carney was a thoroughly decent man who had tasted too much of life himself to continue passing judgment on others. So he forgave.

I don't pretend to have known Jackie Gleason. I never shared a meal with him, never traveled in a car with him. But Danny Kaye was another matter. Not that I *knew* him, not that anyone really knew him. If, however, in 1985 I felt more pity than anger at Gleason's sad antics, surely it was due to my having spent so much time with Kaye five years earlier.

It came about like this. In 1977 and 1978, plans by neo-Nazis to demonstrate in Skokie, Illinois, a Chicago suburb whose largely Jewish population includes scores of World War II concentration-camp survivors, triggered a fiercely emotional response. But even as Skokie's citizens deplored the neo-Nazis, they also were forced to wrestle with one overriding question: Should the constitutional guarantees of free speech for an individual—regardless of how reprehensible his beliefs—be denied in order to protect the well-being of an entire community? In Skokie this controversial issue was debated in synagogues and churches, in public town meetings, behind closed city hall doors and across dining room tables. An academic question had become the stuff of high drama.

CBS developed a television movie (originally titled *Defend to the Death*, later changed to the less-inflammatory *Skokie*) which examined the crisis through the eyes of the neo-Nazis, the city leaders, the American Civil Liberties Union attorneys who were required to defend the neo-Nazis, and the outraged local citizens. The film's heavyweight cast included Brian Dennehy, Ed Flanders, Kim Hunter,

Carl Reiner, John Rubinstein and Eli Wallach. At the head of this ensemble, making his television drama debut as a concentration-camp survivor, was Danny Kaye.

When I was assigned to the project, I knew little about the sixty-seven-year-old entertainer, other than the obvious fact that he had been a presence for as long as I had been alive. He was very famous; I was never *not* aware of him. But I knew nothing about the man, could hardly call myself a fan. His frenetic, rubber-faced comedy style was not for my generation.

High praise to the CBS reference library and to its thorough clippings files. They were all there for the reading, those carefully worded press releases about Kaye's impoverished Brooklyn upbringing as David Daniel Kaminsky, son of an immigrant Ukranian tailor, and how he quit high school to make his way as a performer on the Borscht Belt . . . about his early marriage to songwriter Sylvia Fine, who wrote much of his specialty material . . . and about the stardom he enjoyed on Broadway at age twenty-eight in the 1941 Moss Hart-Kurt Weill-Ira Gershwin musical *Lady in the Dark*. Later that same year he starred in Cole Porter's *Let's Face It*, then moved on to Hollywood. But his greatest success, as all the frayed clippings confirmed, came in his personal appearances:

• KAYE 'STOPS' SHOW FOR BRITISH RULERS, *The New York Times* reported on November 2, 1948, in an account of Danny Kaye's unprecedented conquest of London. "So many Americans have played the Palladium in the last year," the article stated, "that one of the English comedians tonight called it 'the American zone of London.' Of all Americans, Kaye was the most popular and, at this moment, is Britain's favorite comedian." *Life* magazine also reported on Kaye's apotheosis: "For the first time in living memory, the staid British Isles were indulging in a type of worshipful hysteria which affected young and old of both sexes and all classes." Kaye was entertained by George Bernard Shaw and praised by Winston Churchill. The Savoy Hotel added two switchboard lines solely to handle his calls.

• March 11, 1958: PHILHARMONIC SPLITS SIDES WITH DANNY KAYE AT BATON. The glowing New York *Herald-Tribune* review chronicled the shenanigans at one of the comedian's first benefit concerts. (In ensuing years, symphony concerts helmed by Kaye, a dedicated amateur conductor, would raise more than five million dollars for musicians' pension funds.)

But it wasn't only Kaye's career that made for absorbing reading. His very life seemed charged with event:

• December 13, 1962: Danny Kaye Sure is Cut-Up Now. A *Washington Post* story related how Kaye diagnosed his own case of appendicitis while piloting his twin-engine plane from Los Angeles to Washington, D.C., then made an unscheduled stop at the Mayo Clinic in Minnesota for immediate surgery. (Fascinated with medicine, Kaye observed so many operations that he was made an honorary member of the American College of Surgeons.)

• February 13, 1967: Danny Kaye Plays Doctor Role in Air. A New York *World Journal* wire-service report told how, during a commercial night flight from London to Chicago, the pilot asked Kaye to use his medical training to assist a fellow passenger who had suffered a heart attack. Although the woman later died in the hospital, Danny Kaye kept her alive on oxygen for five hours until the plane could land.

• September 25, 1975: A *Washington Post* feature on Kaye's expertise as a Chinese cook (he added a wing to his Beverly Hills home to accommodate a massive Chinese stove) quoted one of his acquaintances: "When Danny took up cooking it had to be Chinese. The other great cuisine is French. Its glory is sauces. They take hours of undramatic slow cooking. Chinese cooking has the excitement of stir-fry. It's quick, it's complicated, it's pure theater."

Stir-fry these stories with the interviews about his movies and about his various CBS radio and television series, and with the articles about his inexhaustible activities on behalf of UNICEF (visiting so many refugee children that he became known as the world's goodwill ambassador and in 1965 was chosen to accept UNICEF's Nobel Peace Prize), and it soon became evident that the word *moderation* did not exist in his vocabulary. Beyond the fact of his accomplishments, it seemed that whatever Danny Kaye did, he was driven to excess.

He was not, however, driven to friendship. When I wasn't reading clippings, I was speaking to those who knew him. One well-known actor described Kaye as "a walking icicle." A noted author recalled having been a houseguest at the Indian Embassy in London in the 1950s when Kaye came to dinner. The author, after having retired early, was startled to be awakened by Kaye, who had trespassed into her bedroom. He implored her to return to the party, " 'because nobody walks out on Danny Kaye.' "

A palpable shudder rippled through the CBS corridors in New York at the mere mention of his name. Before flying to Chicago, I was coached, prepped and all but prayed over by those who had worked with Kaye on his Emmy Award-winning variety series from 1963 to 1967. More than a decade later, their scars still had not healed.

"You can't crowd him."

"You have to give him the feeling he's a free soul. Let him know he's an adult and can make his own decisions."

"Be respectful."

"You must always defer to Danny Kaye. Let him make the decisions. Never take him for granted."

"That bastard! Shoot the son of a bitch."

"Shoot him if you must, but for God's sake don't mention Sylvia!"

In November 1980 I flew to Skokie one day before filming was to begin, as intimidated as Androcles, knowing my head was about to be placed in the lion's mouth. Upon my arrival at the hotel, I chanced to meet Herb Bonis, a quiet, gentle man who had been Kaye's aide for a quarter century. Because his boss wasn't scheduled to work the next day, Herb arranged a courtesy visit.

At the appointed hour he ushered me into their hotel suite. Danny Kaye sat on a plush beige sofa perusing his script . . . and I didn't recognize him! He was as disheveled as a scarecrow after a windstorm. His hair was scattered to the four winds . . . but there was no wind, no breeze, no sound even. As Kaye balefully gazed at me over tiny reading glasses that drooped down onto his aquiline nose, my second thought (my first had been: Who is this?) was the discovery that Ichabod Crane had carrot-top hair.

I extended my hand; he ignored it. Rather, with one outstretched, disdainful finger, he gestured for me to sit. I retreated to the far end of the sofa and waited for the conversation to begin. It didn't. Instead, after an agonizing eternity (thirty seconds, maybe), Kaye rose, slowly shuffled into the bedroom, shut the door behind him, and there remained. I assumed that the visit was over. But Herb was still benignly slumped in his chair. Wouldn't he tell me if I was expected to leave?

Several minutes later, the star ambled back to his perch on the sofa. I mustered a feeble greeting to the effect of, On behalf of CBS, can I do anything for you?

Danny Kaye finally spoke. Staring me straight in the eye, he snarled, "You can tell CBS to get the fuck out of this project."

Herb, seeing my eyes spinning like cherries in a slot machine, interjected that Danny was only kidding.

Kaye wanted a fingernail clipper, so Herb was dispatched to the hotel gift shop. I rose to leave, but the star's menacing right index finger again indicated that I should remain. So we plodded on, in strained conversation. Nothing fazed him until I mentioned Sid Garfield, one of the former CBS publicists who had prepped me for this assignment. Sid's name elicited Kaye's only smile of the afternoon.

"Is Sid still with CBS?" he asked.

No. He left. Now he's with Alexander Cohen.

"You mean he stopped working for a corporate prick and went to work for a private prick."

Silence again choked the room. When next Kaye spoke, it was to reveal himself as a chronic worrier: The script had too many words . . . the audience would not accept him in a serious role . . . the shooting schedule was too tight. . . .

Herb returned, and Kaye proceeded to clip his brittle fingernails. The yellow, nicotine-stained nails whizzed through the air and littered the sofa and floor. That done, he lit another Pall Mall. This man, whose life had been a veritable whirlwind, now seemed to lack the energy to reach as far as the coffee table ashtray. As he half-heartedly stretched his arm in the table's general vicinity, the long cigarette ash dropped to the floor. Kaye did attempt to clean up the mess, but his efforts proved ineffectual.

It was a long hour.

The next day Kaye flew to London to perform once again at the Palladium, this time at a star-studded benefit in honor of the Queen Mother's eightieth birthday. During his absence, *Skokie* entertained a cameo appearance by Lee Strasberg.

After four decades as the icon of the Actors Studio, where his worshipful students hung on his every syllable, the eighty-one-year-old Strasberg suddenly was enjoying a brief fling as a movie star. Though he had only one scene in *Skokie* and worked only one day, the young actors who shared that scene—John Rubinstein and James Sutorius—were excited at the prospect of hearing any words of wisdom this most famous of acting coaches might impart.

All through the morning, the inscrutable Strasberg proved distant, forbidding. Then, unpredictably, he joined the company at lunch. Everyone sat in eager anticipation, but the guru's mind was on politics, not theater. Fifteen days earlier, Ronald Reagan had been elected president of the United States. Strasberg declared that this was indeed an important achievement.

"Why?" someone had the temerity to ask.

Because, Strasberg replied, as if his response was too obvious to require utterance, ever since John Wilkes Booth had murdered Abraham Lincoln, actors had been in disrepute. The election of actor Reagan to the highest office in the land removed that stigma.

An embarrassed silence descended upon the table. Strasberg's wife Anna filled the awkward void with an amusing anecdote about how their young sons Adam and David thought voters should have cast their ballots for Strasberg for president.

James Sutorius asked, "What would you do if you were president?"

"First, I'd get a good script," he cryptically answered. End of conversation.

Lee Strasberg returned to New York City; Danny Kaye returned to Skokie and finally went to work. Although I again needed to speak with him in order to write press copy, Kaye kept avoiding me. Herb finally arranged the interview for a Sunday afternoon—with the proviso that I not take more than twenty minutes.

As I entered the suite, Kaye's opening salvo was a complaining, "Dennis, what do you want that isn't already in the bio?"

Let's not talk about you, I suggested. Let's talk about the film.

Ah, the film. *Skokie* was much on his mind. Kaye was concerned that he not portray his character, Max Feldman, with too thick a European accent. "There's a difference between being Jewish and being Yiddish," he distinguished. "The Yiddish are the immigrants who originally came over. When people have a picture in their minds of unattractive Jews, that's who they're thinking of. That's not this man. This is a nice, quiet man.

"People who were born and raised in America don't understand the contrasts that exist for someone who was born in Europe and later lives in America. I understand that. I was the only one in my family born in the United States, so there was a European tradition in our home. Yet outside the home, I traveled in American culture and society, so I was able to see quite clearly the difference between the two."

He spoke of his makeup test, and of how he had considered giving Max eyeglasses, a mustache. Then he decided, "But none of that makes any difference. All that matters is what you feel when you say the words." By way of demonstration, he began to say the words. Not just Max's words . . . *all* the words. Kaye had memorized not

178

only his own role—he knew every line in the script! He could even recite the scenes he wasn't in. Who learns the entire script? I asked myself. One possible answer: a man afraid.

Hoping to capitalize on the extensive research materials the CBS librarians had supplied, I steered the conversation into a few non-*Skokie* questions.

"What do you have there?" he accusingly asked, pointing at the file in my lap.

Oh, this? Just some clippings.

"Let me see."

As he perused the photostats, Kaye became absorbed by these extracts from his own life. "Herb, come look at this," he called to his assistant, who occupied a bedroom off the suite's front hallway. The value of research, I learned at that moment, is not merely to have done it . . . but also to make sure your subject knows you've done it.

Can we continue? I asked.

"Yeah!" Kaye replied. "Ask me anything you want."

That *yeah* was as magical an opening as Aladdin's *abracadabra*.

He spoke about his television variety series, and about the challenge of working in front of a camera: "A lot of entertainers get hypnotized by the lens. But there's an unnatural quality if you stare at somebody when you talk to them. When people talk to each other, I don't fix my eyes on you and never take them away. I look at you, and then I will look away while I assemble a thought, and then come back to you.

"On our series we used cue cards, because there was simply too much material to memorize every week. But we spent a lot of time determining where to place the cue cards so that they'd be most unnoticed. And we never relied on them. The cards were just reminders, because we'd rehearse our sketches very carefully. Then, before each show, we would say to all the cameramen, 'Hold tight, with a very loose grip,' so that they wouldn't have to jerk the camera in case I decided to be spontaneous and walk somewhere else."

Kaye was proud of his ability to connect with a live audience, even as recently as the preceding week at the Palladium: "The people sat there for three hours, and I was the last one on the bill. I sang a song, and then I said, 'I guess I have spent the happiest days of my life in this theater, in this city, in this country.'" His ruddy-pumpkin face was candled by a sublime smile as he recalled the five years (1948-52) of his annual pilgrimages to the Palladium, highlighted,

not by that first extraordinary booking, but by his second engagement, in 1949, when the royal family broke precedent and sat in
the first row of the orchestra rather than upstairs in the royal box.

"I met them after the show," Kaye recalled. "King George said
to me, 'What would you like to drink?'

"I said, 'Oh, I don't know, sir. A Scotch would be nice.'

"He said, 'Scotch? We don't even get that at home.'

"And I said, 'Sir, you don't know the right people.' "

This was a relaxed, accessible Danny Kaye. But in truth, he was
not a "great interview." His gifts resided in his instincts, not his
intellect. (There was, for instance, the day Howard Rosenberg of the
Los Angeles Times visited the set. The interview with Kaye went
smoothly enough. But the moment Rosenberg departed, Kaye declared, "He's going to write a hit piece, and this is what it will say."
Two days later, when Rosenberg's story appeared, Kaye had had it
pegged, right down to the commas.)

In mid-afternoon DK (that became his sobriquet) needed to do
some shopping at the nearby Old Orchard Mall. I took that as my
cue to leave, but no, he wanted me to drive him. Off we went to
Marshall Field's to purchase a duffel bag. Then, with his face masked
by a golf cap pulled low over his brow, we roamed the mall like two
teenagers. DK stopped often to talk to youngsters. In an era when
children are not supposed to speak to strangers, it was fascinating
to see him make contact with kids so effortlessly.

I was doubly intrigued to witness these exchanges, because one
of the many rumors hovering around Kaye was that his affection for
children was a cruel hoax, that in fact he hated kids. While it is
true that Danny Kaye's publicist, Warren Cowan, succeeded brilliantly
in concealing his client's darker sides from public view, I never saw
any indication that Danny Kaye disliked children. He did, however,
view each child as an individual whose personality was already
formed. Likable kids he liked; lovable kids he loved; hateful kids he
loathed. (One obnoxious five-year-old came close to being punted
the length of the mall. DK also had to be nearly restrained from
throttling the child's neglectful mother.)

We went into a bookstore, where DK expressed his disdain for a
cookbook titled *Cooking without Salt*. "Cooking without salt," he
groused, "is like . . ." The sentence concluded with a profane *non
sequitur* whose relevance eludes me to this day. We perused movie
guidebook listings of some of his films, including *The Court Jester*
(surely his most enduring comedy) and *The Five Pennies* (a biogra-

phy of jazz trumpeter Red Nichols generally dismissed by critics, but a film in which Kaye took enormous pride).

Back at the hotel he insisted that I return with him to his suite, then promptly fell asleep in front of the ever-droning television. I was on the verge of slipping away when he awoke. Now he invited Eli Wallach (whom he had not yet met) to dinner at a local Chinese restaurant. As soon as Wallach arrived at the suite, Kaye produced a red leatherbound photo album which documented his various adventures: here, a photo of the private plane he had once owned (DK, a licensed pilot with instrument, commercial and jet ratings, was once listed in the *Guinness Book of World Records* for having flown to sixty-five cities in five days on behalf of UNICEF); next, a photo of his Chinese stove; then a picture of the Seattle Mariners baseball team, of which he was part owner. Danny Kaye's need to impress Eli Wallach (a fellow Brooklynite, but more important, a *real* actor) was transparent.

As we entered the Chinese restaurant, Kaye passed a startled couple who began to gush with effusive compliments. "Hi, how are you; nice to see you," the star said, and moved on to his table. A minute later the irate couple attacked me in the coatroom, complaining, "How dare he treat us that way?" I was astonished. Kaye had done nothing rude. At worst he'd been perfunctorily polite. But he had not lived up to their expectations. By being merely courteous, he inadvertently hurt people. No wonder he preferred the sanctuary of solitude.

Our first course was a hot-and-sour soup. Kaye glanced at it and, without so much as a taste, said, "There's too much cornstarch." I couldn't help but be impressed by his knowledge of food. "Before you leave Chicago," he told me, "I'll have you eating pelican shit." All too predictably, the restaurant owner soon came to the table and asked to take a photo of Danny with the chef. Kaye obligingly smiled for the camera. As the two men walked away, he muttered, "In forty-eight hours the fucking picture will be in the window."

Back at the hotel, DK—who had taken an instant liking to the ever-cheerful Eli Wallach—phoned Wallach's home in New York. When daughter Roberta answered, Kaye pretended to be a Chicago cop who had arrested her father for drunk driving. The spontaneous improvisation was hilarious. As the conversation drew to a close, and Kaye had identified himself, I heard him ask, "Do you love your father?" Clearly her reply was in the affirmative, because DK added, almost under his breath, "I wish you'd call my daughter."

I finally left the suite at 10:30 P.M., ten hours after having arrived.

The next morning, as the production focused on scenes between Wallach and Ed Flanders, Kaye flew to New York City, where he kept a second home in the Sherry-Netherlands Hotel. Back in Skokie, I had time to puzzle over the transformation that had occurred on Sunday. I was suddenly accepted, included. But what did that mean? Wasn't this Danny Kaye the same irascible person I'd met nine days before? Yes, of course he was, and at the same time decidedly not. It's so much easier to dislike someone who dislikes or, worse, dismisses you. Now I was to shoulder a new responsibility: to come to know, and to grow to admire, a difficult man.

Later that week, Thanksgiving morning arrived wrapped in a blanket of unexpected snow. Stranded in the hotel, Eli and I shared an elaborate holiday lunch at the hotel's rooftop restaurant. "America is an amazing country," Wallach said as he took a lusty swipe at his cranberry sauce, "wonderful, because the geniuses who put together the Constitution left room for stretching." Referring to the divisive issues at the core of *Skokie*, he continued, "America is not one of those houses where every time the earth shakes the house falls apart."

Prior to starring in *Skokie*, Wallach had traveled to his parents' homeland, Poland, to act in a television adaptation of John Hersey's novel *The Wall*, about the futile attempts by Warsaw Jews to stave off extinction by Nazi Germany. "I've seen documentaries that reduce the horrors of World War II to mere statistics," Eli said. "But I try to be involved with projects that tell stories of the spirit, about people struggling desperately to survive. I think they're important stories. Man's hatred to man is, I fear, a constant thing. So any exposure of it, any airing of grievances, is helpful and necessary."

Eli recently had acted in another story of the spirit, the stage play *The Diary of Anne Frank*, in a family-invested Off-Broadway production whose cast included wife Anne Jackson as Edith Frank, daughters Roberta and Katherine as Anne and her sister Margot, and Wallach as family patriarch Otto Frank.

Otto Frank intrigued me, for he was a man forged by catastrophe. In 1933 Frank, a German Jew, felt compelled to emigrate with his family to Amsterdam to escape the systematic wrath of Hitler's anti-Semitic purges. Had there been no war, Frank might have lived out his life as an anonymous, slightly nervous manufacturer of pectin for jam making. But by 1942 Hitler's Third Reich had consumed all Europe. In July '42, after the German occupation of Holland, Otto took his wife and daughters into hiding. For more than two years the Frank family, together with the family of one of his business associates, and later a local dentist, eight refugees in all, lived in the Amsterdam attic above the pectin company's offices. There in the attic, Otto Frank manifested an inner strength, a forceful calm he never knew he possessed.

In August 1944 the hiding place was discovered, its inhabitants herded into concentration camps. After the Allied liberation, Otto—already aware that his wife had died at Auschwitz—returned to Amsterdam and resumed work, behaving, outwardly anyway, as if nothing untoward had occurred in those attic rooms above the office he now reoccupied. But privately he was sustained by the hope that Margot and Anne, who had been transferred far away to Bergen-Belsen, might have survived the ordeal and that father and daughters would one day be reunited.

It was not to be. Months later Otto Frank received the crushing news that he was the sole survivor of the attic. That despairing day when he learned his daughters would not be coming home was also the day that Miep Gies, the heroic woman who had tended to the sequestered families' countless needs during their years of seclusion, and who had found and hidden Anne's diaries after the family's capture, relinquished the journals to Anne's grieving father.

For the first few years, Otto told almost no one about the diaries. They were his personal passport to the past. Then, ever so reluctantly, he consented to a limited Dutch printing (not notably successful; everyone in Holland had horror stories of his and her own). When requests for international publication were tendered, Otto again had to be persuaded. It was still too soon for him to realize that, from the anonymous millions of victims, his family had been chosen as the emblem of understanding. It was as if his daughter, dead at age fifteen, was being born anew. And not only through her words. Photos of her guileless smile gave a face to those otherwise incomprehensible horrors.

All this, Otto Frank did in time come to understand. And so, in 1952, *Anne Frank: The Diary of a Young Girl* was published in America. When it was optioned for adaptation as a Broadway play, this time Otto did not object. He used his share of the profits to maintain the attic as a museum, and he took the time to personally respond to the letters that arrived daily, many of them written by youngsters like Anne, innocents who asked questions for which there are no answers.

"I never met Otto Frank," Eli Wallach said of the patriarch who had died three months earlier, on August 19, 1980, "but we kept in touch with him through Albert Hackett and Frances Goodrich. Otto sent us an opening-night telegram."

I too knew the Hacketts, Albert and Frances, the prolific screenwriters of such films as *Father of the Bride, It's a Wonderful Life* and *Seven Brides for Seven Brothers.* By coincidence, I first met them in January 1979, two nights after having seen the family Wallach Off-Broadway in the Hacketts' play. Albert was seventy-nine, a thin, ebullient man with silver-bristle hair and apple-red cheeks; Frances, surely in her eighties, relied on a walker for mobility.

That night at dinner Albert explained how they had come to write *The Diary of Anne Frank.* Otto, having discovered through his reading of Anne's diaries how little he knew his own daughter, had recommended to producer Kermit Bloomgarden that a woman be involved with the dramatization. Bloomgarden approached Lillian Hellman. She in turn suggested the Hacketts, whom she had befriended after they adapted Dashiell Hammett's *The Thin Man* for MGM.

"When we finished the script," Hackett recalled, "we sent it to Otto in Geneva, and he OK'd it. He never saw the play. He *never* saw the play! He couldn't bring himself to see it. But we had his approval. Then, right before we opened in Philadelphia, Kermit said he'd been watching the rehearsals, and there was a point in Act Two when the momentum dropped. So we added the scene where Mr. Van Daan was caught stealing bread. This incident never happened, but we felt it was consistent with Mr. Van Daan's character. We handed the scene out to the cast on the train to Philadelphia. Lou Jacobi, defending his character, argued, 'But he never did this.' Well, he did it in the play."

Since Otto Frank never saw the play, did he ever find out about the fabricated scene?

"I don't know," Albert answered, "but I do know one thing: He would not have liked it. But structurally we needed it."

After their play won theater's Triple Crown (Tony Award, Drama Critics Circle Award and Pulitzer Prize) in 1956, the Hacketts wrote the initial screenplay for the movie version. "We stuck as close to the play as possible," Frances said, "but it didn't work on film."

"Nor did it help that George Stevens, a very fine director, was not well," Albert added. "During World War II he had been in the army with a camera unit, and he went all through those concentration camps. That took a whole lot out of him. On the *Anne Frank* set he tried to recreate some kind of a tension for himself, some kind of feeling that the war was still on. He even began to eat hardtack! But it's not a good movie."

During the filming Otto Frank was the Hacketts' houseguest in Los Angeles. "I remember one Sunday morning," Albert continued. "The phone rang. This man asked, 'Is Mr. Frank staying with you?'

" 'Yes.'

" 'I knew him in the concentration camp.'

"So he came over. A young man he was. He told us about someone at Auschwitz who was starving. One day Otto gave the man his meal ration. Imagine such a thing, giving up your food to another, when you had so little. This is not something Otto would have told us himself. He didn't have to talk about it. The strength was there."

"Like that line in the diary about the dentist—" Frances interjected.

"Yes. Anne wrote that her father didn't speak to Dussel, the dentist, for two days. We asked Otto why not. His answer was, because Dussel hadn't shaved for two days. You see, even in the attic, he felt that everybody should keep up appearances for the children."

Twenty-four years had elapsed since they wrote *The Diary of Anne Frank*, yet tears flowed down Frances Goodrich's face that January night as she recalled Otto, and Anne, and all those they personified. "What were we doing then?" she plaintively asked. It was another of those answerless questions.

That Thanksgiving evening the phone rang. Danny Kaye, back from New York and in high spirits, cajoled Eli and me into joining him at the rooftop restaurant for another holiday meal. As usual, he was not to be denied.

Our revelry was interrupted by a brash woman who descended on our table and insisted that Kaye sign an autograph for her grandson, who stood mutely at her side. Kaye asked if the boy could speak for himself. When she said yes, he sent the termagant back to her table and tried to establish a rapport with the youth, something I'd seen him do so well with other youngsters. DK joked, "You ought to leave home, be on your own." The kid was only twelve years old; he was not in sync with Kaye's humor. Perhaps he was dysfunctional. Whatever the reason, he just stood there, staring.

DK signed the autograph, handed over the piece of paper, turned back to Eli and resumed the story he'd been telling before the intrusion. As Kaye spoke, the boy took one step back from the table, stared at the rear of DK's vermilion head, shredded the autograph, hurled the pieces onto the floor and silently walked away. Kaye, who could only hear the tearing, continued to talk as if nothing had happened; Eli and I continued to listen as if nothing had happened. But something *had* happened: No harm had been intended. But through some innocent, missed communication, everyone involved in the brief incident had been hurt.

Two days later a new presence appeared on the set. Carl Reiner arrived to portray a spokesman for the Anti-Defamation League. For his first scene, at the Evanston Courthouse, he and DK shared a makeshift dressing room in one of the judge's chambers. They whiled away the hours swapping tales of their youth in Brooklyn. DK told this affectionate story about his father: In the early 1950s, long after his son had found international fame, Papa was scheduled to fly from New York City to Boston, but he arrived at La Guardia Airport to learn that strong winds had grounded all flights. The Ukranian tailor approached the airline attendant and asked, "I'm Danny Kaye's father. I could be hurt too?"

But shared stories were not enough. Out came the validating red leather photo album. Once again Kaye felt the need to prove his worth, the need to impress. Not that Reiner needed impressing. As he told me, "Danny Kaye is the one we all looked up to when we were aspiring young comedians. I'm only nine or ten years younger than he is, but he was the Old Man of Comedy. I still have my recording of Danny singing his unique 'git-git-git-git-gattle-gay' style. I attempted to copy him. I never could get it down, thank God, because there was only room for one Danny Kaye. He has maybe the best musical ear extant, one of the best ears ever gifted to man."

While reading a *Chicago Tribune* review of the current Lyric Opera production of Giuseppe Verdi's *Un Ballo in Maschera*, starring Luciano Pavarotti, Reiner casually remarked that he had never seen Pavarotti perform live. That's all DK needed to hear. He phoned Pavarotti's hotel, was put straight through, and arranged to purchase four house seats (for DK, for Estelle and Carl Reiner, and for me, the chauffeur) for that evening's performance.

Now Reiner was impressed. What he didn't know was that all week long Kaye had been frustrated by his failed attempts to reach Pavarotti. It was sheer serendipity that this one call provided a successful connection.

Alas, this particular Saturday turned out to be the only day of the entire five-week shoot that the actors were held overtime. After having been kept waiting eight hours to begin filming their courtroom scene, Reiner and Kaye finally went to work at 6:00 P.M. and finished at 7:45. The opera began at eight. DK, who was intolerant of tardiness of any kind, was furious—all the more so when, in the car racing downtown, he realized he had misplaced his watch and seven hundred dollars. I assumed the lost items were safely stowed in the pockets of his costume, but a call to the production office only added to the frustration: The costumes were locked away until Monday morning.

By the time we finally reached the opera house, the curtain had already risen. Because we could not be seated, we were invited to watch from the wings. The Reiners delighted in the privilege of being backstage. But for Kaye, something more sublime was transpiring. As he stood hidden in the shadows, Verdi's music slowly carried him to a place I know not where, a place free from fear and aggravation.

When the curtain descended on Act One, the scores of exiting supernumeraries swarmed over Kaye in such uninhibited adulation that he had to be ushered away. We moved on to Pavarotti's dressing room. The tenor's expansive frame filled the doorway. Smiling through doelike eyes, he embraced Kaye, saying, "How wonderful to see you, my old enemy."

Now, finally, we were able to take our seats. No sooner did the opera resume than DK promptly fell asleep. His wheeze was loud enough to distract everyone within a three-row radius. After the opera ended, Kaye wanted to vacate the auditorium as quickly as possible. But Carl Reiner, who was still savoring the experience, would not be rushed. He struck up a dialogue with two newlyweds who were seated in front of him. Such relaxed, spontaneous behavior was alien to DK; apart from children, I never saw him voluntarily enter into a conversation with a stranger.

On the drive home, Reiner, wanting to prolong the memorable evening, suggested that we stop for a late-night snack at Sam & Hy's, a Skokie deli.

"We'll have to sign autographs," Kaye complained.

"It goes with the territory," Reiner coaxed. "Whenever I'm working in New York, I make a point of going into the Stage Deli at least once a month. You have to give the people a thrill."

Kaye caved in.

At one point, while DK visited the men's room, I took the opportunity to query Reiner about his bizarre 1967 Broadway comedy, *Something Different*, which had a disappointing run of only 111 performances. "That's the best thing I've ever written," he ruefully acknowledged. "It's a play that evolved from nothing. I'd written a movie called *The Comic*. Now I was just sitting at my typewriter, marking time, waiting for the worlds of finance to put this picture into place. So I started to noodle, and this play grew out of nothing. No, that's not exactly true. It grew from my dissatisfaction with not being able to understand the new abstract, absurd plays that were being done in New York. I thought I was getting senile. So I started to write an abstract, absurd drama of my own, and it turned out to be *Something Different*.

"When we opened in New Haven, the play had a third act, which was the reason I wrote it. Act Three was a Pirandello-ish play-within-a-play-within-a-play. Four levels. I thought that was the cat's meow. The critics did too. They said, 'If he beats this, he'll have a work of genius.' But I couldn't beat it. I couldn't make the audience sit still for it, especially not the older audience, who thought they were coming to see the same Carl Reiner who had written *The Dick Van Dyke Show* and who weren't prepared to see something so wildly crazy. It was different than anything, and that third act was even more different, because it became dramatic, with actual deaths onstage. Little old ladies were coming up the aisle to shoot me. Only the Yale audiences appreciated it. They were wild for it, and when they heard I dropped Act Three in Boston, they were all upset. Let's face it: Nobody's ever written a three-act play and then dropped the third act. But it wasn't a conventional three-act play. It was a crazy, absurd work. And the reason the experience was so traumatic was because the play was on the edge of being a hit.

"We finally got the play together in Boston. Audiences there bought it, and then the New York previews were sold out, with people falling out of the balconies from laughter. Clive Barnes from *The New York Times* saw a preview. I couldn't have asked for a better performance from the cast, but he didn't understand it. Walter Kerr came opening night, which was a dull performance. He saw the same play, not performed as well because the audience was not as responsive, and he gave it a great review. But his Sunday review didn't run until three weeks after we opened, and by then the boat had sailed. But *Something Different* was one of those events in my life that I

continue to think about. Sometimes I think I'd like to produce it
again. Then I think, no, the subject is too show business. It's the
story of an author who loses his Muse. But why does that have to be
a show-business story? It could be the story of anyone who loses
faith in himself. People lose their Muses in life, not just in theater."

DK returned to the table, and I left for a moment. During my
absence, he and Reiner persuaded the waitress that I was a rising
young star ("the next Tom Selleck"). For the remainder of our meal
I had to sign autographs for waitresses, cooks, hostesses. On the
drive back to the hotel, as the Reiners snickered in the back seat,
DK asked how I had enjoyed my fifteen minutes of fame. Joining in
the merriment, I said, "I see what you guys did. I know you, and—"

Kaye's voice lashed out from the shotgun-seat darkness. "You
don't know me! And don't think for one minute that you do!" A
stunned silence pervaded the car.

By the next day, all was forgotten. Kaye insisted that we go for a
ride in the country. As I would soon learn, during our opera foray
he had decided that my foot was too heavy when I slowed the car at
stoplights. We sought out an isolated back road so he could give me
instruction in braking!

So it went for the next two weeks: by day, the work; by night,
dinners out (where all food was passed around the table Chinese-
style, regardless of the restaurant's cuisine). Soon Eli Wallach was
gone, then Carl Reiner was gone. When Herb Bonis returned to Los
Angeles, DK asked me to move into Herb's vacated bedroom. Living
in the hotel suite, I soon saw another side of Danny Kaye: the in-
somniac, who would stay up into the wee hours of the morning, hoping that the old movies on television would become his soporific.

After *Skokie* finished production, I didn't see DK for nine months.
Then he came to New York to conduct another Pension-Fund benefit
concert with the New York Philharmonic. Only this time, for the first
time, it would air on public television.

The concert was quintessential Danny Kaye. There were moments
when he was so absorbed by the music that his putty face became
beautiful, as though he were in a state of grace. I had seen that face
only once before, backstage in Chicago when he was under Verdi's
spell. Now, despite the harsh glare of the television lights, there were
moments when it was as if the audience wasn't even there. Then,
ten minutes before the end, Kaye, ever on the lookout for someone
to impress, had to tell the audience, "I don't know if you know this

or not—I suppose you have read it somewhere—I don't know how to read music." That too was quintessential Danny Kaye, and so specious. Let's face it: A man who has mastered surgery, cooking, aviation, could learn how to read music if he wanted to. Somehow it served his interest to be able to claim that he could not.

Once the concert was behind him, DK agreed to promote *Skokie* in Chicago, Philadelphia and San Francisco. After the schedule was set, he arbitrarily canceled Philly. A two-city publicity tour wouldn't prove too arduous for most stars—but DK wasn't like most stars. In Chicago he was so rude that the local station manager informed CBS that Danny Kaye was never to set foot in their studio again. Back in New York, he had to be forced to sit with television reporters during the lunch that followed a *Skokie* press conference. As the meal ended, Mickey Rooney bounded into the restaurant for a press conference on behalf of his upcoming television movie, *Bill*. On his way to the dais, Rooney maniacally called out to the assemblage, "My initials are M.R., as in 'mentally retarded.'" Kaye literally raced from the room.

Now began the final chapters of his life.

• In May 1982 he received a Peabody Award for his performances in *Skokie* and with the New York Philharmonic.

• In February 1983 he underwent quadruple heart bypass surgery.

• In December 1984, along with Lena Horne, Gian-Carlo Menotti, Arthur Miller and Isaac Stern, he was an honoree at the seventh annual Kennedy Center Honors. His deteriorating hip caused him to suffer intense pain throughout the ceremony, but when Vin Scully saluted him and said, "You made the whole world laugh," Danny Kaye stood the tallest and the straightest of the five recipients. The following week he underwent hip-replacement surgery.

• In November 1985 he acted in a little-seen episode of the revived *Twilight Zone* series. Three months later he guest starred as a buffoonish dentist on the highly rated *The Cosby Show*. After he received an Emmy Award nomination for that performance, he called me to vent his irritation that the Television Academy would ignore his serious work in *Skokie* and *The Twilight Zone* and then recognize the same old shtick he'd been doing all his life.

On March 3, 1987, Danny Kaye, age seventy-four, died of heart failure, two days after having been admitted to a Los Angeles hospital for internal bleeding and hepatitis. Later that month I had lunch with Eli Wallach. He'd seen a lot of DK while in Los Angeles filming *Nuts*.

"Have you been around death?" Eli asked me.

No.

"Well, I was, during the war. The eyes change. The eyes prepare you. I saw it coming in Danny's eyes. In fact, the last time I saw Sylvia, she said to me, 'He's deciding whether or not to die.' "

I was struck by Eli's comments because, during my brief time around DK, only infrequently had he revealed himself through his eyes. He was more prone to convey his moods through the slump of his shoulders, the curl in his forelock, the drumming of his fingers on a table. Not the eyes. Yet, there was that one night . . .

In November 1981, two weeks after *Skokie* had aired, after the good reviews had quelled his fears—*those* fears, anyway—I arrived in Los Angeles on another assignment. The jet lag had taken its toll, and I was in my hotel room preparing for bed. But on a whim, I called DK to say hello.

"Get your ass over here," he ordered. I dressed, found my way to his Beverly Hills home and walked in on one of those famed Chinese dinners that he loved to cater for his celebrity friends. The Gregory Pecks, the Leslie Bricusses, the David Hedisons were all seated around the circular kitchen table. Roger Moore and his wife would arrive as the group was adjourning to the den. That's where DK got into a discussion with Luisa Moore about comedy. "No, no, no!" he protested. "Comedy doesn't depend on words. Let me show you." To illustrate his point, he screened a ballet sequence from one of his Sam Goldwyn comedies.

That was the beginning. Next he unreeled a cassette of highlights from *The Danny Kaye Show*—DK singing with Ella Fitzgerald, performing with Michel Legrand, a riotous military sketch with José Ferrer. Through it all, DK was enraptured at watching himself. He silently aped every line, every note. Then he played another videotape, and another. The captive audience began to grow restless. If anyone needed a reason to leave, it came when DK and Roger Moore agreed that they'd be willing to stay up until 5:00 A.M. viewing tapes. You never saw a party break up more quickly. As the guests scurried to their cars, Danny Kaye followed us out onto the front walkway, imploring everyone to return. That's how we left him, his eyes filled with confusion and hurt. At least that's what I assume he was feeling.

He was right, of course, late on that Skokie Saturday night when he accused me of not knowing him. I did not. I doubt that anyone did. But I witnessed him. I saw him funny; I saw him sad. I saw him bring joy to people; I saw him bring unnecessary anguish. I was even privileged to see him in thrall. I just never saw him confident.

He was a complicated man.

SIDES:
THE AUDITION

" 'Never sit on a stage when you're auditioning!
Get up; walk around; stand on your head.' "
—FRITZ WEAVER

"I never was upset if producers didn't like my
auditions. I usually agreed with them."
—JON VOIGHT

"An actor must have this enormous ego in order to
perform—and none at all in order to live."
—CHRISTOPHER WALKEN

"So here I am at my age, still auditioning."
—GERALDINE PAGE

James Brolin can laugh about it now, but it wasn't so funny when he was still struggling. "As a young actor," he said, "I'd go on an audition, and for six months I'd tell people I was 'up for' such-and-such a role. Then somebody would say, 'Oh, but they're almost finished shooting that,' and I'd have to change my story. It wasn't so much that I was lying to my friends; I was lying to myself. Anything to keep me going."

It's a rare actor who doesn't blanch at the mere mention of the word *audition*. The audition is the gauntlet, the crucible, that reminds the actor that every role is the first role, and that judgment must always be passed anew.

Tall, angular and erudite, **Fritz Weaver** has spent a lifetime playing tall, angular roles like Sherlock Holmes, Abraham Lincoln and Sir Andrew Aguecheek. Like Gregory Peck, another tall actor, the Tony Award-winning Weaver (*Child's Play* [1970]) received some early training at the Barter Theater in Abingdon, Virginia.

193

"I always acted in high school in Pittsburgh," Weaver said, "but I didn't think of acting as a serious career. I wanted to write. I went to the University of Chicago, and then I was in the graduate program. But all the while, I was acting in plays on the side, and one of them just tipped me over into the whole thing. I decided this is really what I want to do.

"From Chicago I went straight to New York, where I auditioned for the Barter Theater in Virginia. Every year a Broadway star would audition hundreds of young people and would select two, a male and a female, for this special scholarship. The year I auditioned, the star was Fredric March. He didn't have any trouble deciding on the female. That was Rosemary Murphy. But he couldn't choose his male. He had it down to two of us, David Hedison and me, but he had to pick one.

"David and I were up on the stage while Fredric March said to Bob Porterfield, who ran the theater, 'I don't know what to do.' While this was going on, David was prancing around, flirting with everybody, and I was sitting there, very intense, tall and even thinner than I am now, saying to myself, 'I'll be damned if I'm going to try to woo him.'

"David, by the way, is a lovely man. Whenever we're together, we reminisce about this incident.

"Finally March comes back and says to me, 'I'm sorry, I think you're very talented, but I picked David Hedison.' Fighting back the tears, I tore out the stage door as quickly as possible. I was halfway down the street before I realized that Bob Porterfield was running after me, calling out, 'Hey wait, where are you going?'

" 'I lost.'

" 'No, I want you to come anyway. I was hoping he'd pick you, because you're more useful. You can play all kinds of roles. You come anyway.'

"So I came anyway. I toured for two years with the Barter Theater. We beat the roads of Virginia to death, playing high school auditoriums and mining towns way up in the hills. All because Bob Porterfield, bless his heart, came running after me. Then he gave me some good advice, in the form of a stern lecture. He said, 'Never sit on a stage when you're auditioning! Get up; walk around; stand on your head; do *something*. But don't ever sit still like that again.' "

Brimming with youthful optimism, **Jon Voight** never sat still. But, like Fritz Weaver, one of Voight's most important jobs came to him despite his audition.

"When it came time to cast *Midnight Cowboy*," he recalled, as we sat out a Montana rainstorm on a television mini-series location, "Dustin Hoffman was set to play Ratso Rizzo. But Joe Buck was the prize that the rest of us were pursuing. Initially the director, John Schlesinger, auditioned many actors. He gave screen tests to some who were unknown like me and to others who were better known. I came away from my audition very happy. There's an oddball kind of Laurel and Hardy-ness between Joe Buck and Ratso. If you don't have humor under every scene, the story could become maudlin or even seamy. I understood that, and I felt I conveyed it in my screen test. Nevertheless, they decided to give Joe Buck to Michael Sarrazin, who was better known.

"In New York I had a reputation for turning down roles and also for recommending other actors in my place. I could walk away from a part. I never was upset if producers didn't like my auditions. I usually agreed with them. But with Joe Buck, I went in full of confidence. And when I lost that role, my heart hurt. I was sick. For two weeks I actually walked around with a knot in my stomach. Then at the end of those two weeks my agent called and said, 'Hold on, Jon, they may come back to you.' They had trouble making the deal with Michael Sarrazin.

"At this point, an amazing thing happened. I was living up on 107th Street. It was a rainy, rainy day, and I said to this homeless man who was out on the street, an old, alcoholic, punchy fellow who'd been a boxer, I said, 'You've got to get out of the rain. I'll get you a bottle of liquor, but I want you to come to my house and get out of the rain.'

"So I got him into my house, and I made him a bunch of sandwiches. Tuna fish and peanut butter. They must have been awful. In the midst of this, the phone rings. [Voight feigns a thick British accent.] 'Hello, Jon. This is John Schlesinger. We've had some thoughts about perhaps coming back toward you with this project. I wonder if you're still interested.'

"I said, 'Well, of course I am.'

"He said, 'Would you mind coming crosstown and seeing me for a bit, just to say hello again? Could you come right away?'

"Now we're past the audition, right? We're having a meeting, which can be even more frustrating to the actor, because you have no idea what they're looking for.

"I hung up the phone. I said to this guy, 'I have to go now. If you go out in the rain, I want you to take this coat.' I gave him a coat. But I said, 'If you want to stick around, feel free to watch television or do anything you like.' And I left.

"Now, a lot of people would say, 'You're leaving this guy in your house?' Crazy stuff, right? But I thought that the guy would feel good that I trusted him. So I left, and I went and saw John, who didn't have much to say and was very noncommittal. When I came back, the guy was still there. We started talking. He was a sweet, sweet man. He had a wife and five daughters. He hadn't seen them in years. I called his wife for him. We called each of his five daughters. And I told him a little about myself. I said, 'I'm a young actor. I'm trying to get a professional career going. I'm up for a part that could change my life completely.'

"He says, 'Oh, I hope you get it. I pray to God you get it. You're such a nice man. You deserve it.'

"The phone rings. I get up. I say, 'Come on over with me. This might be the call.' The guy comes over with me! His face was all scarred up, because he'd been a boxer and an alcoholic and in the streets for years. But he's rooting for me. So we're standing there together, and I pick up the phone, and I hear the voice say, 'Hello, Jon. This is John Schlesinger.' And I nod to the fellow that this is the call. And John says, 'We've decided to go with you for the project. Do you feel secure in the choice?'

"I say, 'John, I don't think you'll regret this decision.'

"He said, 'Good. We'll start work Monday.'

"So I hung up the phone. I said, 'I've got the part!'

"He said, 'God bless you! God bless you! I'm so happy for you!'

"I'm looking into this guy's beaten-up face. I asked him, 'What should I do now? What's the first thing I should do?'

"He says, 'Call your mother. She'll be so happy to hear.'

" 'Call your mother.' Of course! So now I'm crying, because it was such a beautiful thought. I get on the phone: 'Mom, I got the part in *Midnight Cowboy*! It's a happy, happy day for me. It's the beginning of many things.'

" 'Oh, Jon, God bless,' she says. 'I love you, son.'

" 'I love you too, Mom.' I'm weeping. The guy is weeping. This guy is weeping! The two of us are crying together. Now we go back in the living room. And I'm happy he's there. His presence made a big difference, because he gave me some poise in all this thing. I see his plight and condition, and I know to appreciate my situation no matter what happens. Who knows? Maybe having him there that day made the difference in how I handled myself when I went for the meeting with Schlesinger. Maybe this guy was the difference in my getting the part.

"Anyway, we're sitting in the living room having a little drink, and he looks at me and says, 'I want to tell you something. I got something I want to say to you.' And it came out of a deep, serious place. He waited a long, long time. It must have been a pause of maybe two minutes. And I'm waiting, and waiting. He looks up to me finally with deep, deep sadness, and he says, 'I want to tell you something, but I forgot what it was.'

"Oh my God. It was so beautiful. It was just exactly like me and Ratso, the two of us expressing our affection for each other.

"I never saw him again. I don't even know his name. But he made a great difference, that man. And ten years later, when I filmed *The Champ*, playing a punchy fighter who's doing the best he can for another human being, that old alcoholic boxer was a part of me."

Voight's being cast in *Midnight Cowboy* placed him on a fast track to fame. In April 1976, when the following conversation with **Christopher Walken** occurred, Walken was still on the fringes. His third film, *Next Stop, Greenwich Village*, had just been released. In a newspaper interview, the film's director, Paul Mazursky, described Walken as being "on the verge of stardom." When he heard the quote, the actor replied, "I appreciate his saying it, but I'm very cynical about that sort of remark. I've been 'promising' for ten years. I'll tell you. I had a sort of blow last night that slid off me like water.

"Last week I was flown to California, very classy, and I screen-tested for eight hours for a very important part in a major film. It was very encouraging. I was told at the time by everyone concerned that it was wrapped up. They were talking about what hotel I'd stay at and which restaurants we'd be eating in.

"Then last night I got the phone call, and I did not get the job. For a moment it was like being hit with a hammer. But this morning I'm perfectly OK, because I have developed a very thick skin, and all for the better. An actor has to have a thick skin, because this sort of thing happens all too often. It occurs to me that there is a strange paradox about this business: An actor must have this enormous ego in order to perform—and none at all in order to live. Which is to say that standing on a stage in front of two thousand people and asking them to watch you for two or three hours requires incredible audacity. Yet in the periods between, you have to deal with rejection and business matters in an egoless way."

Every actor's dream is to become successful enough that he or she will never have to audition again. But as **Geraldine Page** observed in 1982, fame and success are no guarantees for a cessation of the hostilities:

"I was very lucky in that, when I was seventeen and decided I wanted to be an actress, I found in the public library in Chicago a book called *So You Want to Be an Actor*. It was a wonderful book, because it put in the most forceful terms all the horrible things that can happen and do happen; and at the end of each chapter, it would say, 'But of course the people who have made it don't let this deter them.' So from early on, I was anticipating the onslaught of all those horrendous aspects, and none of them surprised me. But I certainly did run into them, and I still run into them. I can now say with some authority that it was a very truthful book, even given to understatement.

"I'll give you a recent example. When I read *Agnes of God*, which I'm doing on Broadway right now, I loved this play. It was so theatrical! I said to myself, 'Mother Miriam is for me.' Then my agent had to talk the producers into hiring me! They wanted Irene Worth or Colleen Dewhurst, somebody that they knew could be a mother superior. They had never seen me play an authoritarian figure. The author is supposed to have said, 'She only plays flighty characters.' So here I am at my age [58], still auditioning.

"Now when young people come to me and ask, 'Could you advise me? Should I or shouldn't I become an actor?' I say, 'If you can talk yourself out of it, do talk yourself out of it. The only way you should stay in the business is if you cannot talk yourself out of it. You must love acting for its own sake.

"But if you become an actress to make money, you can make millions and all you'll get is tax problems.

"If you become an actress to meet fascinating people, you will be quickly disillusioned by them.

"If you become an actress to become famous and sign autographs, you'll learn that you have no privacy and will want to shoot yourself.

"No, the only reason to become an actress is because you love it so much that you cannot talk yourself out of it."

CHAPTER SEVEN

OUTSIDER

---

*"Othello had reached the pinnacle of everything he
thought he ever wanted, but he was still an outsider.
That's what did him in."*
—PAUL WINFIELD

This is purely subjective—because there's no such thing as *best*
where performances are concerned—but for me, the most memorable television performance by an actress was given by Geraldine
Page as the old woman in the 1966 adaptation of Truman Capote's
A Christmas Memory. My most memorable television performance
by an actor? Paul Winfield, in the six-hour 1978 mini-series *King*.

As civil-rights advocate Dr. Martin Luther King, Jr., Winfield delivered a titanic performance that should have cemented his position in the front ranks of American actors. But television shows come
and go so quickly; it's rare indeed when any actor's career is affected by a role in a TV-movie or mini-series. As for a black actor . . .
forget it. It's not going to happen, not in this country. So *King* came
and went, and Paul Winfield returned to the ranks. In the post-*King*
decades, his roles too infrequently have been unworthy of an actor
who stood on the mountaintop.

It has been said that film stars dwell in cocoons of their own
spinning, removed from day-to-day reality. But not minority stars,
who must scramble for every job. Today Paul Winfield lives in a handsome home high in the Hollywood Hills, with a panoramic view that

stretches to the Pacific. It is a house that reeks of success. But that emission is misleading, for Winfield is only as successful as his last paycheck. Although outsiders may enjoy productive years, they are never able to glide on the coattails of their credits. Paul Winfield is still scrambling.

"I'll give you the absolute truth . . ." he said as we sat in his sunken living room, surrounded by so many hand-carved African masks you could almost imagine they were eavesdropping, " . . . as I remember it." Then Winfield laughed, a deep, sonorous, boisterous laugh that would continue to punctuate his stories, especially the ones that revealed him as too naive, or too ambitious, or too cocky. More than once he would scoff, "I was pretty full of myself."

Let's start at the beginning, I suggested. You were born here in Los Angeles in 1941.

"Wrong. Oh, that's what the research says, but I was actually born in Dallas, Texas, on May 22, 1939. Here's what happened. My mother, who *was* born in Los Angeles, was the second of three daughters. Her name was Lois Whitfield; she later changed it to Winfield. In 1938 she was going to City College when she met the true love of her life, my father, a handsome, charismatic fellow who was already married and had something like seven children. So my mother and father never were able to marry. When my mother became pregnant, she did not abort me. But her mother, my grandmother, who was very religious, kicked her out. So she went and stayed with her older sister, who was living in Texas, and gave birth to me there. She waited until I got sort of 'cute,' then returned to Los Angeles and showed me to my grandmother. All was forgiven, and we were taken in. But because she was now burdened with me, my mother never went back to school. Instead she married my stepfather, a construction worker named Carney Morris, who was from Mississippi and had finished maybe the eighth grade.

"When I was growing up, I didn't get along very well with my dad. He was my stepfather, but I called him 'Dad' because he was the only father I knew. I've since come to understand a great deal more about the man and have certainly forgiven him. Understanding is forgiving, I suppose. Today I have a clearer appreciation for how numbing manual labor can be. You see these TV fathers who bounce in from some mythical office somewhere, and they have energy. But if you've been collecting garbage cans all day, or digging a ditch all day, you don't come home dancing on your toes with funny things to say. You may be glad to see your family, but you need to rest. From the son's standpoint, there's no way to comfort this guy, because we've got to have food and clothes and money, so I'm sorry, Dad, but you have to go out there and do this all over again tomorrow.

"In the mid-'80s, when I played the unsympathetic father in the film version of James Baldwin's *Go Tell It on the Mountain*, I understood that character because I'd grown up with him. He wasn't a villain, but he was incapable of understanding a son who aspired to more than he did."

And your mother?

"My mother was a lot more educated, and a lot more ambitious, than my father was, and that eventually led to a lot of disappointment in both their lives. In time, she too had to go to work, to help make ends meet. She worked in garment factories where conditions were so bad that she ended up as a labor organizer. She was sort of the Norma Rae of Watts. 'You don't have to put up with this! If we stick together—' Of course, she was fired a lot.

"My mother always encouraged my interest in the arts. We saw lots of movies together. One of the movies I remember most I saw when I was ten years old. For a few years during and after World War II we lived in Portland, Oregon. That's where we were when Stanley Kramer's film *Home of the Brave* opened. Portland was a very segregated city. When you went to the movies, white audiences sat downstairs, and blacks were relegated to the balcony. But *Home of the Brave* was a story about racial discrimination, starring a black actor, James Edwards. We all went to see it. We bought our tickets, and we walked straight into the orchestra; and from that time forth, we stayed in the orchestra. There was no big to-do. There were no riots. But that marked the end of segregated movie theaters in Portland."

In the early 1950s your family returned to California. What was it like, growing up in South-Central Los Angeles?

"The neighborhoods were a microcosm of a functioning United Nations. There were a lot of East European kids, a lot of Estonians, Armenians. And every ethnic community maintained its own culture. Mexicans, for instance, were a big part of our group, because the Mexican families might have ten or eleven kids. But in the summer, if we were all playing outside barefoot, we would not be allowed into a Mexican home without first going home and putting on shoes and a shirt. As for the Chinese kids, you could play with them outside, but you were never allowed into their homes. So we all got along, but we didn't blend together."

What was it that motivated you to want to act?

"Early success, I think. Within the South-Central area, we moved around a lot. I used to tell interviewers that we moved so much because my father's construction work took him to different locations. But the truth was that we'd get behind in paying bills, and abruptly move to avoid the landlord or the grocer. I might attend three different schools in the same school year. As the outsider who had to come in and prove himself, it became harder and harder to make friends. Instead I became something of a loner.

"But at Edison Junior High School, I got cast in a very small part in a play called *Annabelle Steps In*. I had a line in which I had to say 'Jumpin' Jehoshaphat.' It was the first big laugh of the evening, and it brought down the house. All summer long, people would see me and say, 'Weren't you the guy in that play?' Then they'd ask, 'Would you say that line again for me?' And I'd say 'Jumpin' Jehoshaphat,' and they'd say, 'We're having a party this Saturday, why don't you come?' So acting became an entrée into a world I didn't really know how to break into.

"That was junior high school. When I started high school, we were living way out in the Fremont district. The high school there was a disaster. But my mother was determined that I get the best possible education. So she arranged for me to move in with one of her sisters, my Aunt Jean, so that I could attend Manual Arts, a progressive high school in Aunt Jean's district.

"At Manual Arts I enrolled in a marvelous elective class in theater that met after school. Our teacher was getting his master's degree in psychodrama. He used us shamelessly, but it was a great opportunity to be exposed to theater and film. I'll never forget seeing the Tyrone Guthrie film of *Oedipus Rex*, with Douglas Campbell as Oedipus. I was bowled over by that final scene where Oedipus discovers he killed his father and slept with his mother. Campbell delivers an aria that begins with a moan that starts low and ends up on a stratospheric level of pain and hurt and revelation.

"Every Friday we would have Lunchtime Playhouse, where kids could bring their lunches in and we would perform scenes. I was determined to stage that final scene from *Oedipus Rex*. So we got chicken wire, made plaster masks. We couldn't figure out how to make the platform shoes, but a janitor found us some old drapes from the auditorium, and we pinned those around us. And there I was in high school, doing Greek tragedy.

"I also liked to do scenes from Eugene O'Neill, because he wrote with a lot of parentheses that told you what the scenes meant and how to read the lines. Back then, I assumed that if you followed those directions, you must be doing it right. Then one day a kid acted a scene from Richard Wright's *Native Son*. At the end of the story the police are after him, and he comes in through the window, has a final farewell with his mother and then goes out and gets killed. That scene was so real and immediate that it wasn't like acting at all. It wasn't like O'Neill, with all the parentheses. That made a deep impression on me."

Wasn't it while you were at Manual Arts High School that you worked for the Los Angeles Police Department?

"Aunt Jean was secretary to the police commissioner, so she got me a job down at Parker Center, the main LAPD headquarters, as a night clerk in the Records and Identification section. In those days the files weren't on computer. If someone was arrested, I'd have to search through all the stacks looking for the right file. It was very interesting work, because I would read all these cases. The files would actually state, 'This guy, while he was in his holding cell, fell down and broke six ribs and was lacerated about the face.' And it was clear that they'd beaten him. So I developed an antipathy to the LAPD very early on."

You couldn't find any positive sides to the police force?

"No."

There were no good police officers?

"No."

But you never actually crossed swords with the LAPD yourself?

"You didn't have to confront them. They were always *there*. After I began to make some decent money from TV, I went out and bought my first car, a bright canary yellow Pontiac Firebird convertible. It was a very sleek 'look at me' car, which is exactly what I wanted, because I thought I was on my way up. But that car became the object of constant harassment by the LAPD. Especially if I had someone white in the car with me, I couldn't drive more than ten blocks without being pulled over. Eventually I had to paint it black, just to call off the cops."

What was your first big break?

"*The Dutchman*. It came about like this. After high school, college for me became a process of following scholarships. I went to the University of Portland until that scholarship ran out. Then I attended L.A. City College, but they didn't have any money. Got a brief scholarship at Stanford, then came down to UCLA, where I had one for books and a living stipend. While I was studying at UCLA I joined a professional actors' workshop called Theatre West as a student observer. Now we're into 1965. One day at Theatre West—simply out of the goodness of his heart, I didn't really know him—Carroll O'Connor said to me, 'My friend Burgess Meredith is directing two one-act plays by LeRoi Jones at the Warner Playhouse. You should audition.' So I went right down there. I was cast in a featured role in *The Toilet*, and I understudied Al Freeman, Jr., as Clay in *The Dutchman*.

"*The Toilet*, which is set in a high school john, is about the friendship between a black gang leader and a white boy. The play has a lot to do with the hierarchy of these various gang members. One of the best pieces of direction I've ever heard came from Burgess Meredith, when he said to the actor playing the gang leader, 'If you're the king, you don't have to act like a king. It's up to everybody else to bow when you walk by.'

"The production was a big hit and got extended. But Al had to return to New York to do a soap opera, so I took over the lead in *The Dutchman*, which is a two-character play about a chance meeting on a subway between a black guy and a white woman. That was my big break. I played *The Dutchman* with three different actresses— Shirley Knight, Patricia Houston, who has gone on to her reward, and Sheree North, who I think actually was the best of all three. Shirley Knight would do pyrotechnic things like peeling an orange and then smashing it into your face. A viewer might legitimately ask, 'Why does Clay stay on the subway and take all that abuse from this crazy woman?' But Sheree was so voluptuous, sensual and seductive that you could see how she kept him there. She was really scary."

In 1965 didn't a lot of people find LeRoi Jones scary?

"Even the *Los Angeles Times*. They thought the production was inflammatory, so they withdrew our ads. We made such a stink about it that the paper finally ran an editorial, which said that their reason for boycotting us was because the plays could endanger the peace of the city. Two months later the Watts riots broke out and the city was in flames. Not, I might add, because of our production."

Would it be fair to say that the Watts riots had a beneficial effect on your career?

"No question about it. By the mid-1960s, remember, Martin

Luther King's civil-rights demonstrations were bringing blacks into America's living rooms. Before the demonstrations, blacks might as well have lived on the other side of the moon. For many white people, the last black image they remembered was from *Gone With the Wind*, where the blacks were all house slaves and so happy to be there, or maids like on *Beulah*. Now, for the first time, whites were seeing water hoses turned on black people, and dogs unleashed on black children, just for wanting to sit at a lunch counter or, God forbid, for wanting to vote. The realization that blacks were simply opposing the daily humiliation of being denied their humanity, I think, appealed to the basic goodness of most white Americans.

"After the Watts riots, everything in Hollywood began to change. Suddenly we were the flavor of the month. They used to have a Writers Building at Twentieth Century-Fox. I remember walking down the halls of that building and hearing these white guys trying out black street talk, trying to write how black people at that time talked. The producers were white, the directors were white and the writers were all white. But they needed black actors. So the studio doors flung open, and I happened to be there at the right time to play the angry, young, articulate black.

"Actually, some of those more articulate roles were still a few years away. My first role was on an episode of *Perry Mason* at the end of its long run. Initially they cast me as a character who perjures himself on the witness stand. By TV standards, that was a good, meaty role, and I enjoyed doing it. A week later they called back to say they'd decided that for a black character to lie on the stand was too dicey, so they un-cast me and refilmed the scene with a white actor.

"By way of compensation, they gave me a role in another episode, but this time I only had one line. I was a mechanic in overalls who discovered a body in an auto shop. My line was, 'Gee, Pete, he ain't breathin'.' When you only have one line, you become obsessed by it. I rehearsed that line every imaginable way: 'Gee . . . Pete . . . he ain't breathin'!' 'He ain't breathin', Pete. Gee.' But everyone on the set understood the trauma that I was going through. Even the guy who played the dead body, when it came time to shoot my close-up, asked, 'Would it help you if I lie down next to the camera here?'

"I said, 'Sure, why not? That's very nice of you.'

"Now I have to tell you. When I decided to pursue acting, there were essentially three successful black stars: Harry Belafonte, Sammy Davis, Jr., and Sidney Poitier. Two of those three sang and danced, and I didn't do either. My parents simply did not believe I could succeed as an actor. When I went off to college to study theater, neighbors would ask my parents what I was majoring in, and they'd lie and say 'Sociology,' or anything that sounded respectable. But the moment I appeared on TV with one line on *Perry Mason*, the minute they could *see* what I was doing, I'd overhear them bragging to people, 'We always knew he'd be great.' It became very exciting for them."

And how was it for you?

"I was actually sort of ambivalent. After a lifetime of scraping to make ends meet, finally I was being paid decent money for doing TV. That was nice. But I still wanted to do Shakespeare and Chekhov. Not long after my one line on *Perry Mason*, Raymond Burr started up a new series called *Ironside*, and I was offered twelve hundred dollars a week to play Ironside's assistant. By then I had an agent. He kept saying, 'Paul, this is a once-in-a-lifetime deal.' But I couldn't see how I'd grow as an actor by pushing Raymond Burr around in a wheelchair, so I turned it down and went off for a season of repertory at Stanford."

When you returned to L.A. after a year at Stanford, didn't you promptly become the center of controversy in another public imbroglio, with more newspaper editorials?

"I did. And all I wanted to do was to *act*."

What happened?

"In Los Angeles one of the direct outgrowths of the Watts riots was the creation of the Inner City Cultural Center. After my season at Stanford, I was accepted into this new acting company. We opened with Lou Gossett in *Tartuffe*. He was wonderful! But we were playing to student audiences, and the production, which featured a black Tartuffe seducing a white Elmire, upset the school board something terrible. Then, with that uproar still on people's minds, along came *The Glass Menagerie*. Maxine Stewart was Amanda; Bonnie Bedelia was Laura; Larry Kert was Tom; and I was cast as the Gentleman Caller. Once again the school board was up in arms. They wanted me replaced, and I have to concede that they did have a point. It would have been cruel for Tom to have brought home a black gentleman caller when his mother was a southern belle of the old order. So the school board had a point. At the time, of course, I wasn't in favor of this position, because I really wanted the part. My attitude was: Since my job is to interpret human behavior, why should my skin color get in the way? But of course it did. It still does, for that matter, though less than it used to.

"At this point—with the school board after my head, and the newspapers writing editorials—Gregory Peck enters the story. He was one of the Inner City Cultural Center founders, and he was on the board of directors. His reaction to all this sound and fury was, 'If the only problem is Paul's skin color, why don't we change the color of his skin?' That became the solution. Prior to every performance of *The Glass Menagerie*, I went to the Twentieth Century-Fox makeup department and received this two-hour application of white makeup, which Gregory Peck secretly paid for out of his own pocket."

If Peck had not come up with this resolution, how do you think the controversy would have played out?

"They would have gone with traditional casting. I would have been dumped. Even though I would have received my salary, I would not have been allowed to play the part. I would have felt crippled because of my color. I would have felt that I had been discriminated against, and that I could not rise above, or was not equal to, the task. At the early stages of an actor's career, even though we say we're all ego, it's a very fragile ego. Certainly mine was. Rejection due to color would have deprived me of the courage to continue on the way I did, because I had so many other discouragements along the way."

So what Gregory Peck did was a good thing?

"Oh God, it was fantastic! It changed my life completely. It reenforced my belief that I could do anything, that I wasn't going to be held back by my color, my class, my gender. If I wanted a role badly enough and was trained to do it, I would be given the chance to do it."

What was that experience like, playing in whiteface?

"We did five performances a week at ten o'clock in the morning for fifteen-year-old kids. The first few performances, we literally had to stop the play and say, 'This is not a television screen. If you throw things, they're not going to bounce off, they're going to hit us. We are human beings. You are part of this experience, and we need your full cooperation.' But I can truthfully say that the best theater training I've ever had in my life was working my ass off to hold the attention of students at ten o'clock in the morning. By the end of that run, we knew how to get their attention. It's not that the audiences got better; *we* got better. To this day I still meet people who say, 'I was one of those kids who was bussed in and saw my first play at the Inner City Cultural Center, and because of that, I still love to go to the theater.' And that is very gratifying to an actor.

"But the best part of the experience was that after each performance, after the curtain call I would remove my wig, I'd wipe off some of the makeup, and the kids would discover that I was black. Then we would discuss why I had to play the role as I did. Should I have had to do it? Could I have played it in my own natural color? Generally, the black kids believed that I should have done it in whiteface. The black kids were the most understanding about it."

Wasn't it during your second season at the Inner City Cultural Center that a very influential person entered your life?

"Yes. I was playing Walter Lee, the Sidney Poitier role, in *A Raisin in the Sun* with Beah Richards. She was, and is, an amazing actress. At the end of the play, when Beah gets her garden shears— 'You did *what* with that money?'—and Beneatha has to stop her from killing me, Beah may well have lost it and come over and killed me. It was that real. It was towering. It was one of those moments where we both didn't know what was going to happen next, which is the best kind of theater.

"One night Sidney Poitier came to see the play. Actually, he came to see Beah. When Sidney starred in the play on Broadway, Beah was Claudia McNeil's understudy. I think he wanted to finally see her play the part. In 1969 there wasn't a bigger movie star in the world than Sidney Poitier. He was just coming off of *In the Heat of the Night*, *To Sir, With Love* and *Guess Who's Coming to Dinner*. So when he then asked me to be in his next movie, I can't tell you how thrilled I was. I thought to myself, it doesn't get any better than this.

"*The Lost Man* was my first movie. I had no idea what I was doing. Now I'm working with Sidney Poitier, who had to have a special sound man, because he talked so softly that you couldn't hear what he was saying if you stood more than five feet away from him. I'd watch him on the set and think to myself, when are we going to see some acting here? Then I'd view the film, and I'd realize that Sidney knew how to fill up that frame unlike any other actor.

"He was a great teacher. But Sidney doesn't just teach you how to be a film actor; he teaches you how to be a star. He *was* a star, but he knew who was paying the bills, and he always had time for the public. We filmed *The Lost Man* in a hot, humid Philadelphia housing project where we had to wear flea collars around our wrists and ankles to keep from being eaten alive. People would stand for hours behind the ropes just to get a glimpse of him. Then at the end of the day, as exhausted as he was, before he left in his limo, he always went over and shook their hands, thanked them for coming, and signed.

"We'd be eating in restaurants. Sidney would have a fork in his hand, and people would come up and grab his hand. He never got upset. He always put his fork down, took time, and wrote this elaborate, beautiful *Sidney Poitier*. After *The Lost Man* I made a picture called *R.P.M.* with Anthony Quinn. I could tell you a lot of positive things about Anthony Quinn, but if somebody approached him in a restaurant, he'd say, 'Get the fuck out of here. Can't you see I'm trying to eat?' My third film, *Brother John*, was with Sidney again. It was wonderful to be back in his company, because he is a great man. There is nobody like him. Many times after I became a celebrity I found myself in situations where fame seemed to be a burden, and I would ask myself, 'What would Sidney do?'"

Yet in 1974 you were quoted in a newspaper interview as saying, "I liked him more as a gentleman than an actor. . . . He sold out by defining what's saleable."

"And he's never forgiven me. After he read that, he stopped talking to me. In point of fact, I don't remember using the phrase *he sold out*. But the quote appeared under my name, and I have to live with it. At the time, it never occurred to me that Sidney *could* be hurt by anything I said, or would remotely care what I thought about anything. I've never gotten over it, and he's never gotten over it. And I'll always be sorry about that, because what I owe Sidney can't be measured and it can't be articulated."

It's ironic that two of your first three films starred Sidney Poitier, this huge box-office draw, yet neither *The Lost Man* nor *Brother John* was a success. Then you made this low-budget movie about black sharecroppers in the South during the Depression, and *Sounder* provided the turning point in your career.

"And also the turning point with regard to what kinds of black films were being made. *Sounder* was a real landmark in that its success opened the door for a lot of other black films that otherwise might not have been produced."

It's amazing that an actor never knows—

"—how a movie's going to turn out? Right. You never do, which is why you must put everything you have into each one, on the assumption that it's going to be good. Otherwise, why waste your time? But you never know. In my career it has only happened on one film that all the elements—acting, directing, camera work, set decoration, everything—dovetailed in such a harmonious way that the sum of its parts was greater than all the individual elements, and that film was *Sounder.*"

When you went up for your first interview about *Sounder*, you said to the director, Martin Ritt—

" 'Are you really the man who fucked up *The Great White Hope?*' That's true. I didn't know anything about *Sounder*. I went up for the film primarily because I wanted to meet Martin Ritt. The film version of *The Great White Hope* had just come out. I was deeply disappointed in it, and I wanted to ask the director what happened. And I did ask him, and the question actually engaged him."

What did he say?

"He didn't shoulder the blame alone. He said, for one thing, that the film's budget got out of hand. But he also thought that several of the people connected with it—which I suppose included the actors, but primarily Howard Sackler, the writer—that they were too familiar with the material from having done it on Broadway. He said he lost battles about story points that the others simply assumed the audience already knew."

What did Martin Ritt, an immigrants' son from the Bronx, bring to *Sounder*?

"At the time, I didn't know that he had once been an actor. But he understood actors, and he chose to shoot the film sequentially, which is very rare. They built our cabin out in somebody's cow pasture in rural Louisiana. Twice while we were filming, that cabin was blown down by hurricanes. Both times, Marty shut down production until the set was rebuilt and we could continue filming in sequence.

"But the film that was released was not the story we set out to tell. *Sounder* is named for the dog, and in the original script the dog played a much more significant role. But the dog that they cast was so old he couldn't hit his marks. It was hot down there in Louisiana. The dog was hot, and Martin Ritt was hot, and eventually he got tired of wasting his time on this dog. He said, 'Screw that, let's focus a little more on these people,' and I could literally see them moving the camera up from the dog and onto the actors."

And the man who was moving that camera was—

"John Alonzo, who has gone on to film so many great movies, like *Chinatown*. At the time of *Sounder*, John only had a few credits. I can still hear Marty telling him, 'James Wong Howe is really good, but he takes too long to set up a shot and we can't afford that. So we got you, John,' which did not seem to me to be a confidence-instilling remark. But John is in a class of his own. He's excellent, and Marty must have liked him, because he used him again several times, including on *Conrack* and *Norma Rae.*

Wasn't *Sounder* your first experience in the American South?

"Yes, not to mention my introduction to Southern segregation, which was a real eye-opener. It was rampant; you couldn't get away from it. We were staying in a big motel in Baton Rouge. One day, Kevin [Hooks, who portrayed Winfield's son] and I came back from a long, hard day and jumped into the pool. A few minutes later, everyone else got out. We didn't pay much attention to it. We swam a while longer, then went and got dressed. On our way to dinner, we walked past the pool. It was filled with people again. I was naive in those days. I said to Kevin, 'It's just a coincidence. But let's see.' So we got back into our swimming suits, jumped back into the pool, and all the white people got out again. As soon as we left, they returned. It was so stupid, it didn't even upset me. But from that point on, we would make a point of getting into the pool, just to aggravate people."

Sounder brought you an Academy Award nomination as Best Actor. In March 1973 you took your mother to the awards ceremony as your date, didn't you?

"I tried to talk her out of it. I thought she might have more fun watching it on TV, where you can talk while it's happening. But she said, 'I want to see those people up close.' She loved movies, and here she'd lived in Los Angeles most of her life, but with all the race and class divisions, she'd never seen a movie star in person. So I took her, and we had a fine time.

"Right up until she died in 1978, my mother was probably my biggest fan. Her life was filled with disappointments, so if she wanted to live vicariously through me, that was fine. One time we were at a huge nursery in San Francisco called Acres of Orchards. Various people would come up and ask, 'Aren't you Paul Winfield?' And she would take over: 'This is my son. Did you see *Sounder*?' and give them a whole list of my credits. As we were about to leave, a woman approached me. You could tell she knew me from somewhere. I saw my mother getting in gear to deliver her spiel. Just then this woman asked me, 'Don't you drive the Fillmore bus?' My mother did a fast U-turn and headed for the other side of the room. Later on I reminded her, 'You have to take the bitter with the sweet.'

"One of my own memories of that Academy Awards ceremony is that I met Gregory Peck. I really hadn't dealt with him directly during the *Glass Menagerie* experience. But at the Academy Awards he complimented me on my work in *Sounder*, and I said, 'You know, I based my character on your performance in *The Yearling*.' To me, Gregory Peck in *The Yearling* was the most perfect father that had ever come down the pike. He was strong, he was silent, he was sensitive. But he was the head of that household. I saw no reason not to try to get those same qualities into my character, Nathan Lee, who was also a dirt-poor farmer."

Two years after *Sounder* you found yourself back in the deep South making, of all things, a musical version of *Huckleberry Finn*.

"What can I say? I've always wanted to be in a musical. When I was a kid, I related more to Fred Astaire than to Sammy Davis. I knew I couldn't grow up to be Sammy Davis, but those Fred Astaire movies made you feel so good. Life should be like that somehow. But we weren't filming in top hats and tails. We were down in the swamps of Mississippi with water moccasins and the worst kinds of conditions. It wasn't my idea of how you make a musical."

Once again you found yourself in hot water. This time you were framed in Natchez on a drug rap.

"I wasn't framed."

You *weren't* framed? You were caught?

"I was caught. Actually, I was innocent. Here's what happened, and this is the truth. From the moment I arrived in Natchez I didn't like the place, and the longer I stayed there, the worse it got. I went there with the full intention of finding the birthplace of Richard Wright. I assumed there would be some little plaque somewhere commemorating the birthplace of the greatest black American writer. There wasn't. But I did go through many of the beautiful antebellum mansions. They are magnificent homes, and you know that this extraordinary craftsmanship was the work of slaves. Then you go around to the back and see where the slaves lived, and it tears at you.

"So I wrote a letter to a friend of mine in L.A., telling him about Natchez, but also telling him about life on the set, and about how everyone was smoking grass, doing this, doing that. I didn't smoke grass. At that point in my life I was on a health-food kick, under the influence of Cicely Tyson, drinking watermelon juice. But my friend misread between the lines of the letter and thought I was asking for grass. He took it on himself to send me some, and they caught it in the mail. I didn't know where it had come from. That's why I initially told the reporters I was being framed.

"They put me in jail for about an hour. Then they came to me and said, 'Go to this office at two o'clock Sunday afternoon.' I was supposed to meet with the man who would decide whether or not I'd be brought to trial. So I go to this shuttered, louvered office. And there's this white man in a white suit sitting across from me in this darkened room. I never knew who he was, but obviously he was some-one important. And he said, 'Well, it was very unfortunate this had to happen to you. I've been told that you are a good boy, that we should all be proud of you, that you have done great things for your people.'

"And I'm sitting there, and I hear myself grovelling, 'Yes sir,' 'Thank you, sir.' I hated that man, and I hated myself for caving in to him. Eventually I pleaded *nolo contendre*, paid an eleven-thou-sand-dollar fine, and the whole story blew over—except in the black press. They couldn't get enough of it."

Another of your post-*Sounder* jobs was to portray baseball star Roy Campanella, who was confined to a wheelchair after a paralyz-ing auto accident in 1958. What was that experience like?

"Terrifically sad. We filmed *It's Good to Be Alive* at a Veterans Administration hospital in Long Beach, where we were surrounded by all these fellows who were living in their wheelchairs. The guys were very friendly. They didn't mind me asking questions about what happens to their muscles, and how they sit, and what their sex life is *not* like but how the desire is still there. But when we left in the evening, we *left*, and I'd look back through those windows and see them still sitting there, and that really affected me.

"One of the fellows had just gotten a van rigged up so that he could drive. We returned to work one Monday morning, and he wasn't there.

"I said, 'What happened to Joe Walsh?'

" 'Well, you know, he got in that van, and he went off and blew his brains out.'

"Months after we finished the film, we did our photo shoot. I had to put the braces on again and get back in the wheelchair. I thought I had gotten over it somehow, but I started crying again. It's difficult to talk about even now, but to me it is so heroic when a man's indomitable will can find something positive from pain and suffering and deprivation. Roy Campanella was a man who knew things would never get better for him. Yet he still decided to live."

Did you meet him?

"Only once, before we began filming. I was terribly intimidated by him. But I would say that in playing his life, and by walking in his shoes—or *not* walking in his shoes—I got something even more profound than I got from walking in Dr. King's shoes for a brief time.

That film forced me to think about suicide and euthanasia, issues that I hadn't had to deal with."

You didn't have the opportunity to meet Martin Luther King. How did you prepare for that role?

"After I was cast, I asked that I be allowed some research time, which was agreed to. So I went to Atlanta. The first person I met was Daddy King, his father. We were at an airport restaurant on a Sunday, a big, popular place, just packed. Daddy King held court at a large round table. White and black people would come by to speak to him, and he'd have time for all of them and knew them by name. I was sitting next to him, and my hair was a little long, and I had a beard. Finally, near the end of dessert, the people who were accompanying me said, 'Daddy'—everybody called him Daddy—'Daddy King, this is Paul Winfield, and he's going to be playing your son in this movie that you've heard about.'

" 'Oh yes, yes.'

"We shook hands, and I said, 'Anything you want to tell me, Reverend King, I certainly would appreciate your helping me out.' He looked me up and down, looked at my long hair and looked at my beard, and then said, 'Well, there was only one Martin.' End of conversation.

"Coretta King was a lot more helpful. Later during that same trip I went to her home to have tea, just the two of us. I didn't have to be around her very long to see that she is a truly heroic woman. Since Martin's death she has lived a remarkable life, single-handedly raising four children while constantly in the national spotlight. I remember, when I left the house that afternoon, she checked out the street before she would allow me to leave. I said, 'Why are you doing that?'

"She said, 'You know, our phone is still tapped.'

"But while I was there in the house with her, it was very calm and quiet. We talked about her life with Martin. Then she said, 'Come on down to the rec room.' She said, 'You know, I haven't looked at this since they brought it back. It's his overnight bag from Memphis. Would you like to see what's in it?' "

Wait a minute. Let me get this straight. Your meeting with Coretta Scott King took place nine years after her husband's assassination. And in all that time, she had not opened his valise?

"Had not opened it. So she went back behind some shelves in a storage room and brought it out, and together we opened it up. Inside there were maybe three white shirts, one pair of dress pants, some underwear, some handkerchiefs, and parts of speeches he'd been working on. Very basic, very Spartan.

"As we sat there in silence, looking at the contents of this suitcase, I noticed a fireplace. On the mantlepiece was a bouquet of plastic flowers that were themselves wrapped in plastic. Coretta saw me looking at the bouquet, and she said, 'I keep it there because that's the last thing Martin sent me.' She went on to say, 'I collect-called him in Memphis that last night, and he said, "Did you get the flowers?" I said, "Yes, Martin, I did, but you've never sent me *plastic* flowers before. What in the world were you thinking of?" And he said, "I just wanted to give you something that would last.'"

So you think Dr. King knew that death was near?

"Very likely. That notion was confirmed for me when I met with Andrew Young. Andy believed that Dr. King had intimations of his own death, as reflected by the prescience of his speech the night before he died, when he said, 'I may not get there with you.' Dr. King was not scheduled to speak that night. They had to go get him out of bed. He'd already gone to bed, but people wouldn't leave the church. Finally he got there at eleven o'clock at night during a big storm. Andy said the storm would blow those church shutters shut, and every time they slammed, Martin would duck, as if it was a gunshot.

"I asked Andy, 'How did you feel when he was murdered?'

"He said, 'You know, Paul, I felt strangely relieved that all the pressure was off him.' Andy believed that Dr. King was headed for some kind of a breakdown, that the pressure on him was getting to be too much. He had fallen out with President Johnson over the Vietnam War. He was being shunned by other black leaders, who thought he was out of step. Andy didn't know if he'd have the wherewithal to continue."

Once you began filming, didn't you feel a lot of pressure yourself?

"Let's put it this way. It was not an experience I would care to relive. *King* was the first picture Abby Mann ever directed. He did not trust actors, or allow them to bring anything to the piece. Actors would fly into Macon, Georgia, for their three days on the film. We would adjourn to my trailer to have a readthrough of the scene. Everyone's nervous, having just arrived. And Abby would say, 'OK, Joe, you read Tom's part.' He'd start recasting in front of them, which got the actors even more uptight: 'What did I do wrong?' He even rattled Roscoe Lee Browne, the most sanguine actor I know, who never loses his cool.

215

"Even worse was when we'd be ready to shoot. The assistant director would say 'Roll it,' and the sound guy would say 'Speed,' and everybody'd be waiting for Abby Mann to say 'Action.' Instead he'd go up to the actors on the set and say, 'Now remember, in this scene Dr. King is having the most important meeting of the entire movie, and you have to persuade these people to do this, and you over here, you have to convince them to do that, and this is what's gonna happen, and that's what's gonna happen. Now, *Action!*' And the actors would freeze. The entire experience was a nightmare! Several years after *King* aired, I was approached about another Abby Mann project. I said, 'I would have to be dead in the gutter before I'd work with that man again.'"

If there were so many problems, then why is the film so good?

"For one thing, there was a lot of talent involved. Look at the cast: Cicely Tyson, Roscoe Lee Browne, Ossie Davis, Al Freeman, Jr., Steven Hill, Ken McMillan, Howard Rollins. Also, Abby printed *everything* he shot, which is unheard of. Then these teams of editors pulled the thing together. It actually looked so good that, while we were in Georgia filming, NBC said they'd give us two more hours if we could find something more to say, which of course we did."

So Abby Mann was not only directing but also writing a new script?

"Yes. But Abby had been working on that script for something like thirteen years. This was a project in which he was deeply enmeshed, which was the only reason I could find to continue working with him. It got to the point where we'd say 'Good morning' and 'Good evening.' But we could not talk about the scenes.

"The other reason to stay was because we were telling an important story. So many people cared so deeply. The production company would get entire congregations to donate their time and appear in the church scenes. It would be stiflingly hot, no air. And because of the way Abby filmed, it would take hours longer than necessary. But those people would sit there all day, quietly, patiently, totally cooperative. Even now I get chills thinking about them. Between takes, I'd say, 'I get to go out to my trailer and cool off, but you folks are stuck in here. Isn't it a drag?' And they'd say, 'Well, we just wanted to give something back to him.'"

What did that performance do for your career?

"It should have done a lot more. But it doesn't matter. What mattered was that we got it in the can somehow, and somehow, miraculously, thank God, it turned out pretty good. What mattered was that we did justice to the man and also vindicated all the backstabbing that we received from other so-called black leaders, who objected to all sorts of picayune things in the film.

"The Reverend Ralph Abernathy, for instance, called to complain about the scene depicting the first time Martin was taken to jail. I played it the way Dr. King described it in his autobiography, which is that he was scared. Petrified. But so many people wanted me to play him like a born saint, as if he was a new Jesus who had just come down amongst our midst. To me, the greatness of Dr. King's life was that even though he was scared, he then went on to be arrested more than one hundred times. He overcame his fears and proceeded to stand up and be counted. If you're going to depict him as a perfect human being, why bother? Where's the drama in that?"

What did the King family think of the mini-series?

"There was a private screening for the family and friends. When it was over, they were all in the lobby. I was skulking around, *wanting* to be noticed but not forcing it too much, and also nervous about what they would think. The kids came up to me right away and said they thought it was great. Then Coretta came over and said, 'It was wonderful. It was everything we hoped it would be. But come see Daddy King. Daddy wants to talk to you.' I approached him with bated breath. Again, this long pause as he looked me up and down. Then he reached out and embraced me. He held me to his chest and said, 'Fine, you did fine.'"

Let me try to put the mini-series into perspective. It aired in 1978, one season after *Roots*, which had garnered enormous ratings for ABC. Surely one of the reasons NBC added two hours to *King* was in the hope that this would be their *Roots*.

"No doubt."

After *King* aired, its dismal ratings became a big news story. Even the circumspect *New York Times* ran a banner headline that described the show as "a Ratings Disaster." Then an amazing thing happened. A month later, the Nielsen rating service reported that somehow there had been a computer glitch on the three nights that *King* aired, and now they didn't know what the ratings were.

"The whole sequence of events was bizarre. According to Abby Mann, Mr. [Arthur] Nielsen was a very close friend of J. Edgar Hoover's. Hoover of course hated Dr. King, and it is now believed that Hoover initiated a conspiracy to hold down the *King* ratings. If that's true, then Hoover succeeded brilliantly, because the impact that our low ratings had on black TV programming was devastating.

Cicely Tyson was in preproduction with a six-hour mini-series about the Underground Railroad. The minute the *King* ratings came out, her show was slashed to four hours. Other black shows that were already filmed and ready to air languished on network shelves for years. A serious approach to casting black actors began to deteriorate. The next year, for instance, there was a mini-series called *Freedom Road*. The producers said that since Cicely and I hadn't brought in the viewers, they could resort to stunt casting. So the role I might have played instead went to Muhammad Ali, who may be one of the epochal athletes of our time, but that doesn't make him an actor. Ali was supposed to play a carpetbag senator. On the film set he'd say, 'I can't learn all these words, let's just cut 'em,' and the picture turned into a shambles. All these things happened as the direct result of the *King* ratings, which surely were manipulated."

As I look back over the arc of your career, the only role you've played that's larger than Martin Luther King is Othello.

"I feel as if I've spent my entire life playing Othello. I think I've finally got him out of my system."

When did you first play the Moor?

"In college, time and time again. I'd usually be one of the only blacks in the theater-arts programs. I'd play the butlers and the porters. Finally the teachers would decide I deserved a decent role, and it was always Othello, which was fine with me."

And your first professional *Othello*—?

"—was at the Alliance Theater in Atlanta, with Richard Dreyfuss as Iago. The entire run was sold out. The production was so successful that Mr. Coca-Cola himself offered to pay to move it outdoors to a city park, where we played it seven nights for free, with people sitting on the wet, damp grass. I don't want to lie about this, but after it was over they told me that something like a hundred thousand people had attended the play over the course of that week. I'll never forget it, because one of those added performances was on my fortieth birthday. I remember looking out at this mass of humanity and thinking to myself, this really gets you over that fortieth-birthday hump."

You could control that many people with Shakespeare?

"It was amazing. You could hear a pin drop. You would think that the further the audience got from the stage, the more restless they would become. Not at all. They got completely swept up in the play. Well, it's a very powerful story. *Othello* is the most direct-lined plot of any of Shakespeare's plays. If you do it right, believe me, an audience will get caught up in it."

But the time you thought you *really* did it right was in 1984—

"—at the Old Globe Theater in San Diego, yeah. It was a beautiful production directed by Jack O'Brien, who I think is one of the most brilliant directors ever. There were no weak links in that chain. Everyone was good."

Roberta Maxwell played Desdemona in San Diego. Who was your Iago?

"Jonathan McMurtry. He's one of my actor heroes. He's the actor who does repertory day in, day out, playing maybe three different characters in a week. He's the kind of actor who doesn't get paid enough money to be able to send a kid away to college, but who loves being on the stage, has been acting for years, and is still there. I think that's what, in the perfect world, I should be very happy to be doing."

In 1993 you returned to *Othello* for the first time in nearly a decade.

"Yeah, I went out to the Guthrie Theater in Minneapolis for five months. It was a good experience. Before rehearsals began, I thought I knew everything there was to know about Othello. I figured I'd just go out there and reprise the role. But as soon as we began to rehearse, it felt like it was the first time I'd ever played him. I learned so many new things, and realized that I *have* learned so many new things in the nine years since I last played him. Mostly what I've learned comes as the result of having had so many friends and acquaintances die of AIDS. I've attended so many funerals and memorial services that death has become like an old friend. It's so much easier to cry; let's put it that way. I guess it's called getting older. Obituary columns used to be filled with people you never heard of. Now suddenly it's people you know, people you've worked with, people you've loved, people you've depended on for laughter or good times or even a shoulder to lean on, or an ear to listen to, now dead, gone."

Apply that to Othello.

"I understand Othello's despair and loss and heartache so much more than I ever did before. The depth of his despair, the depth of his feelings of loss, hatred, anger, all because he's an outsider. All the things that I felt I was myself all my life. Trying very hard to fit in, and realizing that he never will. Othello had reached the pinnacle of everything he thought he ever wanted, but he was still an outsider. That's what did him in. Anyway, it's a great part, and I'm glad I took him on again at the Guthrie."

One senses that you are more fulfilled on the stage than in front of a camera.

"I have reaped great benefits from both. Movies introduced me to the black world. Until I made *The Lost Man* in Philadelphia, I had never been to a slum. Until I made *Sounder* in Louisiana, I had never visited the South. So film acting has allowed me to expand my horizons. But there's no substitute for standing on a stage in front of a live audience, even if the work is so ephemeral that once you leave the theater it's gone, never to be reproduced again.

"Maybe this is one of the reasons why I collect all these African masks. I surround myself with objects because I can't hold on to my own work. When I was a kid in college, you couldn't get me to help build the stage flats. I was an *artiste*. Manual labor was what my father did, not me. But as I've matured, and seen a lifetime of performances vanish into air, I've begun to take great pride in those few things I've built that you can touch. In my first house I built a wall bookcase that was maybe twenty-five feet long. It took four of us to push it into place. And I would come down at night and just stare at my bookcase, and think to myself, this is going to last.

"I have a walnut table from North Africa that's over six hundred years old. How can you think, I *own* this? I'm simply a custodian. For the time being, here in this house, it's being taken care of and preserved by me until it gets passed down to someone else who will love it the same way someone loved it when it was first built. It's an incredible table, solid walnut. The top is three inches thick. But it's *there*, and it's been there for six hundred years, and it will be there for another six hundred years. No actor can say that about his craftsmanship.

"This is probably one of the reasons why Harrison Ford's head is screwed on so tight. One of the dividends that came my way after the Watts riots was that for a brief time I became a contract player at Columbia Pictures. Harrison Ford was in the class with me. He was a great guy. When we weren't working as extras in TV shows, he was a gardener over in Laurel Canyon. He worked as a contractor, putting up Sheetrock, whatever it took to survive. A quarter century passes, then we worked together again on *Presumed Innocent*. By then he was the highest-grossing box-office star in movie history, but he was still essentially Harrison Ford. I'm sure that he's as grounded as he is because he's spent a lifetime balancing the tangible and the intangible."

So if you're talking to college students, do you tell them, "Don't be afraid to pick up a hammer and build a flat"?

Paul Winfield laughed his boisterous, ego-pricking laugh, then replied, "I'm not sure how serious your question is, but I'll give you a serious answer. No, I don't. That's something you have to come to on your own. Tactile pride is one of those lessons that only life can teach you. But what I do tell kids is that if they want to become actors, they should do it because they *have* to, not because they *want* to. Acting has to be all-consuming, something that they cannot leave alone. Otherwise it will eat them up and spit them out. This business is too hard.

"That's what I tell kids. As for me, it was great to be a young actor in the '60s, as the doors were opening. But a part of me would rather be a young actor today, when the selection is so much broader, and I could be out there competing for the roles that Denzel Washington gets, the roles that have nothing to do with color."

Last question: Did you keep anything from the *King* production as a souvenir, something you could hold onto?

"Not a thing. All I have left are the memories."

SIDES:
The Mysterious *X*

---

*"Ladies and gentlemen, I would like you to meet
a fellow human being."*
—DOROTHY McGUIRE

*"For an audience to be able to watch a character
who loves himself—what a joy."*
—KEVIN KLINE

*"You can't help but say 'Yes! Yes! Yes!' in the theater, because
you know it's a very hard way to live your life in reality."*
—FRANK LANGELLA

The following exchange was overheard on a movie set in Georgia, after two women had stood all day in the summer heat watching the tedious, repetitive process of filmmaking:

EXASPERATED FAN:	Why do they have to film the same scene over and over and over?
HER SAGE FRIEND:	Are you kidding? Do you know how many movie theaters there are in this country?

Actually, as most of us know, it doesn't quite work that way. There's only one final film, the master print, from which every other copy is struck. From Maine to California, we're all seeing the same movie.

Live theater, on the other hand, has more aches and pains than a man in his mid-fifties (escalating ticket prices, dwindling audiences, demanding unions). Yet because it is *live*, it offers a dynamic for danger that a locked-in film cannot provide. Occasionally at the theater you don't even have to wait for the houselights to dim before the danger erupts.

In 1963 I witnessed a fistfight in the Imperial Theater lobby after it was announced that Zero Mostel would not be appearing that evening in *Fiddler on the Roof*. In 1977 an even more astonishing event occurred. Prior to a performance of Tennessee Williams' *The*

223

Night of the Iguana at New York's Circle in the Square (no cast substitutions here; everything was status quo), inside the theater an agitated woman suddenly began irrationally shouting that *she wanted to see Dorothy McGuire!*, who was starring as Hannah Jelkes opposite Richard Chamberlain's Reverend Shannon.

Discomfited audience members tried to ignore the addled patron, as if she were a panhandler you don't want to acknowledge. They anxiously hoped that someone would remove her before the play began. But before that could occur, **Dorothy McGuire** emerged from the wings, quieted the woman with a few private words, then addressed the audience: "Ladies and gentlemen, I would like you to meet a fellow human being."

Although no one who was there that night is likely to forget McGuire's acute sensitivity, two decades later the actress was quick to downplay her behavior. "I might not have responded in the same way had I been performing in another play," she told me. "But when you act in *The Night of the Iguana*, you come to realize that the iguana is a symbol for all the iguanas in our own lives, all those people who are so ugly that we don't want to touch them. Here was a woman crying out to be touched, and so I did. But I don't take any credit for what happened, because at the time I was under the spell of Tennessee Williams."

Although Dorothy McGuire is best remembered for her film roles in *Gentleman's Agreement*, *A Tree Grows in Brooklyn*, *Three Coins in the Fountain*, *Old Yeller* and *Friendly Persuasion*, she first came to prominence on Broadway when audiences fell in love with her in *Claudia*. In 1943 she went to Hollywood to repeat that stage success for the movies. Even before *Claudia* was released, she married photographer John Swope (who had tried his hand at acting alongside Jimmy Stewart and Henry Fonda with the famed University Players on Cape Cod). In 1947 McGuire joined forces with Gregory Peck and Mel Ferrer to cofound the La Jolla Playhouse. She was never far from the stage.

"I feel at home onstage," she said. "Don't ask me why. The mysterious *X*."

Later, as she sought to define the indefinable poise of stars like Peck, Stewart and Fonda, she again fell back on the phrase "the mysterious *X*."

What is the mysterious *X*? I asked.

"It's a term that was gifted to me by a student at my daughter's college in Sedona, Arizona. It was one of those periodic parents' events. Perhaps it was even commencement. I no longer remember. But I was there, and I attended an art exhibition. There was one sizable brown and white painting that I very much admired, so I started talking to the young artist. I said, 'Tell me about your painting.'

"He said, 'We were down at the lake one day, and everybody was doing watercolors.' He evidently got bored doing watercolors. So he took his canvas, submerged it into the lake, and up came mud on the canvas. He left a lot of the mud just as it was. It looked like the moon with a nimbus. I was intrigued by his experiment, and it elicited many questions.

"I said, 'Is the painting an explosion of earth coming from the universe?'

" 'Yes, Mrs. Swope.'

"I said, 'Is that—?'

" 'Yes, Mrs. Swope.'

"I sensed that the artist in him was getting bored with my questions, but I pressed on. I asked, 'What is this element over here?'

"And he said, 'That, Mrs. Swope, is the mysterious *X*.'

"That idea was hung into my psyche forever. The mysterious *X* is that creative quality that should not be indexed. It is simply there, and it puts its arms around you."

Perhaps the mysterious *X* also enters into the understanding that every actor must reach about this mystifying vocation that he cannot *not* pursue. Like so many actors, it took **Kevin Kline** years to come to some kind of accord with what he does . . . and why he does it.

The turning point in Kline's career occurred in 1978, when his vibrant performance as vain film star Bruce Granit in the Hal Prince-directed musical *On the Twentieth Century* transformed this hitherto unknown actor into a Broadway presence.

"Bruce Granit was a 1930s movie star who takes ego to a ridiculous extreme," Kline recalled, "so I went to the audition with my hair slicked back and wearing a double-breasted jacket, baggy pants, an ascot and white shoes. I had never dressed for an audition before, but actors should do that. Casting directors don't know your work, so you have to show them. It also made sense because with this character you had to work from the outside in, because on the inside Bruce was nothing.

"I got the role, but my nervousness over the audition was a breeze compared to the traumas of the first rehearsal. I was so scared, I couldn't sleep the night before. That morning when I walked into the rehearsal hall, I had my name on a chair next to Madeline Kahn. It was like: Hey! I'm sitting up here with the stars. Six photographers were monitoring our every move, which made me feel very conspicuous. I'd seen photos of Hal Prince talking to the casts of his earlier shows, and I suddenly felt, I've been here before. It was scary.

"Then Hal began to speak, and his opening remark was, 'Before we read through, I have a couple of cuts. They affect Bruce and Lily.' The first line he cut had been my biggest laugh at the audition.

"I said to Madeline, 'Great, he's cutting my part.'

"She says, 'Don't worry about it. It's just a castration complex you have. All men have it. You'll get over it.'

"I thought to myself, this is one weird broad. But she was very funny, and her comments helped me that morning.

"After that first reading, I didn't work for a week. But even though the stage manager told me rehearsals were closed, I went anyway. I thought to myself, I'm in this production; I want to see what's going on. You should always know how you fit into the whole. The night before I finally began to work was more nerve-wracking than ever. But that next morning I put on my same double-breasted jacket and the same art deco tie, and I filled my pocket with confetti. When it was time to make my entrance, I walked onstage and threw a handful of confetti in the air.

"Doing all those crazy things taught me a valuable lesson, which was so important two years later when I came to do the Pirate King in *The Pirates of Penzance*. The lesson is this: The more an actor owns his part, the more satisfied he'll be. When I was a young kid touring with the Acting Company in Shakespeare and Gorky and Chekhov, I thought that actors couldn't be creative, that we simply interpreted the writer's words. But roles like Bruce Granit and the Pirate King helped me to understand that I am a creative artist, and that through my work I can make a statement about how I feel about life.

"Throughout the run of *Pirates* I used to find myself apologizing for the show. I'd say, 'It's silly and mindless and just entertainment.' But the truth was that during those two runs I came to realize the importance of sheer entertainment. Bruce Granit was a narcissistic jerk, and the Pirate King was a hapless, misguided pirate. But they both lived life fully, and they both liked themselves, and that's why audiences liked them. For an audience to be able to watch a character who loves himself—what a joy. Because most of us spend our lives hating ourselves."

Theater as therapy? That too is part of the mysterious *X*. **Frank Langella** had his own thoughts about the need for live theater when, in 1978, we spoke after a Saturday matinee of *Dracula* at the Martin Beck Theater. Langella, who was enjoying a personal triumph in the title role, already had given scores of interviews. Now as he spoke, it was clear that he was reciting his preprogrammed line of chatter. And why not? He was tired; he still had a second show ahead of him that evening. But in an attempt to shift him off automatic pilot, I asked about his performance as Cyrano de Bergerac, which he had played in Williamstown, Massachusetts.

Langella's eyes blanked. "Oh God," he finally replied, "I don't know what to tell you."

Wasn't it one of your most successful roles? I prodded, already knowing the answer.

"Yes, it was," he confirmed as he stirred to life. "I think successful for the same reason that this play is successful, which doesn't necessarily have to do with me. It has to do with my belief about audiences and what they need.

"I think that, for the last ten or fifteen years, we have been living in an era of such mechanization, such nonhuman contact, and such a flattening and leveling out of the human spirit that, if an audience gets a chance to be in the same room with a man of heroic dimension like Cyrano or Dracula, and if they get to see him played at a heroic level, it unleashes in them all the passion and desire and want and excitement that they had in youth.

"When we're young, we all dream of being the best baseball player or ballerina or doctor that could ever be. But as we get out into life we start getting pummeled, and more and more of our dream goes away. Then we look up one day and realize we've lost that heroic thing we set out to do. We find ourselves in a commonplace life. Then we turn on the television set and see commercials telling us over and over again that we should be like everybody else and have two cars and use the same shampoo and the same deodorant, and our lives get rolling-pinned out.

"So imagine the impact of going to the theater and hearing Dracula say, 'I am the king of my kind, and no one will stop me from being that!' Or you hear Yul Brynner say, 'I am the King of Siam!' Or you hear Cyrano say, 'I will fight against injustice and prejudice and the impurity of life!'

227

"When that happens, you can't help but be overwhelmed by it, and you can't help but say 'Yes! Yes! Yes!' in the theater, because you know it's a very hard way to live your life in reality. So when our *Dracula* audiences leap to their feet and scream and yell, they're not clapping just because they enjoyed our performance. They are clapping because some spirit in them has been unlocked and unleashed.

"That's why I think Cyrano was such a colossal success for me. Maybe there's something in me that understands that as an artist. I'm not even talking about talent or ability now. I'm talking about maybe a quality in me that loves that spirit in all of us so much, and somehow it communicates itself to an audience."

Yes, it's more than danger that draws us to the theater. The dynamic also includes the reaffirming embrace of the mysterious *X*.

CHAPTER EIGHT

CYRANO

---

*"The simplicity—achieving more with much, much
less—that's the nightmare."*
—JOSÉ FERRER

I was tempted to title this chapter, "Actor's Actor." Not because
José Ferrer was a better actor than the other contributors to this
book; he'd be the first to concede he was not. But through the sheer
reach of his career, he is the locus who connects nearly everyone
here represented.

• In the 1930s the unknown young actor was busy accruing credits in such short-lived Broadway dramas as *Missouri Legend*, which
starred Lillian Gish's sister, Dorothy, and in long-run comedies like
Brother Rat. That's what he was appearing in when Henry Fonda
brought fellow Nebraskan Dorothy McGuire backstage. "She was the
prettiest little girl you could ever want to see," Ferrer once recalled,
"the kind of girl we all wanted to fall in love with."

• In the early 1940s Ferrer replaced Danny Kaye on Broadway in
a Cole Porter musical . . . In the mid-'40s, when fellow outsider Paul
Winfield was only three years old, Ferrer was making Broadway history as Iago in *Othello* . . . In the late '40s Ferrer directed Gregory
Peck in a production of *Angel Street*. "We had done it at the La Jolla
Playhouse in a production staged by the original Broadway director," Peck said. "But when we decided to take it on the road for ten

---

229

weeks, we wanted to give the production more vigor, so we got Joe Ferrer."

• In the 1950s he directed Jessica Tandy in the trend-setting two-character Broadway comedy *The Fourposter* . . . Though he never worked with Sterling Hayden, in 1951 they both testified in the same hearing room before the House Committee on Un-American Activities.

• In the 1960s Ferrer's first original Broadway musical, *The Girl Who Came to Supper*, had to be rewritten on the road because of John Kennedy's assassination.

The associations are there, lots of them. But I didn't title this chapter "Actor's Actor" because the most enduring connective, the one that links Ferrer to Stacy Keach and Richard Chamberlain and Frank Langella, overrides all the others. It is not merely the act of having played Cyrano de Bergerac that unites these actors. More important, it is the fire in the belly that bonds them together. Why does an actor reach for Cyrano? Because he knows that the tale of the sensitive Frenchman with the garish proboscis is pure theater. During those few hours that Cyrano struts and strides and loves and yearns, auditoriums once again become temples.

For my generation—on stage, film, television and even long-playing records—José Ferrer was the mellifluous standard against which those other worthy actors were measured. After years of having admired Ferrer's Cyrano, when I met him in 1972 I was taken aback to discover that Joe (and he was always *Joe* to anyone who worked with him—not Mr. Ferrer, not José, just plain Joe) pretty much dismissed his most famous and influential role.

Which of your stage performances are you proudest of? I asked.

"Iago," he replied without hesitation, "because the words were so great, and Jim Downs in *The Shrike*, because my own emotion was so intense."

Not Cyrano?

"I discount Cyrano, because *Cyrano* has been a star maker in every country in the world. If you have any talent at all, you always come out of it very, very famous."

Yet the longer I knew him, and the more I observed him, the more evident it became that Joe's own persona was fraught with parallels to the swaggering swordsman. Both were iconoclasts who drew sustenance from their individualism, intellectuals who tended to distrust their admirers. If Cyrano relished a confrontation with falsehood, prejudice, compromise, Joe confronted them too. If

JOSÉ FERRER

Cyrano's final enemy was vanity . . . well, Joe was the first to acknowledge that he was not falsely modest. Exaggeration personified, he was the blazing sun and the dark side of the moon; he was humility and arrogance, pilgrim and sinner. Like Cyrano, he wore the masks of tragedy and comedy with equal understanding and panache.

The canvas of José Ferrer's life was painted with bold, primary colors. (And by the way, his still-mangled last name is correctly pronounced *FerRER*, as in RARE, not "Ferrar," as in car.) Born to wealth in Puerto Rico in 1912, by age six Joe was a child prodigy, an accomplished classical pianist who performed Mozart and Bach. He was also six when his family moved to Manhattan. Until he was twelve, Joe was shuttled between the two disparate islands, the two contrasting cultures. He took up fencing—an avocation that would serve him well in later years—at age ten. Although he was graduated from high school and passed the entrance exam to Princeton at fourteen, wiser heads at the university refused to allow the brilliant, precocious student on campus until he was sixteen. He spent much of those next two years at a private boarding school in Switzerland, polishing his foreign-language skills (he spoke six), excelling as a sculler. He was into anything and everything—except theater. As he would later write, "I'm one of those people whose family had absolutely no theatrical background."

At Princeton Joe and classmate Jimmy Stewart both were enrolled to study architecture. "Jim's thesis was the design for a small-town airport," Joe recalled. "There weren't any rural airports in the 1920s. Had he stayed with it, Jim might have made an important contribution to the evolution of aviation in America. He was a very, very gifted architect. I was very *ungifted*."

Ungifted, perhaps, but rarely bored. He formed a popular six-piece jazz band, José Ferrer and his Pied Pipers, which eventually grew to fourteen instruments. Joe played piano and saxophone, could fill in on the clarinet in a pinch, and sang. He was so preoccupied with extracurricular activities that (to his father's chagrin) it took Joe five years to graduate. During that fifth year he was persuaded to audition for the annual Triangle Club musical. Cast in the leading role, Joe instantly fell in love with theater. Now he knew what his career would be.

CYRANO: *I have been wandering—*
Wasting my force upon too many plans.
Now I have chosen one.

231

LE BRET: *What one?*
CYRANO: *The simplest—*
             To make myself in all things admirable!

Out of a sense of obligation to his father, Joe began his graduate study in romance languages at Columbia University. But it was
difficult to focus on his thesis, "The Role of the Peasant in Belgian
Literature," while roommates Jimmy Stewart and Myron McCormick
were auditioning for Broadway plays. In the summer of 1935 Joe
put the Belgian peasants behind him forever and made his way to
Suffern, New York, west of Nyack, where fellow Princetonian Joshua
Logan was running a summer theater. Joe talked his way into an
all-purpose job as assistant stage manager, poster delivery boy and
occasional walk-on in such plays as *Caesar and Cleopatra* starring
Helen Hayes. Forty years later he would remember Suffern as "the
happiest summer of my life."

Forty-one years later, in her memoir *My Side*, Ruth Gordon also
recalled Suffern. After starring in a play there, she told her lover,
producer Jed Harris, that her driver, a young kid named Joe Ferrer,
was destined for success.

"What do you base it on?" the ever-skeptical Harris asked.

"He drove me so nicely."

"What's that got to do with anything?"

"How you *do* things is what counts and all he's asked to do is
drive me and he does it great."

Joe must have done something right, because Suffern led to his
first Broadway job: third assistant stage manager, plus a two-line
role as the Second Policeman, in *A Slight Case of Murder*, a new comedy by Howard Lindsay and Damon Runyon. Although in the mid-
1930s the Depression still held a stranglehold on America, Broadway was thriving. Scores of plays were produced every season, and
most had scores of roles. *A Slight Case of Murder* had a cast of forty-
eight. No matter that it closed after sixty-nine performances; José
Ferrer was now a professional, cocky with inflated confidence.

THE MEDDLER: *But do you dream of daring—?*
CYRANO: *I do dream*
                Of daring . . .

Between 1935 and 1940 he appeared in nine Broadway plays.
Among the highlights: a small, splashy role in Maxwell Anderson's
Key Largo, starring Paul Muni . . . Guthrie McClintic's production

of *Missouri Legend*, which, despite its short run, featured a remarkable ensemble, including Dorothy Gish, Russell Collins, Dan Duryea, Dean Jagger, Karl Malden, Mildred Natwick and Joseph Sweeney . . . *Brother Rat*, the hit farce set at the Virginia Military Institute. When Joe auditioned, he promptly recognized a kindred spirit in the play's young casting agent, Garson Kanin, who shared Joe's energy and ambition. Kanin would remain one of Joe's dearest friends for the rest of his life.

In 1938, during summer stock in Connecticut, Joe fell wildly in love with nineteen-year-old Uta Hagen, a gifted actress who had scored a success as Nina with Alfred Lunt and Lynn Fontanne in *The Seagull*. He wooed her with a determination that was not to be denied; they were married that December and had a daughter.

Two summers later, in 1940, Joe was back in stock, this time as the director of the Westchester Playhouse in Mt. Kisco, New York. The opening entry, Marcel Pagnol's satire *Topaze*, starred Walter Slezak in the title role. Ten days before the opening, Slezak, already bored with the play, asked if they couldn't stage *Charley's Aunt* instead. The young director diplomatically explained "that Brandon Thomas hadn't really conceived the role of Lord Fancourt Babberley for a fat, middle-aged Austrian," so they stayed with *Topaze*. But Slezak's suggestion planted a seed in Ferrer's fertile mind—with this difference: Joe envisioned a *Charley's Aunt* that would showcase, not a middle-aged Austrian, but rather an ambitious Puerto Rican.

He wasted no time in persuading Josh Logan to direct him in a Broadway revival that exuded the high spirits of a Triangle Club show. "On opening night," Joe later recalled, "I went onstage, and the first person I saw was Walter Slezak, sitting in the front row. I kept one eye on him all night long. He knew I was watching him, because he was alternately clapping and then shaking his fist at me." Thirteen years later, Joe would repay Slezak by starring him in the hit Broadway comedy *My Three Angels*.

Charley's Aunt opened on October 17, 1940. The next morning twenty-eight-year-old Jose Ferrer awoke to discover he was a star. That's how quickly it can happen. For the next nine months he clowned his way through a tour de force so physically rigorous that he shed five pounds at every performance. Joe gloried in his newfound celebrity, yet he also knew that fame ensured an actor nothing. When *Charley's Aunt* closed the following summer, he made a bold decision. He rejected the coveted starring roles that finally were coming his way (comedies and farces, mostly, which called on him to repeat his performance) and instead set out to become an actor-manager, developing and producing his own projects.

With his very first venture, Joe learned how much of producing is out of the producer's control. *The Admiral Had a Wife* was a frothy comedy about naval officers stationed at Pearl Harbor, Hawaii. Starring Uta Hagen, and with a cast that featured Alfred Drake and Mildred Dunnock, its Broadway opening was set for December 10, 1941. On December 7, the Japanese attacked Pearl Harbor, triggering America's entrance into World War II. That same day, Joe shelved the show.

Once again José Ferrer was another out-of-work actor looking for a job. He found one that spring when he and Uta were cast as Iago and Desdemona in Margaret Webster's daring new *Othello*, to star the charismatic baritone Paul Robeson. Never before had a black actor played the Moor in the United States—which is to say that never before had a black man kissed a white woman on an American stage. The controversial production was able to muster only two bookings. But its debut at the Brattle Theater in Cambridge, Massachusetts, proved a sensation. At the curtain call, the cheering, stomping, opening-night audience, liberally peppered with Harvard students, compelled the entire cast to return to the stage for a spontaneous singing of "The Star-Spangled Banner"! A bidding war ensued among producers who wanted to move *Othello* to Broadway, with the Theatre Guild claiming the prize.

Due to Robeson's concert commitments, the New York opening was delayed for fourteen months. Joe filled the time by codirecting and -starring with Uta in *Vickie*, a slight farce about women pressed into war jobs. *Vickie* eked out a six-week run. Then in January 1943 he replaced Danny Kaye in Cole Porter's *Let's Face It*. Already on its last legs, the musical closed three weeks later, but it gave Joe what he most sought—the opportunity to sing in a Broadway musical. (In an ideal world, he would have been born with the voice of Ezio Pinza. To my knowledge, Joe never took an acting class in his life, but the money he doled out for singing lessons could have supported a small principality. He never did sing like Pinza. But those singing lessons helped his speaking voice to evolve into an instrument of precision, range and beauty.)

Othello rehearsals resumed in August 1943. After one day, the Theatre Guild fired both Ferrers, who had requested modest salary increases. They were replaced by Stefan Schnabel and Virginia Gilmore, who also lasted only one day—at which point Robeson refused to continue unless the Ferrers were rehired. (Two years before Joe's death, he remarked one evening at dinner, "I'm often asked to speak to acting students, and this is what I tell them. I say, 'You're going to get fired. Everyone gets fired. Olivier got fired, Gielgud got fired, I got fired and you will too.' Know at the outset of your career that it's going to happen, and it needn't deter you.' ")

Rehearsals resumed, and then *Othello* went out of town. "One of my most vivid memories of the pre-Broadway tryout," Joe recalled, "was a letter I received from the celebrated Robert Edmond Jones, who may have been a revolutionary scenic designer back in 1915, but who designed a rotten set and rotten costumes for this production. He wrote me a letter—I still have it—which said, in effect, 'I know you're doing your best, but your best isn't good enough. You might consider how John Barrymore, who always wanted to play Iago, would have acted the role.' Barrymore had just died the year before.

"Jones and I were staying at the same hotel, but he mailed me this letter, didn't even stick it under my door. After I read it, I confronted him, and I said, 'You have been rough with me, so I'm going to be just as rough with you. You are living in the past. John Barrymore is dead. Now get used to that idea, because he is dead. He can no longer play Iago. If he could, I'd bow out, you would have him, and everything would be peachy-dandy. But you're stuck with Joe Ferrer. You are stuck with no longer having John Barrymore. So never mind what he would have done. I want to worry about what I can do, and I don't want to hear any more of this kind of talk ever again.' Jones and I never spoke again after that, except to nod hello."

> CYRANO: *Watching you other people making friends*
> *Everywhere—as a dog makes friends! I mark*
> *the manner of these canine courtesies*
> *And think: "My friends are of a cleaner breed;*
> *Here comes—thank God!—another enemy!"*

Joe found his own way to Iago. In his first Shakespearean role, he succeeded in making villainy accessible and immediate. As theater guru Sanford Meisner would state more than four decades later to Paul Robeson biographer Martin Bauml Duberman, "The good performance in that production was José Ferrer." Not that such praise carried much weight with the likes of Robert Edmond Jones. "Throughout my career," Joe once told me, "I was always viewed by the theater establishment with a sort of mistrust, as if I was some kind of flash in the pan. Perhaps they were right. I was never responsible for a big sellout movie or a big sellout play. Even when I had four plays running on Broadway simultaneously, I didn't feel any security. I thought they were all freaks. In the long arc of my career, the accumulative *quality* of my work has stood me in better stead than the actual *success* of it."

Our conversations about *Othello* occurred in 1972. Joe was directing the American premiere of Christopher Fry's verse drama *A Yard of Sun* at the Cleveland Play House, where I was the public relations director. At the time we both were reading Margaret Webster's *Don't Put Your Daughter on the Stage*, which included her account of *Othello*, an account that occasionally varied from Joe's recollections. For instance, in her memoir, Webster (who, in addition to directing, also played Emilia) wrote of *Othello*'s Broadway opening, "I hadn't been on the stage two minutes before I knew for certain that it was going to be all right."

"I'm glad Margaret Webster knew it was a smash after two minutes," Joe carped. "Nobody else did. We all worked our butts off till the curtain came down, hoping against hope. It was a fantastic evening. But we all stood backstage afterward and people came up and said things to us and we didn't believe them.

" 'Two minutes.' That's romanticizing. You try telling that to the Lunts and see what they say. They'll throw you out of the house. An actor is out there fighting for his life till the curtain hits the ground, and you don't know. You don't know! I know the Lunts didn't, because I've talked to them. Miss Cornell never knew. Paul Muni never knew. I sound like something out of yesterday, mentioning these names from the past, but today's actors don't have the consecutive theater careers that those stars had."

Othello (still the longest-running Shakespeare production in Broadway history) ran for 296 performances. But what about Margaret Webster's contention that, although Paul Robeson "understood Othello, he could never play him"?

"I can never be less than grateful to Margaret Webster," Joe replied. "After all, she did put that production together, and she did cast me. But she had to be terribly naive to think that he *could* play Othello. What were his acting credits? What was his apprenticeship? What was his training? Did she think of doing *Othello* because he was a great actor, or because it was an opportunistic thing of casting a famous Negro with a great voice and *some* acting talent? It was a piece of justifiable opportunism on her part.

"Why *should* Paul Robeson be a good Othello? When actors through the centuries who spent thirty and forty and fifty years learning their trade can't play Othello, when Edwin Booth couldn't master it, why should an actor who's done maybe three or four parts in his entire life—*The Emperor Jones, Show Boat* and a couple other things—why should he suddenly be able to master Othello? Of course he couldn't play Othello. *But . . .* when he *felt* like it, and when he wanted to infuse it with energy, something *magic* happened on the stage. But he didn't *want* to very often, didn't feel like it very often, because his interests were political and social. So there were a lot of performances that weren't very good, and then there were some other performances that were very good."

At the conclusion of its record-breaking Broadway run, *Othello* embarked on a coast-to-coast tour that played in forty-five cities in seventeen states and Canada. "With the exception of one or two towns," Joe said, "we sold out something fearful. Of course, we could not tour in the South, but in 1944 *all* America was segregated. The rule which Paul imposed, and which Uta and I subscribed to, was: no segregation in the house. A black could sit anywhere. Sometimes the local theater managers would say, 'We'll divide it down the middle. They'll have equal opportunity, but—' Nothing doing. There they were, whites sitting next to blacks."

How often did you find yourselves the victims of prejudice?

"There weren't any flailing fists. Mostly it was a cowardly kind of prejudice, where people would back down if you stood up to them. Or it was the anonymous prejudice that poisoned the hate mail Uta constantly received. The only place where there was a real incident was at the Claypool Hotel in Indianapolis. This was November 1944. The election between FDR and Wendell Willkie had taken place the preceding week. We arrived late at night. Uta and I were given a big suite on the seventh floor and Paul had a suite on the ground floor. No sooner did we get up there than the phone rang. It was Paul. He said, 'Come on down and look.'

"So I went down. The hotel had given him a three-or-four-room office suite which had been used as the Republican Party campaign headquarters. There were still typewriters on the desks. There was no bathroom, no closet, no bed; they'd set up a cot. So we went out and talked to the night manager, and he said, 'We're full up. That's the only thing we've got.'

"And I said, 'This isn't a prejudice thing?'

" 'Oh no!'

237

"I said, 'In other words, if you had space you'd give it to him?'

" 'Heavens, yes.'

"So I said, 'Fine. Then my wife and I will sleep down here, and Mr. Robeson can have our suite.'

"Well, the guy was white to begin with, but he became a lot whiter. There was nothing he could do. He just swallowed spit."

During the Broadway run, Joe told an interviewer that he and Uta wanted always to act together in the same shows, "so I can keep Stage-Door Johnnies away from her." But it wasn't the Stage-Door Johnnies he needed to worry about; Joe's competition was onstage. In mid-performance one night, Robeson and Hagen were standing in the wings waiting to make an entrance when he suddenly, as the actress told biographer Duberman, "took his enormous hand—costume and all—and put it between my legs. . . . [I] was being assaulted in the most phenomenal way . . . and I got unbelievably excited." So began a two-year affair that continued through the Broadway run and accelerated on the road. It also signaled the end of Joe and Uta's marriage, the end of his fantasy that José Ferrer and Uta Hagen might become Broadway's next Alfred Lunt and Lynn Fontanne.

Though his friendship with Robeson soured, the facts speak for themselves: *Othello* changed José Ferrer. Never again would he fritter his talents on a *Vickie* or an *Admiral Had a Wife*. Although he would not neglect to entertain, henceforth he would also strive to be a creative force, to use his profession to explore his conscience.

> CYRANO: *What's that you say? Hopeless? Why, very well!*
> *But a man does not fight merely to win!*
> *No—no—better to know one fights in vain!*

Joe's first post-*Othello* project was to produce and direct *Strange Fruit*, Lillian Smith's stage adaptation of her controversial, best-selling 1944 novel about a love affair in a small Georgia town between an educated black woman and a weak white man. The play closed after sixty performances.

"I made a lot of mistakes on *Strange Fruit*," Joe said, "but the big reason why it didn't work is that the audience was put on trial. *Strange Fruit* had a cast of thirty-four. The whole town was onstage. The audience got to know everyone, and they liked them. Then, when a Negro was going to be lynched, and all these good people the audience had grown to like during the last ninety minutes either approved of the lynching or simply closed their eyes and pretended the lynching didn't take place, each audience member was forced to ask himself, 'What would I do under those circumstances? How would I react?' Those are tough questions, and most audiences who pay top dollar to see a Broadway show don't want to be asked tough questions, so they stayed away in droves.

"The same thing happened fifteen years later in 1959 with *The Andersonville Trial*. It's the trial of that poor clay pigeon Henry Wirz, the commandant of the Andersonville Prison Camp in Georgia, who was the only person hanged for war crimes after the Civil War. The North had prison camps just as bad as the South. But the thinking was, if we blame these terrible camps on this poor devil Wirz, *who's a foreigner*, then we can allow ourselves off the hook. So the Union, in effect, lynched him. *The Andersonville Trial* demanded a moral position from the audience. Audiences like to watch the characters onstage squirm, but *they* don't want to squirm. And when they are asked to make a moral decision—when they themselves are put on the witness stand and asked by a play, 'Now tell yourself the truth: How do you feel?'—they hate it."

Throughout his career, Joe's relationship with audiences was ambivalent. While he'd have been thrilled by a blockbuster success, at the same time he would have been suspicious of the audiences that clamored to attend such a hit. "The people who infuriate me," he once said, "are the ones who pay big bucks to see Van Cliburn or Artur Rubinstein or Vladimir Horowitz, walk out saying 'We love good music,' and then won't donate a nickel to their local symphony orchestra. They don't love good music, or good theater or good dance. They love *names*.

"Over the course of my career, I've acted in shows that played to small audiences of five, ten, fifteen people. Actors in the cast would say, 'Why bother?'

"I said, '*Why bother?!* They came when nobody else came. We kill ourselves for them.' I've spoken to casts: 'A sold-out house means everybody said, "Oh boy, that's the hot ticket to buy." But here are some people who, when most people didn't want to come, *came*. We owe them.' "

CYRANO: *The word is sweet—*
What will the deed be?

Joe first had the notion to revive *Cyrano de Bergerac* in 1940, during the run of *Charley's Aunt*, before he had the wherewithal to make it happen. "I thought I could bring something new to *Cyrano*," he said. "Some of the actors who had succeeded in the role before I got to it had played into the lushness of the language, as if Cyrano was a traditional Parisian. But he wasn't. The real Cyrano was from Gascony, down on the border with Spain. I wanted to use my own Spanish blood to play against the obvious sentimentality that can overwhelm the play."

As soon as *Strange Fruit* opened in November 1945, he set out to mount the Edmond Rostand classic. Producer Ferrer went all out: He commissioned delightful original music by Paul Bowles; he surrounded himself with a company of thirty-five actors; visually, his *Cyrano* was spectacular . . . and all to no avail. In May 1946 Josh Logan saw the play during its pre-Broadway tryout in Boston He took Joe out to a post-performance dinner, plied him with wine and then pronounced his ominous verdict. "The problem with this production," Logan bluntly announced, "is Cyrano. There are times I can't even find you on the stage. You've been so consumed by your chores as a producer, you haven't protected yourself as an actor." Joe promptly released his director and took the helm himself. He told the cast, "From now on, I'm going to be front and center in every scene, at all times. And when I am, *nobody move.*" With the restaging now required, Joe was unable to bring the production into New York before the end of the season. He shut it down, then resumed in the fall.

Cyrano de Bergerac opened on Broadway in October 1946 to rapturous reviews.

One month later, in a trenchant summary of the season to date, Brooks Atkinson wrote in *The New York Times,* "No one can observe without a slight feeling of dismay that almost half of the new productions of the season have been revivals. . . . Perhaps we should not be astonished. All during the war [World War II] we knew that the end of hostilities would find the world exhausted, bitter, reactionary and without direction. Since wars leave the world drained of spirit, it would be unreal to expect the theatre to be rich in a vitality that is lacking in every other human activity." That said, he reaffirmed his opening-night appraisal that "No performance of this year has been so robustious as the Ferrer *Cyrano.* . . . [I]t is beautifully orchestrated in balanced rhythms, style and excitement. This is the grand manner in the romantic theatre—modernized by the keenness of Mr. Ferrer's thinking."

The world may have been exhausted, but Joe was not. Throughout the run he behaved with the tireless alacrity of the most dedicated actor-manager. He directed his company's younger actors in Maxwell Anderson's *Elizabeth the Queen* at the Equity-Library Theater. Three months into the run of *Cyrano*—for the first time in Broadway history—he imaginatively scheduled two special Thursday matinees at which the leading actors swapped roles with their understudies. Joe played a porter and a starved poet.

Cyrano de Bergerac was a hit, but not a success. It closed after 195 performances. Although Joe lost most of his investment (he had mortgaged his house to finance the play), it was money well invested, because now Hollywood took notice. His 1948 film debut, as the Dauphin to Ingrid Bergman's Joan of Arc, earned him an Academy Award nomination as Best Supporting Actor. Joe couldn't have been too disappointed about losing to Walter Huston in *The Treasure of the Sierra Madre*, because he revered Huston as "one of the greatest actors who ever lived." (Other favorites: Rex Harrison and Henry Fonda. Despite Fonda's fame, Joe deemed him "the most underrated actor in America." John Wayne, while perhaps not a favorite, also earned Joe's respect. "In the right role," he once told me, "Wayne is a giant.")

Joe approached the movies with (eager) trepidation, explaining to a columnist, "I knew I could get lost in Hollywood with this puss of mine." As an April 1951 profile in *The New York Times* described, "His hair is thinning; he has big ears, a large nose and, although he is not fat, two chins, both of which recede." To put it kindly, John Barrymore he was not. After his success in *Joan of Arc*, Joe knew that Hollywood would want to typecast him as neurotics and villains. Sure enough, in his next film, *Whirlpool* (1949), he starred as an evil hypnotist out to seduce Gene Tierney. In *Crisis* (1950), he was an ailing South American dictator (charming, but a dictator all the same) whose illness could only be treated by Cary Grant.

Then, also in 1950, he starred in the film version of *Cyrano de Bergerac*. Stanley Kramer produced his movie on the cheap, as if for no other reason than to preserve Joe's stage success. The sets look cheesy; the costumes, threadbare. The supporting players are mostly undistinguished. Yet, through all this ordinariness shines one radiant performance . . . whittled-down from its original incarnation, to be sure; but still witty, still poignant, still heroic.

Joe did not agree. "I saw a preview at the Westwood Theater," he said, after some prodding. "At the end of the preview I left the theater in tears, because I didn't like what I saw. In the decades since then, I've had occasion to see it once or twice. I sit there for fifteen minutes, writhing in agony at how inadequate I consider myself as an actor, and then I leave. Why put myself through that?

"The truth is that I had a miserable time filming *Cyrano*, but until you brought the subject up, I had completely forgotten about those unhappy experiences, because the movie has done so many good things to me and for me. Normally when people mention *Cyrano*—and they still do, all the time—my initial response is to think of the tons and tons of benefit that I've received from that film. It would never occur to me to say, 'Oh hell, that was a terrible experience.' "

As always, Joe's antidote for depression was work. In November 1950, one week after the film opened, he phoned Gloria Swanson, whom he didn't know but who at the time was basking in the current success of *Sunset Boulevard*. Right there on the telephone, he coaxed her into costarring with him in a revival of Charles MacArthur and Ben Hecht's 1932 screwball comedy, *Twentieth Century*. They wasted no time. Thirty-one days later, on December 24, the production opened a two-week run at New York's ANTA Playhouse and instantly became, in Joe's words, "the only smash hit of my career." (He was even playing the John Barrymore role!) *Twentieth Century* moved to a commercial theater, where it sold out for the next six months. When Ferrer and Swanson left the production in June, they were replaced by Robert Preston and Binnie Barnes. *Twentieth Century* closed four weeks later.

In February, with tickets to *Twentieth Century* already a scarce commodity, its two stars were both nominated for Academy Awards. (The scalpers were euphoric.) Four days before the awards ceremony, *The New York Times* described Joe as "currently the hottest property in show business." Then, one day before the ceremony, he was subpoenaed to testify before the House Un-American Activities Committee.

CYRANO: *How Fate loves a jest!*

Initially created in 1938, the HUAC did not find a purpose for its being until the onset of the Cold War in 1947. When, that same year, the committee tangled with the Hollywood Ten, Joe was acting on Broadway. That was the year he won the first Tony Award ever bestowed, for his performance in *Cyrano de Bergerac*, the year that Princeton gave him an honorary M.A. degree.

But by 1950, the Cold War was escalating out of control. On January 31, President Truman authorized development of the hydrogen bomb. Nine days later, in Wheeling, West Virginia, Sen. Joseph McCarthy (Rep.,Wis.) elevated innuendo to a fearsome new level when he proclaimed, "I have here in my hand a list" of State Department employees who were known members of the Communist Party. No one ever saw that list. No matter, because on June 25 the Korean War began.

Now, with young American soldiers dying desolate deaths in an undeclared war in faraway Korea, and with McCarthyism and Cold War rhetoric combining to paralyze the nation with dread of the unknown, the HUAC swung into action. No, they didn't pursue the names on McCarthy's list. Instead they again turned their sights on Hollywood. This time they sought to ferret out those actors who would destroy the American way of life. José Ferrer—not only "the hottest property in show business" but also a known associate of the radical Paul Robeson and a foreigner to boot (forget that Puerto Rico was a U.S. protectorate)—was an obvious target. The only flaw in the committee's perverse logic was that—unlike Sterling Hayden, who preceded him before the tribunal by six weeks—José Ferrer was not then, and never had been, a Communist.

The night after he was subpoenaed, Joe won the Academy Award as Best Actor for *Cyrano de Bergerac*. (Swanson lost to Judy Holliday in *Born Yesterday*.) He donated his Oscar to the University of Puerto Rico.

Because in those perilous times accusation was tantamount to guilt, a Damoclean sword now hung over Joe's head, threatening to destroy his career. Nevertheless he threw himself into his work. While continuing to star in *Twentieth Century*, he produced and directed *Stalag 17*, the World War II prisoner-of-war comedy-melodrama. On May 8, 1951, its triumphant "opening night" was actually a Tuesday afternoon so that Joe could attend without missing his own evening performance. *Stalag 17* became the first of his four concurrent Broadway plays during 1951 and '52.

Two weeks later, on May 22, 1951, with attorney Abe Fortas at his side (thirty years later he would portray Fortas in the television movie *Gideon's Trumpet*), and with the very future of his ascendant career at risk, Joe testified before the HUAC. For several hours he was raked over the coals about his association with fund-raising charities and benefits:

> *Mr. Tavenner* [Frank S. Tavenner, Jr., HUAC Counsel]:
> There was a committee known as the American Committee
> for Protection of Foreign Born.

The Committee possesses information indicating that your name was listed as a sponsor of a dinner given by the American Committee for Protection of Foreign Born held April 17, 1943, at the Hotel Biltmore in New York City.

Do you recall sponsoring that dinner and attending it?

Mr. Ferrer: Dorothy Thompson, William Allen White and Edward G. Robinson were among the people who spoke at that dinner. In connection with the foreign-born, Mr. Tavenner, I would say that I would probably be predisposed emotionally to help the foreign-born in any legitimate cause in this country, because of the fact that I am a Puerto Rican. . . .

Mr. Tavenner: The Committee is in possession of information indicating you were the guest of honor at a meeting sponsored by the Joint Anti-Fascist Refugee Committee in San Francisco on March 10, 1945. Do you recall that?

Mr. Ferrer: If it was the one at which Walter Huston spoke, then I do recall it, yes, sir. . . . I suspect the purpose was . . . action against Franco. We who call ourselves liberal Democrats considered Franco a dictator, a man who was against democratic processes, as Hitler had been and as Stalin is today, and any time there was an occasion to oppose him, I, for one, rather unquestioningly did so . . .

Mr. Tavenner: The Committee is in possession of information indicating that on June 22, 1944, you were introduced as a guest speaker at a Negro function. Did you take part in that meeting?

Mr. Ferrer: The chances are I did. I worked with a great number of Negro artists in the theater. I have seen them suffer injustices, and I am extremely sympathetic to their situation. . . . One of the speakers at that rally was Mayor La Guardia.

On and on the hearing droned. As the inquisition drew to a close, the committee set out to exact its pound of flesh:

Mr. Kearney [Bernard W. Kearney, Rep., NY]: Do you still believe in the abolishment of the House Un-American Activities Committee?

Mr. Ferrer: No, I do not. I do think the House Un-American Activities Committee today is not only fulfilling an extremely important function, which I know that the FBI has been doing all along, but I know they are doing it in a way which I consider much more fair, much more decent . . .

Mr. Jackson [Donald L. Jackson, Rep., Cal]: Do I understand, Mr. Ferrer, that you advocate and endorse the outlaw-
ing of the Communist Party?
Mr. Ferrer: Yes, sir, I do. Definitely. Emphatically.

Still they were not finished. Joe was recalled to appear again
the following day:

Mr. Moulder [Morgan M. Moulder, Dem., Mo): Do you care
to elaborate on   what action you could take to repudiate
your activities along that [the Communist] line?
Mr. Ferrer: At this point I have publicly repudiated any
and all Communist links and sympathies. I have never had
any, and I would like to say my statement was issued in the
spirit of a complete repudiation and to clarify all positions
along that line.

The committee members bullied, intimidated and threatened
until Joe recanted Communist leanings he never had. It was not his
finest hour.

"I've been approached several times to talk about that experience,"
he said thirty years later. "I invariably refuse to comment. Suffice to
say, it was a very personal and a very, very painful experience."

It did, however, allow him to return to work, and work he did.
With *Cyrano de Bergerac* in national release, Joe produced a long-
playing record version. "José Ferrer in highlights from the motion
picture," the dust sleeve proclaimed. In fact, those highlights were
not taken from the film track; they were newly recorded. Paul Bowles'
background music was reinstated, as were the Broadway actors. Forty-
five years later, this gorgeous LP remains one of his finest achievements.

That summer, as a favor to his friend Hume Cronyn, Joe returned
to the straw-hat circuit to take over the direction of the Broadway-
bound comedy *The Fourposter*. In its own small way, this too was an
innovative production. Two-character plays simply weren't done on
Broadway. Hume Cronyn and Jessica Tandy changed that forever. With
Stalag 17 still selling out, *The Fourposter* settled into a two-year run.

ROXANE: *Am I so far above you now?*
CYRANO: *So far—*
           If you let fall upon me one hard word,
           Out of that height—you crush me!

245

Although Joe's immense talent was a given, some people feared that his relentless production schedule could take a toll. Such non-stop activity, one observer predicted, "can lead only to the booby hatch." That was precisely where Joe's next project was headed. *The Shrike* by Joseph Kramm tells the story of Jim Downs, a decent enough man who has failed in his attempt at suicide. Now confined to a hospital mental ward, he is doomed to systematic destruction at the hands of his overdominant wife. She is The Shrike.

"I read that play a year or two before I actually produced it," Joe recalled, "and I loved it. Whenever I talked to people about it, they'd say, 'It has to do with suicide, who wants to see that?' So I put it aside and forgot about it. But in time it swung back up to my conscious level. So I called the play's agent, and she said, 'Jed Harris has it, but his option is up next week. If he doesn't renew, I won't remind him and you will get it.' (This was the same Jed Harris to whom, seventeen years earlier, the prescient Ruth Gordon had predicted Ferrer's success.)

"In the play, Jim Downs is a failed stage director. Apparently Jed's intention was to star John Garfield and have the play rewritten as a story about a blacklisted actor who attempted suicide because he couldn't get work. To my way of thinking, that would have cheapened the play into a specific of the early 1950s instead of leaving it as it is, which is a kind of universal: A man, whatever his circumstances, comes to the end of his rope and tries to end his agony. At any rate, Jed's option fell through, I grabbed the play and away we went."

Joe might have rejected the idea of linking the play to the blacklist, but his production was a clear response to his harrowing HUAC experience. As Walter Kerr defined it in the New York *Herald-Tribune*, "[*The Shrike* is] a cold and merciless examination of the processes by which an intelligent and normally sensitive human being can be utterly destroyed."

"At the outset, Joe Kramm kept insisting that his play was not autobiographical," Ferrer said. "Then eventually he admitted to me that it was. He *had* attempted suicide. In 1948 he got a lot of attention for directing a Broadway play called *Hope Is the Thing with Feathers*, but no work came of it. He was estranged from his wife, an actress named Isabel Bonner, and living with his girlfriend. Unable to make a clean break from Isabel, Joe finally reached a level of despondency where he took the same number of pills as are detailed in the play. By sheer chance, Isabel found him, and they got him to

Bellevue Hospital in time. They kept him there for a while, and then he was put into the custody of Isabel, the very same woman he was trying to leave. I always felt there was some strange deep affinity between Joe and Isabel because, even though he was back living with his girlfriend, Isabel then helped Joe to write the play. He would ask her, 'What happened here when I was unconscious? What did you do? What did they say?' And she would fill in the gaps.

"When we were casting, Joe came to me and said, 'My wife wants to play herself. Isabel wants to play the female lead opposite you.'

"I said, 'Well, she can't.'

"He said, 'Why not?'

"'Because,' said I, treading gently on vulnerable toes, 'I need some kind of a name to bolster up the marquee, because Joe Ferrer isn't going to be enough. Your wife is a wonderful, wonderful actress—' which she was not '—but I need a name.' That satisfied them. We hired Judith Evelyn, the original lady from *Angel Street*. Meanwhile, Joe wrote in a new part for a woman psychiatrist, and Isabel Bonner was cast in that role, as well as understudy for Judith.

"We went into rehearsals. The problems with the play were absolutely minimal. I had *The Shrike* on its feet in a week, at which point my general manager said to me, 'I think you ought to have a week out of town.' So we arranged to go to Philadelphia. Meanwhile Joe Kramm came to me again. This time he said, 'Joe, my girlfriend— we've got to get her into the play. She's a talented actress.'

"I said, 'How will your wife feel?'

"He said, 'No problem at all. She knows and understands.'

"So I gave this girl a bit part as a nurse, and off we went for a one-week run at the Walnut Street Theater. As soon as we arrived in Philadelphia, Joe Kramm came to me a third time, and he said, 'Joe, you've got to get rid of my girlfriend.'

"'Why?'

"'Because my wife won't act on the same stage with her.'

"I said, 'Joe, why do you put me through this? I didn't want to have your wife in the show. I *certainly* didn't want to have your girlfriend in the show. You told me they could coexist together, and now you tell me "fire the girl." What am I supposed to do?'

"He said, 'I don't know, but that's the way it is. You have to work it out.'

"I was at the time married to Phyllis Hill, a good actress. So I went to Phyllis and I said, 'Listen, I've got to fire this girl. Will you step in and play the nurse?'

"She said, 'Fine.'

"So I then went to the girl and said, 'I have to fire you, because I want my wife to have a job in this play.' I had to protect Joe, because he was still living with this woman. So she spat and screamed and told me what a terrible person I was, but I got rid of the mistress. We came back to New York and opened at the Cort Theater on January 15, 1952, on what would have been our twenty-seventh day of rehearsal. We never used up our four weeks' rehearsal time. We ran for 161 performances, and Judith Evelyn didn't miss a single one, so Isabel Bonner never got to play herself on Broadway.

"Now here's the kicker. Three years later, Joe Kramm, who wanted the play done anywhere, at any cost, by anybody, had it done in Los Angeles, with Dane Clark playing Jim Downs and with Mrs. Kramm, Isabel Bonner, finally getting to play her own part. And one night, in the last scene of the first act, she had a massive brain hemorrhage and *died onstage*. Which is a terrible story, except that at least she died in her own boots, doing what she'd always wanted to do, which was to play herself on the stage."

Although *The Shrike* received rave notices and won the Pulitzer Prize, it was never a crowd pleaser. "The play was too grim to be popular," Ferrer said. "It elicits enormous guilt on the part of the audience: men, for their weakness; women, for their predatory instincts. Women would leave the theater ill because they would subcutaneously, subliminally, sub-everything, recognize themselves and reject the image. Margaret Webster couldn't sit through it. Gloria Swanson couldn't sit through it. They both saw exactly what they were: They saw themselves as harpies. But they couldn't admit to it, so they each, independently, on different nights, walked out."

How would *The Shrike* fare if it were revived today?

"It would be as riveting as it was in 1952. But it doesn't get revived, in part because of its large cast, but primarily because it's a play about hopelessness."

As Jim Downs, Joe confronted enormous challenges. For starters, he had to persuade audiences that he was a failed stage director. (This at a time when he was the busiest director on Broadway.) Then he was required to spend most of the evening sitting immobile in a city hospital ward. There were no audience-pleasing pratfalls, as in *Charley's Aunt*; no great words, as in *Othello*; no rapier theatrics, as in *Cyrano de Bergerac*; no hammy charm, as in *Twentieth Century*. He was forced to find a new level of intensity within himself. Then he had to sustain that deeply emotional level while doing as little as possible.

"An actor can only put himself through so much before it begins to take a toll on his psyche," Joe said. "Regardless of how emotional your role's demands are, if you eviscerate yourself every time you step on the stage, that's not skill, that's insanity. A professional actor, like an athlete who runs the mile or a boxer who fights fifteen rounds, learns over a period of years how to create emotion and how to dig into his resources. Of course it's effort. But as your techniques become more available to you, the effort becomes less. I once told an interviewer that technique is the key to the door that lets you into the room of inspiration. Once you're inside that room, the effort may become less, but the moral involvement becomes higher."

How do you define the moral involvement?

"The moral involvement is not resorting to fireworks, but resorting instead to the most invisible means. The simplicity—achieving more with much, much less—that's the nightmare. A great, great pianist said to me recently, 'Artur Rubinstein not only becomes better, but he also plays with less and less effort as he grows older.' Artur Rubinstein is an artist in his eighties, and it's becoming *easier* for him to play the piano. Well, it *should* become easier. And by becoming easier, he then can demand more of himself.

"If you run the mile with difficulty, it'll take you seven or eight minutes. If you run the mile with comparative ease, it'll take you five or six minutes. But if you're able to run the mile so easily that there's nothing to it, you're under four minutes. That's when your moral demand is: When I'm exhausted, I'm at 3:57; can I do 3:56? Have I demanded of my legs what they have left in them? More important, why am I running the mile in the first place? That's the moral question. If you're running the mile simply to beat someone else, that's fine for a kid. And if you're running the mile to beat the four-minute barrier, that's OK too at a certain level. But if you're running the mile because running the mile is the greatest thing you can do, because it takes you to a new height of exhilaration, then you owe it every single goddamn fiber in your being. The moral demand is that the more easily you run the mile, the more you must give."

When did you develop your sense of morality?

"I got it from my father and from being Latin. The Spaniard is the greatest sinner and the greatest Catholic. I'm always terribly aware of the moral involvement. That doesn't mean that I live up to it, because I'm as venal as anybody else. But when I don't live up to it, I'm the first one to say it. Be clear here: I'm talking about morality as a professional, not as a person. It's too difficult to discuss human morality in this Anglo-Saxon society, which pretends to impose morality but which in fact cloaks immorality.

"To me, a Fellini film is the most moral film a man can see. What do *La Dolce Vita* and *Satyricon* say? They say, 'Commit every sin, obey every base impulse, and eventually reach purity by turning your back on those impulses. You no longer need them.' That is true morality. What people confuse for morality in this society is merely a set of imposed rules: Don't do this; don't do that. Morality is a growing process, and morality in art is the purification of oneself, where you achieve more and more while *appearing* to do less and less.

"I once saw John Gielgud do *The Winter's Tale*. My memory of John Gielgud is that he stood alone in the near center of the stage and almost never moved during the entire play. I wept. I was shattered. I came out of that theater a better human being because of the moral values that he established. Now, this is a man who is a homosexual, who's been caught with people in Underground toilets, and we know all about that. To me he is a great, great artist and a great man.

"I had bought a Toulouse-Lautrec pencil drawing for myself. I had gone to Paris and found it. And I went to John Gielgud, and I said, 'If I told you I thought you were great . . . everybody tells you that. So here's something I bought for myself that I treasure, and I'm giving it to you because I've got to find some way of telling you how much I admired you in *The Winter's Tale*.' He gave a performance that was an example of professional and artistic purity. I don't know how else to put it.

"Purity doesn't mean the absence of curlicue and elaboration. Certainly no one is more elaborate than Bach. But when I say *moral*, I mean *pure*, and I think of Louis Jouvet, who used to do nothing and burn up everybody around him. Gielgud did that to me in *Hamlet* in 1936, and then in 1952 he did it to me in *The Winter's Tale*. When he plays the parts that are right for him, he always does it. He did it in *Home*. In *Home* he towered over Ralph Richardson, for my money, and Ralph Richardson towered over the rest of the cast. They were two giants, but one giant was a little taller than the other giant. Gielgud is like a piece of radium that just stands there, and everything around it gets touched.

"Every actor has to strive to find his own moral imperative within himself. It's not something you can articulate, but it's there. I'll give you an analogy. Many years ago, just to fill some time, I spent a couple months on a gastronomic tour of Europe, traveling from great restaurant to great restaurant. After every meal I would ask the chef for the recipe to what had struck me as the high point of the repast. As you might expect, they all said, 'No, no, no, that's our house secret.' Then one day after an artful meal, I made my request to the French chef, a wizened old fellow with a sourdough face. He said to me, 'Only one recipe? I will give you all my recipes. I will tell you all the ingredients I put in a dish and how long to cook it. I will tell you all my secrets. And if you can prepare it as well as I can, then the last forty years of my life mean nothing.' "

In 1952 the New York Critics Awards for Best Producer, Best Director and Best Actor all went to José Ferrer for *The Shrike*. "That meant something to me," Joe said. "One time only, nine critics came together and unanimously selected the same person as Best Actor, Best Director, Best Producer, all for the same production. They didn't give me an award, there was no dinner, they didn't even send me a certificate in the mail. It was simply announced in *Variety*. But I'm very proud of that."

Concurrent play number four, John Hodiak and Kim Hunter in *The Chase* by promising young dramatist Horton Foote, opened three months after *The Shrike*. "*The Chase* got me started," Jason Robards recalled. In the early 1950s, Robards—like John Ericson, Murray Hamilton, Robert Lansing, Ralph Meeker, Tom Poston, Kim Stanley and Tom Tryon—was a struggling young actor whose career was aided by Ferrer. "I'd gone to the American Academy with Tom Poston, and Tom, who was a tumbler as well as an actor, had ended up in *Cyrano*. So one day Tom said, 'Go up and see Joe. He's casting *The Chase*, and you might get something.' I didn't even know if Joe would see me. He was really on top of everything, and he didn't know me. I was just another unemployed actor looking for a job. But I went up there, and he had me right into the office, and Horton was there, and Joe said, 'Let's put him on as understudy and stage manager.' So I started with Joe as second assistant stage manager and understudy to John Hodiak."

Although *The Chase* was the least successful of Joe's productions (the last to open, the first to close), nevertheless in April and May 1952 he was represented on Broadway by four plays at the same time. He directed all four, produced three and starred in one.

"Joe was the last of the actor-managers," said Robards. "The actor-manager approach to theater was already out of style when Joe came on the scene, but he brought it back into style. He was a fantastic person to be around, an acting marvel, a great director. He was hysterically funny, he loved to sing, he had great charm. Above all, he was very well educated. He was brilliant. He could talk about anything.

"When *The Chase* closed, I thought I'd be out of work again. But Joe kept me in the family. He took me over to *Stalag 17*, where I did a lot of understudying. Between Broadway and the road, I was with *Stalag 17* for almost two years. Another time I bumped into Joe, and he said, 'Listen, I'm doing a movie of *The Shrike*. You and Poston come down and walk through Forty-first Street for me.' He gave us two days' work as extras. We made thirty bucks. It's good for starving actors to get thirty bucks. Those were formative years for me. When I think back on them now, and when I recall how nearly every young actor who came to New York after World War II must have worked for Joe, and how generous he was about giving work, I still can't get over it. It's as if he'll always be my boss. Forever."

Joe truly may have believed, as he told me two decades later, that his four concurrent Broadway plays "were all freaks." And it might even be true that he "didn't feel any security." But at the time, he behaved like a man on top of the world, a dervish of limitless energy whose career might last forever.

Indeed, 1953 would prove to be another whirlwind year. In February, while directing Walter Slezak, Darren McGavin, Jerome Cowan and Henry Daniell in the hit Broadway comedy *My Three Angels*, Joe received his third Academy Award nomination, this time for his performance as Henri Toulouse-Lautrec in the John Huston film *Moulin Rouge*. Then in April he went to Hawaii to star opposite Rita Hayworth in *Miss Sadie Thompson*. (As Joe later explained to an interviewer, *Miss Sadie Thompson* was part of the lingering residue of his HUAC experience: "I had been grilled and cross-examined by Ward Bond and other Hollywood 'heroes' who decided I was all right. But Hedda Hopper, one of the great 'patriots' of her day, was still fighting a rear-guard action against me. So when my agent said, 'Rita is Columbia's hottest star and if Harry Cohn will put you into a picture with her, it would dispel any lingering hesitation anyone else might have about hiring you,' I accepted the job on that crass, opportunistic basis." Little surprise that Joe did not deliver a persuasive performance.)

Five years earlier, Joe had hoped to follow his Broadway success as Cyrano by starring in the new Cole Porter musical *Kiss Me, Kate*.

He lost that role to Alfred Drake and had to settle instead for the leading role in a slight comedy, *The Silver Whistle*, which ran for 217 performances on the strength of Joe's star turn as a lovable bum. While an actor's ego can be stroked by the knowledge that he is the sole reason for a show's success, nevertheless *The Silver Whistle* was not *Kiss Me, Kate*. So in June and July 1953 Joe starred in the Porter musical at a Dallas summer theater. While in Texas, he was divorced from actress Phyllis Hill. One week later he slipped across the state line into Oklahoma and married singing star Rosemary Clooney.

In August Joe directed Olivia de Havilland at the La Jolla Playhouse in *The Dazzling Hour*, a comedy he hoped to take into New York. (It was not to be.) Then in September he played a lead role in *The Caine Mutiny*, which would become the second-highest-grossing film of 1954. (That year's number-one box-office hit was *White Christmas*, which costarred his new bride.)

"I think I was the first actor cast in *The Caine Mutiny*," Joe said. "Originally I was approached about playing Captain Queeg. I thought I was too young for the part. So I said, 'I want to play Barney Greenwald, and I want it in my contract that Humphrey Bogart plays Queeg.' The film took three months to shoot, and I didn't work till the last two weeks. When I met Bogart, the first thing he said was, 'I understand you've been trying to take my part away from me.' His technique when he met a person was always to attack and see how they reacted. He would flush out phonies that way. I said, 'Take it away from you? You ought to get down on your knees and thank me for allowing you to play it.' He loved that."

Joe did not, however, love *The Caine Mutiny*. "In Herman Wouk's novel," he said, "Barney Greenwald is a major character. I identified with him deeply. He was a Jew who had been discriminated against throughout his naval career. So when he was asked to defend this poor kid who had mutinied against the captain of his ship, Greenwald was taking on the entire navy establishment. The novel explains all this in detail, but his motives and development were completely excised from the film. But despite all my disappointment with that script, the reason I took the role was for the final scene in the movie, where I threw the champagne into Fred MacMurray's face. That scene was about something."

(Flash forward twelve years to 1965. Nicol Williamson, England's newest angry young actor, is about to make his Broadway debut in John Osborne's *Inadmissible Evidence*. Kenneth Tynan described what happened next in his book *The Sound of Two Hands Clapping* [1976]: "When the play reached America after its London run, David Merrick wanted to fire [director Anthony] Page during the Philadelphia try-out. Nicol defended his director, and a noisy argument broke out backstage. 'As a rule [said Williamson], I detest people who get into fights. They are *thunderously* boring, and that kind of behaviour is *fantastically undesirable*. But Merrick had to be insulted, and insults must be delivered with style. I was holding a glass of Budweiser. Suddenly, I remembered how José Ferrer had thrown champagne over Fred MacMurray at the end of *The Caine Mutiny*. He didn't chuck it at him, he flicked it forward like this.' Gesture as of a man throwing a dart. 'So I said, "I won't stoop to spit in your eye," and let him have it with the beer.'" The director was not fired.)

"I would hate to explode Mr. Williamson's image of my stylish acting," Joe said, when he heard the story. "But here's what happened. Before we filmed that scene, I said to Fred, 'I want to be able to hit you on the first take. I don't want you to have to stand there and get drenched in the face ten times while I practice on you.' So I had the prop man get me a champagne glass and a pitcher of water. Then we hung up a sheet, and I took a piece of charcoal and drew the outline of a head and shoulders at Fred's height. For half an hour I practiced different ways of flicking that glass. Whatever I did that impressed Nicol Williamson was done simply because it turned out to be the most efficient way for me always to hit the target."

My Three Angels . . . *Miss Sadie Thompson* . . . *Kiss Me, Kate* . . . *The Dazzling Hour* . . . *The Caine Mutiny*. But Joe was not yet done with 1953.

> CYRANO: *I will take . . .*
> *Oh, not very much! A grape . . .*
> *One only! And a glass of water . . .*
> *Clear!*
> *And . . . half a macaroon!*

There are all kinds of gestures; like Cyrano, Joe gloried in the grand gesture. Back in May, he had encountered Jean Dalrymple, a board member for the New York City Center, on a street corner. She informed him that the financially strapped theater was involved in a two-hundred-thousand-dollar fund drive and requested a donation. "I'll give you a thousand dollars right now," Joe replied. "But if you want me to, I'll come back in the fall and put on a drama season for you." The offer was accepted. In November, with *The Caine Mutiny* behind him, Joe returned to New York to produce, direct and star in an eight-week, four-play season.

He opened with a lavish new mounting of *Cyrano de Bergerac*. Young film star Grace Kelly, fresh from Africa, where she had costarred with Clark Gable in *Mogambo*, auditioned for Roxane, but Joe instead cast Arlene Dahl. She would be the favorite of all his Roxanes.

"*Cyrano* makes the modern theatre look pallid," Brooks Atkinson wrote of Joe's revival in *The New York Times*. "Mr. Ferrer is a theatre man extraordinary, and this is his most exuberant show."

He followed *Cyrano* with the somber *The Shrike*, with most of the original cast (Judith Evelyn, Isabel Bonner, et al.) intact, then took on the Bard. No, he didn't reprise Iago (Joe didn't want this to be exclusively a "greatest hits" season), but he did hire Margaret Webster, his *Othello* director, to stage *Richard III*. In reviewing the production, Atkinson suggested that to include *Richard III* in an already-taxing season "is to defy the fates as recklessly as Richard does in the play. Not that Mr. Ferrer ever flinches from the impossible. He dotes on the impossible and usually demolishes it with honor."

Joe's final offering was a holiday gift to New York: He revived *Charley's Aunt* for Christmas and New Year's weeks. When the final curtain came down on January 3, 1954, the eight-week season had garnered a profit of nearly $90,000 . . . $91,000 after Joe returned his thousand-dollar director's salary. It was a bravura display of showmanship unequaled in Broadway annals. Such an ambitious endeavor has never been attempted again.

> CYRANO: *I could not choose my place to fall—*
> *The earth spun round so fast—*

José Ferrer was forty-one years old; half his life still lay ahead. But, unbeknownst to him, that triumphant City Center season would mark the apogee of his career. Not that he would ever retire; he would continue to act and direct for the remainder of his life. His favorite work, and some of his best work, was still to come. But only rarely would he again be the actor-manager, making things happen. All too soon he would be waiting for the phone to ring.

The downturn in Joe's fortunes was almost directly concurrent with his marriage to Rosemary Clooney. She lived in Beverly Hills; he lived in New York. So he pulled up his roots and moved to L.A. too. Was this move merely another choice in a lifetime of choices? Or was it a seduction? If the latter, Clooney was not the seducer;

glamour and riches were. As Joe once remarked to me, without complaint, "Anytime you're paid to make a movie, you're paid more than you're worth." He had worked hard; perhaps he felt he deserved some easy money.

Whatever the reasons, beginning in 1954 his priorities changed. In Los Angeles he sired five children. Between 1954 and 1957, as both director and star of five consecutive films (*The Shrike, Cockleshell Heroes, The Great Man, I Accuse!, The High Cost of Loving*), Joe learned that what passes for thoughtful entertainment in the theater is not so acceptable in the dream factory. Each film was imaginatively cast (*The High Cost of Loving* introduced Gena Rowlands; *The Great Man* gave burlesque clown Ed Wynn his first dramatic role and a new acting career), but they weren't films that 1950s audiences were eager to see. Collectively they merely succeeded in ascribing to the Academy Award-winning actor the label "box-office poison." Between 1958 and 1961, he wasn't offered a single movie role.

Meanwhile, in 1958, after a four-year absence, he returned to Broadway as both director and producer of *Oh Captain!*, a splashy new musical starring Tony Randall. *Oh Captain!* was not without merit. (Johnny Mathis got a hit song out of its ballad "All the Way.") Yet, having lost his movie audience, perhaps Joe steered the show to where he thought the audience's musical taste was—and perhaps he aimed a little low. Brooks Atkinson, the same reviewer who a decade earlier had hailed Joe as "the most able, the most stimulating and the most versatile actor of his generation in America," now complained, "Mr. Ferrer has been away from Broadway too long. New York is a big town now." The rebuke was a stinging wake-up call. During the next two seasons Joe would endure three more consecutive Broadway failures (*Edwin Booth, Juno, The Andersonville Trial*), but all three failed due to problems unresolved, not because of pandering to dubious taste.

In the early 1960s Joe's marriage to Rosemary Clooney unraveled—twice. (His fourth and final marriage, to Stella Magee, lasted for twenty years, until his death.) Then, his first original starring role in a major Broadway musical, a personal milestone he had sought throughout his career, was marred by the assassination of President Kennedy. In *The Girl Who Came to Supper* Joe starred as Grand Duke Charles, Grand Regent of Carpathia. The opulent production was enjoying a successful Philadelphia tryout when JFK was killed in Dallas. Composer-lyricist Noel Coward immediately had to excise

Joe's brightest song, a wry number about assassination titled "Long Live the King (If He Can)." Just as *Camelot* was the first Broadway musical to open after Kennedy's election, so *The Girl Who Came to Supper* was the first musical to open after his murder. With the nation still in mourning, it closed fourteen weeks later.

Ironically, an assassination story rekindled Joe's flagging film career. In the early 1960s the only features he was allowed to direct, the sequel to *Peyton Place* (1961) and the second remake of *State Fair* (1962), were pariahs no one else wanted. (After *State Fair* he would never direct another movie.) But in '62 he starred in *Nine Hours to Rama*, a drama about the assassination of Mahatma Gandhi.

"After we finished *Nine Hours to Rama*," Joe said, "I stayed on in London. One day I bumped into Sam Spiegel in Berkeley Square. Since his death, Sam has become something of a legend, and deservedly so. He was a short, gross *arriviste* who wanted to be quality, who wanted to travel first class, and who succeeded in doing so. He lived like a pasha. So I bumped into Sam, and he said, 'You're just the guy I'm looking for.' Sam was producing *Lawrence of Arabia*, and he wanted me to play a sort of degenerate Turkish bey.

"This huge script arrived, and I couldn't find my part. It turned out to be three pages and a half dozen lines. I was very hurt. I said to my agent, 'Why is Sam Spiegel trying to humiliate me? Why does he insult me?'

"But Sam was insistent. They'd been filming for nine months, so he showed me thirty minutes of footage they'd already assembled. I could see it was something quite special, but I didn't realize how special till I arrived on the set in Seville. I only filmed for three days, but working with David Lean and Peter O'Toole was almost like being part of a string trio. There wasn't much talk on the set, but we three were so in tune with each other that we didn't need to talk. I've made fifty pictures in my career. But if I had to be judged as a film actor by one performance, I would want to be judged by my five minutes in *Lawrence of Arabia*."

> DE GUICHE: *Have you read* Don Quixote?
> CYRANO: *I have—and found myself the hero.*

It wasn't long after *Lawrence* that Joe, who had spent so much of his life tilting at windmills, spent several years starring in the popular musical *Man of La Mancha*. Cervantes/Don Quixote became his favorite stage role. He played it more than eight hundred times in the late 1960s, mostly on tour but also for two months on Broadway.

Man of La Mancha was still a near, fond memory when he arrived at the Cleveland Play House in 1972. The day we met (and always thereafter) Joe carried an immense shoulder bag crammed with books. That particular day, he was reading *Of a Fire on the Moon*, Norman Mailer's meditation on man's venture into space. "Mailer has diarrhea of the pen," Joe enthused with an admiration tantamount to awe.

As I would learn, Joe respected all writers of good books, not to mention good writing about books. He once handed me a *New York Times*, folded open to one of Christopher Lehmann-Haupt's lucid reviews of an obscure tome dealing with some arcane topic. "He can review *anything*!" Joe extolled. Then, in a moan approaching despair: "How can one person know so much?!"

Knowledge accrues as the result of a lifetime of reading, I replied. Who should know that better than you?

At the time, I was a book reviewer for the *St. Louis Post-Dispatch*. Joe was so smitten by the notion of receiving free books that I arranged for him to become a reviewer too. How he delighted in this new forum wherein he could wax eloquent on a vast array of genres, from French mysteries (I think he tried to read every mystery ever written) to sports essays to travel anthologies, without drawing attention to himself. Hiding behind his Latin pseudonym, *Pertinax Surly*, Joe could even take his best friends to task without fear of censure. When Rex Harrison published his autobiography, Pertinax Surly chided, "His story comes out bland . . . It's not that one wants a scandal sheet or behind-the-scenes dirt, but somehow we are given a movie-set facade without a real house behind it."

A movie-set facade without a real house behind it. Joe might have been describing the facade of his own declining career, or that of any fading star whose celebrity is no longer sustained by a foundation of work.

In 1978 he returned to the New York stage for the first time since *Man of La Mancha* eleven years earlier, to replace Ellis Rabb in David Mamet's *A Life in the Theatre*. Joe, who had always championed young writers, welcomed the challenge of acting in the Mamet play. "I'm enjoying it more and more," he told me early in the run, "because Mamet gives the actor an invisible vessel to fill. When you first read the play, there seems to be nothing there. Once you get on the stage, the form appears. It's all the more fulfilling because nothing is spelled out in advance. The play is fraught with mystery and suggestion."

Joe signed for six months, but the Off-Broadway production closed after three. He took the closing hard, and too personally. From that point on he turned down every Broadway offer that came his way. This same actor who once had welcomed the opportunity to replace Danny Kaye in *Let's Face It*, knowing full well that the show would die soon after he took over ("I had nothing to lose, and I might have surprised a lot of people"), now rejected replacement roles in *Deathtrap* and *I'm Not Rappaport* for fear that they might shutter during his watch. He even passed on the lead in the much-anticipated Broadway premiere of the London hit *The Dresser*, complaining privately, "They're only offering it to me because I'm a failed, weary, blown-out actor like the character in the play."

Whenever such self-pitying moroseness overtook him, he would retreat to the nearest golf course (his passion). Then the mood would pass, and he would concede, "I have an insatiable hunger. I'm like the guy who keeps gorging himself. This profession is such a party, such a ball. I don't want it to end." And he'd pursue another job, often in the movies. Performances for Carl Reiner (*Enter Laughing*), Mel Brooks (*To Be or Not to Be*) and Woody Allen (*A Midsummer Night's Sex Comedy*) allowed him to return to his comedic roots.

He was also the butt of an asterisk surrounding one of the most popular movie comedies of the 1980s. One summer day in 1982 Dustin Hoffman left the *Tootsie* set in his drag makeup and costume and, with Charles Durning, attended a meeting at Woody Allen's office. "After the meeting, we're going down in the elevator," Durning recalled. "It stops at the ninth floor, and who should get on but Joe Ferrer. I knew Joe from *To Be or Not to Be*, so we started talking. But this was a golden opportunity for Dustin to test his disguise. He started fawning over Joe and finally accosted him with a proposition that I wouldn't want to see in print. Suffice to say, when Joe heard it he instinctively grabbed for his genitals, out of sheer fear and self-protection. Just then the elevator doors opened, and Dustin flitted out. Joe turned to me and said, 'That's the ugliest woman I've ever seen in my life. Who is she?' When I told him, he got so angry he chased Dustin all the way up West Fifty-seventh Street, shouting, 'You son of a bitch!'"

Charley's Aunt had met Tootsie; the torch was passed.

In 1989, after it was announced that Gérard Depardieu would star as Cyrano de Bergerac in the first movie version since Joe's forty years before, the two actors, who had never met, happened upon each other on a beach at Cannes and warmly embraced. Another torch.

I occasionally ran into Joe on film sets. In 1983 he guest starred in the CBS mini-series *George Washington*, for which I was the publicist. Between scenes at the historic Governor's Palace in Williamsburg, Virginia, Joe, dressed in his eighteenth-century costume and wig, sat at the two-hundred-year-old harpsichord and performed Bach études from memory.

That year, 1983, proved a busy one. Not only was Joe president of the Players Club in New York City, but the preceding December he had become artistic director of the ailing Coconut Grove Playhouse in Florida. In one of those grand gestures he so loved, he accepted an annual salary of one dollar. But already, despite his largesse, he was being attacked in the local press for bringing "name" actors to the theater. "I've never known why one should cast aspersions at name-actors," Joe scoffed to me. "No actor aspires to anonymity; he aspires to fame."

But Joe aspired to more than that. While mini-series and feature films paid his bills, they didn't feed his needs. Joe didn't lack for work; what he lacked was sustenance, the opportunity to purge his actor's soul. He lacked those roles that would challenge his professional and artistic purity. Although Joe believed that as an artist grows older, he should be able to demand more of himself morally, the roles he was playing in the 1970s and '80s didn't demand much of anything. So what he determined to pursue, as he had back in the late 1940s and early '50s, was the kind of play that would stretch his moral involvement to new heights.

CYRANO: *If my nature lacks the germ that grows*
Towering to heaven like the mountain pine,
Or like the oak, sheltering multitudes—
I stand, not high it may be—but alone!

The new plays to which he committed himself in his later years were experimental, obscure and always uncommercial. Joe went to Pittsburgh for Tom Thomas' three-character play *The Interview*. Off-Off-Broadway he directed *Lewlulu*, a bizarre comedy by Puerto Rican playwright Pedro Pietri. After acting in Jay Broad's two-character *White Pelicans* on Long Island, Joe was so intrigued by the script that he reopened it Off-Broadway and costarred with Morgan Freeman. Yes, it closed in two weeks, but then, Joe had never been very good at placing a price tag on morality. As he told *The New York Times*, "I walk a tightrope between what pays off in my pocket and what pays off in my gut."

JOSÉ FERRER

CYRANO: *I fight on! I fight on! I fight on!*

In 1988, at age seventy-six, he finally made his acting debut in England at the Chichester Theatre Festival in Jean Anouilh's *Ring Round the Moon*, then returned there two years later for a musical version of Eugène Ionesco's *Rhinoceros* directed by Peter Hall. In 1989 he scored a critical triumph at the Berkshire Theater Festival in Stockbridge, Massachusetts, in *Tête-à-Tête*, a two-character play about the romance between Jean-Paul Sartre and Simone de Beauvoir (Constance Cummings). In 1990, what would be his final stage role was also one of his most satisfying experiences, for he got to sing the Ezio Pinza role (!) in the musical *Fanny* at the Paper Mill Playhouse in New Jersey.

Why is music so important to you? I once asked him.

"It has afforded me unspeakable pleasure all my life," he replied. "I was taken to hear Caruso sing when I was six years old. An experience like that leaves an impression. I would have enjoyed very much a life in music. The only way to have music *and* theater is musical theater."

Soon after *Fanny* closed I was privileged to be able to offer Joe a role in *The Perfect Tribute*, a television movie I had written. Since he'd always been supportive of my work, I thought he would be eager to appear in the film. But when we tendered our offer, he brusquely asked, "Where are you shooting? I won't come to Los Angeles." ("L.A. is a terrible place," he later elaborated, "when you've been on top but aren't any longer.")

We filmed in Atlanta. Joe played Edward Everett, the famed orator who, on November 19, 1863, delivered the two-hour keynote speech prior to Abraham Lincoln's two-minute Gettysburg Address. Joe's protégé Jason Robards portrayed Lincoln. The scene in which Lincoln and Everett meet at the Gettysburg train station marked the first time Joe and Jason ever acted together. That night at dinner Joe spoke with paternal pride of Robards' performance: "Lincoln stepped off the train and gave me his attention for about five seconds. Then his mind was onto something else. I've met a few presidents in my life, and that's exactly what they do."

Clearly there was an affectionate bond between the two actors. "I become like a helpless baby when I'm around Jason," Joe said, wiping tears from his eyes after hearing Robards' hilarious account of how Fredric March forgot his lines on the opening night of *Long Day's Journey into Night*. "When I'm on my deathbed, I hope to have

Jason at my left ear and Burgess Meredith at my right. That way I know I'll die laughing."

But before he died (or, as Joe phrased it, "before my career ends"—which was essentially the same thing), he craved one more Broadway success. It seemed an impossible dream. Then, wonder of wonders, in August 1991 *The New York Times* reported that the following March, after a twenty-eight-year absence, José Ferrer would return to Broadway, not as a replacement, but as one of the stars of Herb Gardner's new play, *Conversations with My Father.* When, several months later, I learned that Joe had withdrawn "due to reasons of health," I muttered to myself, "He's not ill; he has cold feet again." But he *was* ill, and he died in Coral Gables, Florida, on January 26, 1992, two weeks after his eightieth birthday.

> CYRANO: *Perhaps*
> *A little before dark, I must go . . .*

When I heard the news that sad Sunday afternoon, I played Joe's enduring *Cyrano de Bergerac* LP again and again. As his mellifluous voice swelled through my apartment ("When I think/I tremble, and the bell swings and rings—*Roxane!*"), I closed my eyes and relived the most memorable performance I ever saw him deliver. It wasn't Cyrano; it wasn't even scripted. But it was quintessential Ferrer.

In 1987 Joe was to be honored at a luncheon sponsored by the Friends of the Theatre Collection of the Museum of the City of New York. Joe had pretty much soured on awards in his later years, and he nearly forgot to attend the lunch. He was on his way to play golf when a phone call reminded him that he was due at the Marriott Marquis Hotel at noon. Expecting to greet twenty or thirty people, Joe was jolted when he was ushered into the grand ballroom and found it overflowing with the living history of Broadway, hundreds of professionals, all there to pay tribute to José Ferrer . . . and he had prepared nothing to say.

When at last the award was bestowed, Joe stepped to the podium and, in a virtuoso display, addressed the audience for forty minutes. *Forty minutes!* Forty *improvised* minutes, during which he paid homage to every other actor in the room, one after the other. When, for instance, he spoke of Marian Seldes, Joe mused, "How can I describe this woman's grace? I can only compare her to a meal we once shared where the food was wonderful, and the Burgundy wine, exquisite. A shaft of sunlight passed through the restaurant window and landed on our table. Seeing this, the owner came to our table and, gently guiding Marian's finger, slid her glass of wine so that the sun shaft ended in the glass. The beauty of that gesture completed the grace of the experience. *That* is what Marian Seldes brings to the lives of those who know her."

As Joe so effortlessly waved a white plume of eloquence over Marian, and Helen Hayes and Lillian Gish, Hume Cronyn and Jessica Tandy, Arlene Dahl and Tony Randall (in effect, sharing his tribute with those who honored him), the audience was rapt. Even the waiters along the wall were hanging on every phrase. As I watched, and listened, I thought to myself, what an extraordinary man! Some might contend that José Ferrer had been *too* ambitious, that his hamartia was in believing he could fly too near the sun. But, my God, how he had flown!

I thought to myself, what a career! In an instant (only that, for the very concept was mind-boggling) I considered the infinite words that had come trippingly off Joe's tongue during the past fifty-two years, a lifetime of words that had accumulated and resonated in his mind, and that ultimately became the very measure of the man who now held us in thrall.

And, I thought to myself, what a profession! For a moment I even wondered if I'd made a dire mistake back in college when I'd chosen *not* to pursue acting. For who would not want to participate in the pretense? Who would not want to join this unique band of brothers?

But there was no time to dwell on that, for now Joe was speaking with unabashed love about *his* brother—his *theater*-brother—Garson Kanin, and about his *theater*-father, Joshua Logan. As José Ferrer looked out over the assemblage, his words were a benediction that embraced the extended family who sat before him, reminding us all that, beyond the families we're born into, there stirs within each of us the need to create a family of our own choosing, a creative family peopled by heroes who challenge, stimulate and provoke us, and who encourage us as we strive to reach for understandings beyond our reaching.

It isn't a true family . . . merely truer than blood.

FOR FURTHER READING

Most books either begin or conclude with acknowledgments, the author's on-the-record opportunity to thank those who have helped him in his labors. But when I set out to write my acknowledgments, I realized I was thanking the same folks I'd singled out in my earlier book, *Shoptalk*. Truth to tell, those good people know who they are, and they already know how I feel about them, so I don't deem it necessary to repeat the list.

Instead, I want to acknowledge several books about (in most instances, by) actors that have held great sway over me. If you've enjoyed *Actors Talk* and want to "read more about it," as we used to say at CBS, any of the following are well worth your time.

When I was young and still dreaming of a career as an actor, *Actors Talk about Acting* (1961), arranged and edited by Lewis Funke and John E. Booth, was the mother lode of interview books. It was in these absorbing pages that José Ferrer first came to life, and Paul Muni, and the Lunts.

When the Lunts sat for their interview, they were starring at the New York City Center in Friedrich Dürrenmatt's *The Visit*. Lynn Fontanne shares the following observation:

> I remember once somebody being given a piece of bad news. And that person was quite silent for a long time, and then he said, "I see," and no more—there was no more—and it was the most moving thing that a person could say. . . . That man saw; he literally meant what he said, "I see," and took it and didn't cry, or anything. It was perfectly awful. Alfred has to do it in this play . . . and whenever he elaborates on that—which he does sometimes when he is tired . . . and he

says, "Oh, I see," or he says, "Yes, I see,". . . if he says that, it isn't as good. If he just says, "I see," it is wonderful.

Her comment was intended as a lesson in acting economy; but in time, I came to prize it as my first lesson in playwriting. To this day, I cannot read or hear the phrase *I see* without thinking of Lynn Fontanne.

The first actor's memoir that held me rapt was *Letters from an Actor* (1967), William Redfield's behind-the-scenes account of Richard Burton's *Hamlet* in 1964. In the early '60s the scandalous love affair between Richard Burton and Elizabeth Taylor was *the galvanizing event*. When, after having starred with Taylor in *Cleopatra*, Burton chose to turn his back on "show-business whoopsie" and return to Broadway in a modern-dress (rehearsal clothes) *Hamlet* directed by John Gielgud, this was major news. To a college student far off in Bloomington, Illinois, for whom New York City might as well have been a million miles away, Redfield's witty, insightful book was the next-best thing to being there.

Here is George Rose (First Gravedigger) complaining of director Gielgud: "Once he went so far as to tell me that he didn't understand my acting at all because it was too common for him but that he would try to stop me when he thought I was *not* being amusing! When John trusts an actor, he can be horribly cruel." Here is Hume Cronyn (Polonius) analyzing the production: "What went wrong this time is that he [John Gielgud] had a notion. It's a good notion, I think, but he never matured it into a concept." And here is the ever-trenchant Redfield himself (Guildenstern), reporting on the woman in the audience who didn't know *Hamlet* quite as well as she thought she did when she whispered to her companion, "Look at *them*! That's Rosencrantz and Frankenstein!"

Charlton Heston, like William Redfield, came to book writing through letter writing. Heston's first memoir, *The Actor's Life: Journals 1956-1976* (1978) is drawn from his evocatively personal diaries. The volume's very first page offers a valuable lesson: "Early in 1956, I started keeping a work journal. . . . [T]he journals have taught me a lot . . . [T]he main thing I've learned is this: *It's not always the way you remember it was.*"

The moral? Keep a journal.

During my twenty-three years as a book reviewer for the *St. Louis*

Post-Dispatch, I think I read every actor's memoir published. More than two decades later, my straight-out favorite is Marian Seldes' *The Bright Lights: A Theatre Life* (1978), which is so full of illumination that a glow seems to emanate from its pages even before you open it. But here a contradiction: The book is timeless, as charged with savvy innocence as *Alice in Wonderland*. Yet at the same time, the one flaw in Seldes' memoir is that it was written two decades ago, back when she was still apologizing for not having evolved into her generation's Katharine Cornell. What we've since come to appreciate is that our generation didn't need another Katharine Cornell. Marian Seldes is who she is: actress, mentor, encourager. She owes us a second memoir, as gracefully written as the first.

Perhaps the most unheralded actor's memoir, and one of the sweetest, is Gabriel Byrne's *Pictures in My Head* (1994). His heartfelt account of growing up in Dublin, where part of his youth was spent pretending to be Sterling Hayden in *Terror in a Texas Town*, offers images worthy of Hayden himself. Not Hayden the actor, Hayden the author.

Elia Kazan will be best remembered as a director of stage and film. But he began his career as an actor; and, like Sterling Hayden, he wanted most to be a writer. Kazan's 1988 autobiography, *A Life*, like Hayden's *Wanderer*, is an unyielding search for the marrow of the man. Kazan's laser-beam prose brands friends and foes alike with startling candor. He remembers Harold Clurman as "the greatest critic of our theater . . . I was envious of his knowledge and his insights and loved him to his last day on earth." By contrast, Lee Strasberg "had a gift for anger and a taste for the power it brought him. . . . In order to be close to this tight knot of a man, one had to knuckle under. Others did; I did not." Then there is Marlon Brando, directed by Kazan in both *A Streetcar Named Desire* and *On the Waterfront*. "His gifts go beyond knowledge," Kazan writes. "No one altogether directs Brando; you release his instinct and give it a shove in the right direction."

For me, the single most helpful sentence in this massive volume concerns Kazan's landmark production of *A Streetcar Named Desire*: "I claim nothing exceptional for the way I put *Streetcar* on the stage except that it's not the way anyone else would have done it."

Despite the plethora of actors' memoirs, only a handful have actually attempted to describe the elusive *process* of acting, of creating a role. Two of the most successful are *Year of the King* by Antony Sher and *Double Bill* by Alec McCowen.

Year of the King (1987) is the exhilarating chronicle of Antony Sher's journey in creating a landmark Richard III at the Royal Shakespeare Company. The book is littered with refreshing insights like this one: "Back at home, a video treat—two episodes of David Attenborough's *The Living Planet*. You can find any character by watching animals."

Alec McCowen's gorgeously written *Double Bill* (1980) recalls the evolution of his successful performance in *Hadrian VII*. Prior to London's West End and Broadway, it began at the Birmingham Repertory Theatre:

> I remember vividly going up the stairs, alone, to the director's office backstage at the Birmingham Repertory Theatre, for that first reading of *Hadrian*. Steeling myself to meet new people, a new company, and feeling the dreadful uncertainty of my ability to speak a line of dialogue with any expression—or even sense. Feeling alone, ill-advised, and inadequate. Feeling my throat dry and the muscles of my face twitch as I prepared to smile and meet the company. Failing to feel the comfort of past experience, feeling exposed, afraid and, above all, stupid. Why am I daring to do this?

Why am I daring to do this?

Back in 1965, when I was a student at Illinois Wesleyan University (learning that my future did not include acting), I had a little something to do with booking speakers. After seeing Alec Guinness on Broadway in Sidney Michaels' play *Dylan*, I invited poet and Dylan Thomas biographer John Malcolm Brinnin to visit IWU. (If you want to read a searing, lyric memoir, read Brinnin's *Dylan Thomas in America* [1955].) Through a scheduling snafu, the Religion Department booked a theologian for a three-day symposium that directly conflicted with Brinnin's visit. Yet, by the end of the three days, I noticed that Dr. Stone, one of the religion professors, was attending Brinnin's lectures rather than those sponsored by his own department. After both speakers departed, I confronted Dr. Stone with my observation.

"Well," the good doctor replied, "our man had all the answers, but your man had all the questions."

As the person who asked most of the questions in *Actors Talk*, I want to acknowledge the time I was given, and the seriousness with which I was taken, by my subjects. I hope I didn't burden them with too many of those questions for which there are no answers. But I certainly enjoyed the asking.

INDEX

Abernathy, Ralph, 217
Actor's Life: Journals 1956-1976, The (Heston), 266
Actors Talk about Acting (Funke and Booth), 265
Admiral Had a Wife, The (Barrington), 234, 238
Agnes of God (Pielmeyer), 198
Aidman, Charles, 66
Albee, Edward, 32-33, 51-52
Aldredge, Tom, 19
Alford, Phillip, 97
Ali, Muhammad, 218
All About Eve (film), 91
All American (musical), 50
Allen, Woody, 48, 112, 259
All Quiet on the Western Front (TV film), 147
Alonzo, John, 210
Altman, Robert, 17, 111
American Film Institute, 95
American Musical Theater: A Chronicle (Bordman), 51
Andersonville Trial, The (Levitt), 239, 256
Angelou, Maya, 106
Angel Street (Hamilton), 229, 247
Annie Hall (film), 33, 48
Apple Cart, The (Shaw), 43
Arena Stage, 15, 17
Arkin, Alan, 13, 16
Around the World in 80 Days (musical), 39

Art (Reza), 29
Asphalt Jungle, The (film), 109-10
Astaire, Fred, 212
Atkinson, Brooks, 88, 164, 240, 255, 257
Avakian, Aram, 15

Badham, Mary, 97-98
Baranski, Christine, 19
Barnes, Clive, 20, 188
Barrymore, John, 20, 92, 235, 242
Barrymore, Lionel, 80, 150, 156, 166
Barter Theater, 87, 193-94
Bassett, Angela, 100
Beacon Hill (TV series), 43-44
Becket (Anouilh), 106
Belafonte, Harry, 205
Beloved Infidel (film), 74
Bennett, Michael, 55-56
Bertolucci, Bernardo, 111
Bickford, Charles, 75-76
Big Country, The (film), 70, 75-76
Birth of a Nation, The (film), 138-39, 144-45
Blacks, The (Genet), 106
Black Stallion, The (film), 149
Bloomgarden, Kermit, 134, 184
Blue and The Gray, The (TV film), 8-9, 22, 69-71, 85, 101, 107-08, 127
Bogart, Humphrey, 166, 253
Bolger, Ray, 51

271

Bondi, Beulah, 150-57, 164, 165
Bonis, Herb, 176-79, 189
Bonner, Isabel, 246-48, 255
Bostwick, Barry, 53-62
Bowles, Paul, 240, 245
Boys from Brazil, The (film), 72, 96
Brando, Marlon, 10, 161-62, 267
Bravados, The (film), 74
Breakfast at Tiffany's (musical),
    51-53
Breakfast of Champions (Vonnegut),
    98-99
Bridges, Harry, 114-15
Bright Lights, The (Seldes), 42, 267
Brinnin, John Malcolm, 268
Broken Blossoms (film), 138, 140,
    149
Brolin, James, 193
Brooks, Mel, 50-51, 259
Brother John (film), 209
Brown, John Mason, 88
Browne, Roscoe Lee, 106, 215-16
Brynner, Yul, 227
Burr, Robert, 12
Burrows, Abe, 51-52
Burton, Richard, 8, 12, 42, 45, 54,
    106, 266

Caine Mutiny, The (film), 253-54
Caine Mutiny Court-Martial, The
    (Wouk), 103-104
Caldwell, Zoe, 53
Calley, John, 16
Cambridge, Godfrey, 106
Camelot (musical), 38, 64-66, 106,
    257
Campanella, Roy, 213
Campbell, Douglas, 202
Canterbury Tales (musical), 42, 46
Caribe (TV series), 21
Cariou, Len, 42, 49
Carney, Art, 171, 173
Carnovsky, Morris, 113
Carroll, Madeleine, 109, 117,
    124-25
Carson, Jeannie, 64-65
Catch-22 (film), 15-16

Chamberlain, Richard, 51-53, 224,
    230
Champ, The (film), 197
Charley's Aunt (Thomas), 233, 239,
    248, 255
Chase, The (Foote), 251-52
Chesterton, G. K., 46
Chicago Tribune, 186
Chichester Theatre Festival, 261
Chorus Line, A (musical), 55-57
Churchill, Winston, 174
Cleveland Play House, 236, 258
Clift, Montgomery, 90
Clooney, Rosemary, 253, 255-56
Close Encounters of the Third Kind
    (film), 149
Clurman, Harold, 267
Cobb, Lee J., 15, 130-31
Coburn, James, 116
Coco (musical), 42, 46-47
Coconut Grove Playhouse, 260
Cohen, Alexander, 177
Colman, Ronald, 140
Comegys, Kathleen, 169
Conversations with My Father
    (Gardner), 262
Convy, Bert, 132-33
Cooper, Jackie, 165-66
Coppola, Francis Ford, 111
Cornell, Katharine, 88, 236, 267
Cowan, Warren, 180
Coward, Noel, 43, 45, 142, 256
Crane, Stephen, 119
Crist, Judith, 94
Cronyn, Hume, 157, 161, 163-64,
    245, 263, 266
Cyrano de Bergerac (Rostand), 4-5,
    21, 123, 227-28, 230, 239-42,
    248, 251, 255, 262
Cyrano de Bergerac (film), 241-43,
    245

Dahl, Arlene, 255, 263
Daily News, 89, 172
Dallas (TV series), 145-46, 149
Dalrymple, Jean, 254
Dance a Little Closer (musical), 49, 51

Danton's Death (Buechner), 13
da Silva, Howard, 12, 40-41, 113
Davis, Bette, 91, 110, 140, 150
Davis, Sammy, Jr., 205, 212
Days of Glory (film), 90,108
Dear Me (Ustinov), 7
Death of a Salesman (Miller),
    129-31, 133
Deer Hunter, The (film), 33
de Hartog, Jan, 12021, 163-64
Delicate Balance, A (Albee), 32
Denial of Death, The (Becker), 115
Dennehy, Brian, 173
Dewhurst, Colleen, 19, 198
Dexter, John, 133-35
Diary of Anne Frank, The
    (Goodrich and Hackett), 182,
    184-85
Dirty Sally (TV series), 151
Disney, Walt, 144
Doc (film), 17
Doctor's Dilemma, The (Shaw), 88
Dodsworth (Lewis), 79
*Don't Put Your Daughter on the
    Stage* (Webster), 236
Double Bill (McCowen), 268
Douglas, Kirk, 90, 131
Douglas, Melvyn, 169
Dove, The, 96
Dracula (Deane and Balderston),
    227-28
Drake, Alfred, 234, 253
Dresser, The (Harwood), 259
Driving Miss Daisy (film), 164
Drood! (musical), 49-50
Dr. Strangelove (film), 110, 115-16
Duberman, Martin Bauml, 235, 238
Duel in the Sun (film), 72, 77, 82,
    142
Duke, Patty, 168-69
Dunnock, Mildred, 130, 234
Durning, Charles, 19, 95, 259
Dutchman, The (Jones), 203-4
Dylan (Michaels), 268
Dylan, Bob, 95, 106
Dylan Thomas in America
    (Brinnin), 268

Edwards, James, 203
Enchanted April (film), 31
End of the Road (film), 14-15, 16
Equus (Shaffer), 42, 133-35
Evelyn, Judith, 247-48, 257

Fat City (film), 18-19
Faulkner, William, 110
Fellini, Federico, 250
Ferrer, Jose, 21, 38, 49, 163, 191,
    229-63, 265
Ferrer, Mel, 90, 226
Fiddler on the Roof (musical),
    132-133, 223
Finney, Albert, 8, 12
Firth, Peter, 133-34
Fitzgerald, F. Scott, 4, 74
Flanders, Ed, 173, 182
Folger Library Theater, 28
Fonda, Henry, 90, 103-4, 131, 149,
    224, 229, 241
Foote, Horton, 65, 100, 110, 251
Ford, Harrison, 220
Fortas, Abe, 243
Fourposter, The (de Hartog), 120,
    163-64, 230, 245
Frank, Otto, 182-85
Frankenheimer, John, 96, 110
Frasher, James, 138, 146-47, 149
Freeman, Al, Jr., 100, 204, 216
Freeman, Morgan, 260
Front, The (film), 112

Gable, Clark, 14, 20, 22, 23, 62,
    90, 149, 255
Gardner, Ava, 71, 87
Garfield, John, 246
Garfield, Sid, 177
Garner, James, 66, 103-4
Garnett, Tay, 80
Gentleman's Agreement (film), 73,
    90, 94, 224
George Washington (TV film), 60,
    168, 260
Gielgud, John, 8, 29, 45, 141, 158,
    160-61, 235, 250, 266
Gillette, Anita, 51

INDEX

Girl Who Came to Supper, The
  (musical), 230, 256-57
Gish, Dorothy, 138-40, 142,
  147-48, 229, 233
Gish, Lillian, 38, 137-50, 153, 161,
  164, 165, 263
Gish, Mary, 138-39, 142-43, 148
Glass Menagerie, The (Williams),
  206-08
Gleason, Jackie, 171-73
Godfather, The (film), 111
Goldwyn, Sam, 154-55, 191
Gone With the Wind (film), 77, 205
Goodrich, Frances, 184-85
Gordon, Ruth, 53, 77, 232, 246
Gossett, Louis, Jr., 106, 167, 206
Go Tell It on the Mountain (TV
  film), 201
Graham, Martha, 86-87
Grant, Cary, 76, 241
Granville-Barker, Harley, 160-61
Grapes of Wrath, The (film), 156
Grease (musical), 54-55, 57, 59, 61
Great Expectations (TV film), 29
Great Man, The (film), 256
Great White Hope, The (film), 210
Griffith, D. W., 138-40, 142-45,
  148, 149
Grimes, Tammy, 38, 42
Grizzard, George, 32-33
Grodin, Charles, 105
Gumpert, Emil, 117-118
Gunfighter, The (film), 72-73, 75,
  94, 99
Guns of Navarone, The (film), 70,
  72-73, 76, 93
Guthrie, Tyrone, 133, 202
Guys and Dolls (musical), 38

Hackett, Albert, 184-85
Hadrian VII (Luke), 268
Hagen, Uta, 33, 233-34, 237-38
Hallinan, Vincent, 114
Hamilton, Margaret, 39, 157
Hamlet (Shakespeare), 12, 19-20,
  21, 33-34, 42, 45, 141, 266
"Handsome Johnny" (Gossett), 106

Harris, Jed, 232, 246
Harris, Julie, 12
Harrison, Rex, 241, 258
Hathaway, Henry, 74
Havens, Richie, 106
Hawkins, Jack, 158, 160
Hayday, Brian, 26, 27, 29
Hayden, Andrew, 121-23
Hayden, Sterling, 107-27, 230,
  243, 267
Hayes, Helen, 149-150, 155, 232,
  263
Hayward, Leland, 86, 90
Hayworth, Rita, 252
Heckart, Eileen, 142
Hedison, David, 191, 194
Hemingway (TV film), 27
Hemingway, Ernest, 4, 72
Henry IV, Parts I and *II*
  (Shakespeare), 14
Hepburn, Audrey, 80
Hepburn, Katharine, 46-47, 77
Heston, Charlton, 81, 266
Hewes, Henry, 11
Higgins, Michael, 133
High Cost of Loving, The (film),
  256
High Noon (film), 99
Hill, Arthur, 32-33
Hill, Phylliss, 247, 253
Hill, Walter, 22
Hirschhorn, Naomi, 66
Hitchcock, Alfred, 73, 74, 78, 161
Hobson's Choice (TV film), 147
Hodiak, John, 103-4, 251
Hoffman, Dustin, 14, 18, 28, 195,
  259
Holbrook, Hal, 156
Holly Golightly (musical), see
  Breakfast at Tiffany's
Hollywood Reporter, 163
Homeier, Skip, 94
Home of the Brave (film), 201
Hooks, Kevin, 211
Hoover, J. Edgar, 112-13, 217
Hopkins, Anthony, 133
House Un-American Activities

Committee (HUAC), 40, 110, 112-14, 242-46
Howe, James Wong, 14, 212
Huckleberry Finn, 38, 212-13
Hudson, Rock, 90
Hughes, Barnard, 19
Hunt, Linda, 19
Hunter, Kim, 162, 173, 251
Huston, John, 18, 92-93, 109-10, 252
Huston, Walter, 80, 92, 130, 138, 241

Illinois Wesleyan University, 3, 268
Indians (Kopit), 15, 17
Inner City Cultural Center, 95, 206-8
Inspector Calls, An (Priestley), 29
Into the Woods (musical), 41
Ironside (TV series), 206
It's a Wonderful Life (film), 150, 156
It's Good to Be Alive (TV film), 213
I Walk the Line (film), 95, 96

Jackson, Anne, 182
Jackson, Donald, 245
Jackson, Kate, 138, 148
Jackson, Samuel L., 100
Jacobi, Lou, 184
Jaws (film), 111, 116
Jones, James Earl, 19, 20, 106
Jones, Robert Edmond, 235
Jones, Tommy Lee, 108
Journey into Light (film), 116
Julia, Raul, 19, 57

Kahn, Madeline, 226
Kanin, Garson, 77, 233, 263
Kaye, Danny, 171-82, 185-92, 229, 234, 259
Kazan, Elia, 73, 129-31, 161-62, 267
Keach, James, 9, 22
Keach, Stacy, 7-30, 37, 230
Keach, Stacy, Sr., 9, 10, 11, 14
Kearney, Bernard, 244

Kelly, Grace, 255
Kennedy, Arthur, 117, 130-31
Kennedy, John F., 63-66, 95, 230, 256-57
Kerr, Walter, 246
Keys of the Kingdom, The (film), 72, 90, 94
Killing, The (film), 110
King (TV film), 199, 215-18
King and I, The (musical), 23, 38
King, Coretta, 214-15, 217
King, Daddy, 214, 217
King, Henry, 73-74, 86, 140
King Lear (Shakespeare), 15, 23, 28, 160-61
King, Martin Luther, Jr., 82, 199, 205, 213-15
Kismet (musical), 42-43, 47-48
Kissinger, Henry, 79
Kiss Me, Kate (musical), 38, 253
Kline, Kevin, 57, 59, 225-27
Knight, Shirley, 204
Kramer, Stanley, 201, 241
Kramm, Joseph, 246-48
Kubrick, Stanley, 110, 115-16

Lady in the Dark (musical), 174
Lancaster, Burt, 90
Langella, Frank, 227-28, 230
Lansbury, Angela, 31, 53
Last Angry Man, The (film), 167
Laughton, Charles, 7, 80, 103, 145
Lawrence of Arabia (film), 257
Lean, David, 257
Lehmann-Haupt, Christopher, 258
Let's Face It (musical), 174, 234, 259
Letters from an Actor (Redfield), 266
Lewis, Emmanuelle, 100
Life, A (Kazan), 161-62, 267
Life in the Theatre, A (Mamet), 258-59
Lincoln Center, 13, 15, 33
Lindbergh, Charles, 63
Lithgow, John, 45
Logan, Joshua, 50, 232-33, 240, 263

London Academy of Music and Dramatic Arts, 12
Long Riders, The (film), 22, 26
Los Angeles Times, 180, 204
Lost Man, The (film), 208-9, 220
Lulu in Hollywood (Brooks), 141
Lunt, Alfred, and Fontanne, Lynn, 45, 88, 233, 236, 238, 265-66
Lyndeck, Edmund, 39-42, 53

MacArthur (film), 72, 78-79, 96
Macbeth (Shakespeare), 28, 33-34
MacBird! (Garson), 13-14
MacMurray, Fred, 109, 150, 253-54
Macomber Affair, The (film), 72, 91
Magee, Stella, 256
Mailer, Norman, 258
Make Way for Tomorrow (film), 155
Malden, Karl, 89, 162, 233
Man for All Seasons, A (Bolt), 42, 45, 106
Mann, Abby, 215-17
Man of La Mancha (musical), 38, 257-58
March, Fredric, 92, 130, 194, 261
Mark Taper Forum, 21
M*A*S*H (film), 17
Mason, James, 105, 146
Matthau, Walter, 105
Maxwell, Roberta, 133-35, 219
Mayer, Louis B., 149
Mazursky, Paul, 197
McCarthy, Joseph, 243
McClintic, Guthrie, 86, 88, 141, 232
McCowen, Alec, 268
McGavin, Darren, 42, 252
McGuire, William Biff, 64-66
McGuire, Dorothy, 90, 150, 224-25, 229
McMurtry, Jonathan, 219
Mencken, H. L., 145
Mengers, Sue, 20
Meisner, Sanford, 86-87, 235
Meredith, Burgess, 147, 204, 262
Merrick, David, 51-53, 254
Mickey Spillane's Mike Hammer (TV series), 9, 23-25, 27, 29
Midler, Bette, 54
Midnight Cowboy (film), 195-97
Miller, Arthur, 130, 190
Miracle Worker, The (Gibson), 168-69
Miss Sadie Thompson (film), 252
Mitchum, Robert, 76, 145, 150
Moby Dick (film), 72, 91-93
Moby Dick (TV film), 76-77, 99
Moby Dick (play), 84
Moore, Mary Tyler, 51-53
Moore, Roger, 191
Moran, D. Perry, 123-126
Morning Star, The (Williams), 88-89
Mostel, Zero, 132, 223
Moulder, Morgan, 245
Moulin Rouge (film), 252
Movie Movie (film), 59
Movies, Mr. Griffith and Me, The (Gish), 142
Mulligan, Robert, 98
Muni, Paul, 130, 142, 167, 232, 236, 265
Municipal Opera (St. Louis), 38-40, 42, 50
My Brilliant Career (film), 105
My Fat Friend (Laurence), 42, 45-46
My Side (Gordon), 232
Mystery of Edwin Drood, The, see Drood!
My Three Angels (Spewack), 233, 252

Nathan, George Jean, 141, 145
Neighborhood Playhouse, 85-87
Neill, Sam, 104-5
New Leaf, A (film), 48
New York City Center, 254-55, 265
New York Herald, 141
New York Herald-Tribune, 174, 246
New York Journal American, 89
New York Shakespeare Festival, 12, 14, 19-20
New York Sun, 89
New York Times, The, 20, 88, 138, 164, 174, 188, 217, 240-42,

255, 258, 260, 262
New York *World Journal,* 175
New York World's Fair (1939), 85
New York World-Telegram, 88, 89
Nichols, Mike, 15-16, 19
Nichols, Red, 87, 181
Nick & Nora (musical), 60-61
Night of the Hunter, The, 142, 145
Night of the Iguana, The (Williams), 224
Nine Hours to Rama (film), 257
Nixon, Richard, 40-41, 96, 111
Nolan, Lloyd, 103-4
North, Sheree, 204
Nothing in Common (film), 172
Nureyev, Rudolf, 39

O'Brien, Jack, 219
O'Connor, Carroll, 204
Oedipus Rex (film), 202
Of a Fire on the Moon (Mailer), 258
Oh Captain! (musical), 256
Old Gringo (film), 96
"Old Man" (TV drama), 110
Old Vic, The, 12, 29, 44
Olivier, Laurence, 7-8, 11-12, 19,
    23-24, 31, 38, 45, 98, 106, 235
Omen, The (film), 96
Only the Valiant (film), 74-75
On the Twentieth Century (musical), 59, 225-27
Open Book, An (Huston), 92, 110
Oregon Shakespeare Festival, 11
Osborne, John, 98, 253
Othello (Shakespeare), 218-19,
    229, 234-38, 248, 255
O'Toole, Peter, 8, 257

Pacino, Al, 18, 49
Page, Geraldine, 42, 198, 199
Pakula, Alan, 80-81
Papp, Joseph, 12, 19-20
Paradine Case, The (film), 78
Pavarotti, Luciano, 186-87
Peck, Gregory, 38, 69-101, 107-8,
    140, 142, 161, 191, 193, 207,
    211-12, 224, 229-30

Perfect Tribute, The (TV film), 71, 261
Perry Mason (TV series), 205-6
Pickford, Mary, 139, 141, 154
Pictures in My Head (Byrne), 267
Pinter, Harold, 106
Pirates of Penzance, The (operetta),
    48, 59, 226
Plowright, Joan, 31-32, 106
Plummer, Christopher, 12, 38
Poitier, Sidney, 95, 167, 205, 208-9
Pork Chop Hill (film), 72-73
Porterfield, Bob, 194
Poston, Tom, 251
Powell, William, 140
Power, Tyrone, 90
Presnell, Harve, 64
Priestley, J. B., 163
Prince, Hal, 41, 59, 225-26
Purple Plain, The (film), 91

Quinn, Anthony, 209

Raisin in the Sun, A (Hansberry),
    106, 208
Raitt, John, 4, 38
Randall, Tony, 256, 263
Rashad, Phylicia, 41, 100
Reading Prison, 9, 24-27
Reagan, Nancy, 27
Reagan, Ronald, 113, 177-78
Redfield, William, 266
Redgrave, Lynn, 45
Redgrave, Michael, 45
Reflections in a Golden Eye (film), 43
Reiner, Carl, 174, 186-89, 259
Reynolds, Debbie, 64
Richard III (film), 11, 23
Richard III (Shakespeare), 28, 49,
    255, 268
Richards, Beah, 208
Richardson, Ralph, 8, 250
Ritchard, Cyril, 39, 42, 53
Ritt, Martin, 112, 210
Robards, Jason, 251-52, 261-62
Robber Bridegroom, The (musical),
    54, 57-59, 61

INDEX

Robbins, Jerome, 132
Robeson, Paul, 234, 236-38, 243
Roman Holiday (film), 70, 75, 79, 91, 93
Romeo and Juliet (Shakespeare), 33, 35
Rooney, Mickey, 190
Roots (TV film), 71, 105, 156, 217
Rose, George, 42-50, 266
Rosenberg, Howard, 180
Ross, Duncan, 34
Rowan (Dan) and Martin (Dick), 39-40
Rowlands, Gena, 256
Royal Shakespeare Company, 12, 17, 268
Rubinstein, Ártur, 239, 249
Rubinstein, John, 174, 177
Ryan, Robert, 19-20, 132
Ryder, Alfred, 12

Sarrazin, Michael, 195
Saturday Review, 11
Scarlet Letter, The (film), 141, 148-49
Scarlet Letter, The (TV film), 148
Schlesinger, John, 195-97
Schneider, Alan, 32
Scofield, Paul, 106
Scott, Martha, 89, 150
Scully, Vin, 190
Seldes, Marian, 42, 133, 262-63, 267
Sellers, Peter, 115
Selznick, David O., 75, 77-78
1776 (musical), 40-41
Shaffer, Peter, 133, 135
Shaw, George Bernard, 174
Shaw, Robert, 111
Shenandoah (film), 99
Sher, Antony, 268
Shoot Out (film), 74-75, 95
Show Boat (musical), 38, 237
Shrike, The (Kramm), 230, 246-48, 251-52, 255
Shrike, The (film), 254, 258
Silver Whistle, The (McEnroe), 253

Simmons, Jean, 53
Simon, John, 14, 33
Sinatra, Frank, 110
Skokie (TV film), 173, 177-78, 190
Sleeping Dogs (film), 105
Slezak, Walter, 233, 252
Slight Case of Murder, A (Lindsay and Runyon), 232
Snows of Kilimanjaro, The (film), 72
Something Different (Reiner), 188-89
Sons and Soldiers (Shaw), 89
Sounder (film), 209-11, 220
Sound of Music, The (musical), 38
Sound of Two Hands Clapping, The (Tynan), 254
Spartacus (film), 7
Spellbound (film), 78, 93
Spiegel, Sam, 257
Spoon River Anthology (Masters), 66-67
Stalag 17 (Bevan and Trezinski), 243, 252
Stanislavsky, Konstantin, 87, 158
Stanton, Harry Dean, 98
Stanwyck, Barbara, 48, 53
Stark, Ray, 18
Steinbrenner, George, 93
Sternhagen, Frances, 133
Stevens, George, 155, 184-85
Stewart, Jimmy, 54, 62, 90, 150, 152, 156, 224, 231-32
Sting, The (film), 111
Stix, John, 166-67
St. Louis Post-Dispatch, 258, 266-67
Strange Fruit (Smith), 238-40
Strasberg, Lee, 177-78, 267
Stravinsky, Igor, 49
Streetcar Named Desire, A (Williams), 161-62, 267
Street Scene (Rice), 154
Street Scene (film), 154
Streisand, Barbra, 61
Sullivan, Barry, 104
Sutorius, James, 177-78
Swanson, Gloria, 242-43, 248

INDEX

Sweeney Todd (musical), 41

Tandy, Jessica, 156, 157-64, 165,
  230, 245, 263
Taste of Honey, A (Delaney), 31
Tavenner, Frank, Jr., 243-44
Taylor, Elizabeth, 12, 45, 266
Thin Ice (TV film), 138, 143, 146,
  148
Thomas, Danny, 131
Thomas, Richard, 147
Thorn Birds, The (TV film), 53
To Be or Not to Be (film), 259
*To Dance With the White Dog (TV
  film),* 157,164
Toilet, The (Jones), 204
To Kill a Mockingbird (film), 70, 72,
  80, 93-98, 99
To Kill a Mockingbird (Lee), 94-96,
  100
Topaze (Pagnol), 233
Torn, Rip, 4, 98
Track of the Cat (film), 152
Tracy, Spencer, 73, 77
Traveling Executioner, The (film),
  17-18
Trial of the Catonsville Nine, The
  (film), 96
Truman, Harry, 78-79, 113, 242
Twelve O'Clock High (film), 72-73, 90
Twentieth Century (MacArthur and
  Hecht), 242-43, 248
Tyrone Guthrie Theater, 33, 133,
  159, 219
Tyson, Cicely, 106, 212, 216-217

Un Ballo in Maschera (Verdi),
  186-87
University of California at Berkeley,
  10-11, 83-84
Unseen Enemy, An (film), 139,140
Unsinkable Molly Brown, The
  (musical), 42, 64
Unsinkable Molly Brown, The
  (film), 64

Valley of Decision, The (film), 80,
  161
Van Ark, Joan, 100
Van Patten, Joyce, 66-67
Virginia (film), 108,109
Visit, The (Durrenmatt), 265-66
Voight, Jon, 16, 38, 194-97
Voyage (Hayden), 118-119

Walken, Christopher, 33-35, 38, 199
Wallach, Eli, 174, 181-182, 184-86,
  189, 191
Wallach, Roberta, 181, 182
Waltons, The (TV series), 166
Wanderer (Hayden), 108-10, 115,
  118-119, 267
Wanderer (schooner), 110, 114,
  117, 119, 127
Warfield, William, 38
Warner, H. B., 116
Washington Post, 175
Waterston, Sam, 19
Way Down East (film), 138, 140,
  149
Wayne, John, 10, 74, 241
Weaver, Fritz, 38, 193-94
Webster, Margaret, 234, 236, 248,
  255
Welles, Orson, 17-18, 92
Wellman, William, 152
White Pelicans (Broad), 260
White Sister, The (film), 140, 149
Who's Afraid of Virginia Woolf?
  (Albee), 32-33
Widmark, Richard, 90
Williams, Billy Dee, 166-68
Williams, Tennessee, 224
Williamson, Nicol, 8, 253-54
Willis, Bruce, 98
Willow and I, The (Patrick), 89
Wind, The (film), 141
Winfield, Paul, 38, 199-221, 229
Winn, Kitty, 19
Wise Child (Gray), 49-50
Witness (film), 150
World in His Arms, The (film), 70
Wright, Richard, 203, 212
Wyler, William, 75-76, 79, 155

Wynn, Ed, 256

Yeager, Chuck, 60

Yearling, The (film), *72, 90, 94, 212*
Year of the King (Sher), *268*
Young, Andrew, 215